HRISHIKESH GITA

UNVEILING THE ETERNAL PATH TO MORAL RESPONSIBILITY

HRISHIKESH MISHRA

BlueRose ONE.com
Stories Matter
New Delhi • London

BLUEROSE PUBLISHERS
India | U.K.

BlueRose ONE
Stories Matter
NewDelhi • London

For permissions requests or inquiries regarding this publication, please contact:

BLUEROSE PUBLISHERS
www.BlueRoseONE.com
info@bluerosepublishers.com
+91 8882 898 898
+4407342408967

ISBN: 978-93-6452-797-2

Cover design: Daksh
Typesetting: Tanya Raj Upadhyay

First Edition: January 2025

Dedicated

to

My Respected parent & teachers, family members,

And the curious youth

who encouraged me to publish such a book.

Especiallydedicated

to

My wife- Anita Mishra

My son- Dr. Venkatesh,and

My daughter-Er. Aprajita,

Who contributed their valuable insights and

efforts to ensure that this book

appeals

to

The curious youth as well.

The Blessing

The ***Srimad Bhagavad Gita*** encapsulates the essence of the Upanishads, which form the foundational repository of Indian philosophical wisdom. The primary purpose of this sacred text is to guide humanity, particularly those troubled by sorrow arising from attachment and those inclined to abandon their moral responsibilities. Lord Krishna imparted the Gita to the warrior Arjuna on the battlefield of Kurukshetra, offering it as a divine nectar of wisdom for the benefit of humanity.

This profound teaching was delivered to Arjuna at a critical juncture. While surveying the assembled armies, Arjuna saw revered figures, including his teacher Guru Drona and his grandsire Bhishma Pitamah, standing on the opposing side. Overwhelmed by grief and inner conflict, Arjuna's heart faltered. Laying down his bow, Gandiva, he retreated to the back of his chariot, expressing his desire to withdraw from the battle.

Witnessing Arjuna's turmoil, Lord Krishna diagnosed his mental state as Kalaivya (cowardice or impotence) and sought to reignite his warrior spirit. With complete faith in Lord Krishna, Arjuna turned to Him for guidance in this critical moment, seeking clarity on his moral duty.

At first glance, it might appear that the teachings of the *Srimad Bhagavad Gita* were intended to urge Arjuna to engage in war. In reality, Arjuna was already prepared to fight but was paralyzed by grief and attachment, leading him to consider renouncing the battle. Lord Krishna addressed Arjuna's sorrow by elucidating the immortality of the soul and revealing His ***Viswa Rupa*** (Universal Form). Krishna demonstrated that the great warriors on both sides of the battlefield—including Bhishma, Drona, and Duryodhana—were already defeated in the cosmic scheme by divine will. Thus, attachment to the outcomes of the battle was meaningless.

Empowered by this divine wisdom, Arjuna's doubts were dispelled, and his determination was restored. He stood ready to fulfill his duty as a warrior with unwavering determination.

Arjuna then said:

नष्टो मोहः स्मृतिर्लब्धा त्वत्प्रसादान्मयाच्युत।
स्थितोस्मि गत सन्देह करिष्ये वचनं तव।।

Nashto mohaḥ smṛtiḥ labdhaḥ tvat-prasādān mayācyuta,
Sthito 'smi gata-sandehaḥ karishye vacanam tava.

"My delusion is gone, and my memory has been restored through Your grace, O Acyuta. I am now free from doubt and will act according to Your instructions."

The same eternal wisdom that Lord Krishna imparted to Arjuna was later narrated by Sanjaya to King Dhritarashtra, thanks to the divine vision granted by Maharishi Vyasa. In his conclusion, Sanjaya affirmed that the side with Arjuna, the great archer, and Yogeshwar Krishna would undoubtedly achieve victory, glory, and eternal success.

Arjuna symbolizes enthusiasm, while Lord Krishna represents consciousness. Both enthusiasm and consciousness are essential to succeed in the battle of life.

The true message of the Gita is that success is attainable only through the harmonious presence of enthusiasm and consciousness.

The *Srimad Bhagavad Gita* was originally written in Sanskrit, the sacred language of India. However, in modern times, knowledge of Sanskrit is limited to a few. To make its timeless teachings accessible to a wider audience, Hrishikesh Mishra has translated the verses of the *Srimad Bhagavad Gita* into Hindi, presented in the poetic forms of *doha* and *chaupai,* while also providing its essence in English.

Through the discourse of the *Srimad Bhagavad Gita,* the omnipotent Lord Shri Krishna awakened Arjuna to his duty, unveiling the eternal path to moral responsibility. Hrishikesh Mishra's translation, titled *The Hrishikesh Gita: Unveiling the Eternal Path to Moral Responsibility,* serves as a beacon for spreading the teachings of the *Srimad Bhagavad Gita* to people across the world. It is my blessing to share this divine wisdom universally through such thoughtful presentations.

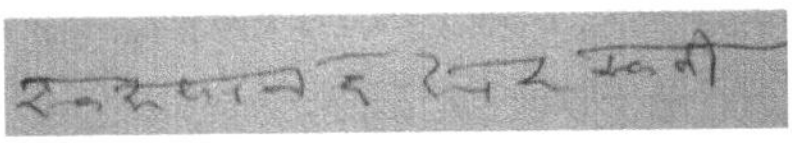

The great shankracharya
(Dwarkapithadheswar)
Shree Swarupanand jee Sarswati

Appreciation

It is often said that man is a social animal. Curiosity is a unique quality bestowed to a man by nature, which sets humanity apart from other creature. This innate curiosity drives humans to act and explore. The essence of *karma* (human effort) is reflected in how individuals perform their tasks and duties.

Human behavior is profoundly influenced by the intensity of mental thoughts, which are shaped by external circumstances. For instance, a person's actions during moments of peace differ significantly from their actions during moments of anger.

The experience of *karma* establishes boundaries for human actions, within which they are deemed virtuous and superior. Indian sages have referred to these boundaries as *Decorum.* The curiosity and Decorum awaken individuals to their moral duties and responsibilities. The *Srimad Bhagavad Gita* serves as a guide for understanding and fulfilling these moral responsibilities.

Control over one's mental attitudes is crucial for performing such duties effectively. A person whose attitudes align with the principles of Decorum is regarded as a true human being. Conversely, someone who transgresses the boundaries of Decorum, driven by unrestrained attitudes, is considered immoral.

The Hrishikesh Gita: Unveiling the Eternal Path to Moral Responsibility, authored by my elder son Hrishikesh Mishra, is a Commendable effort to elucidate the core principles of *Sanatan Dharma.* It offers invaluable insights into the essence of Indian philosophy, fostering a deeper understanding of human welfare and moral responsibility. I sincerely appreciate this noble endeavor, which seeks to contribute to the betterment of humanity.

Radhakant Mishra

Divine Attachment

In Sanatan Dharma, the mother is regarded as the first guru (A teacher). She shares a profound and mystical bond with her child, through which she imparts *sanskars* (moral values). When a child performs good deeds, it is natural for the mother to feel joy and pride. Struggle serves as the medium through which knowledge is acquired. Knowledge gained through struggle is called experience, and this experience paves the way to success.

In my view, the purpose of the Gita is to convey that the ultimate goal of human life—liberation—is attainable only through the struggle .The divine bond with God helps a person to get success. Devotion is essential to strengthen this bond. It is not necessary to renounce worldly life to cultivate devotion; however, it is vital to establish a deep, spiritual connection with God. This divine bond is the experiential path to liberation, the ultimate purpose of human existence.

Throughout the Gita, Lord Krishna repeatedly emphasizes to Arjuna that freedom from the cycle of the material world is achieved through *nishkama karma* (selfless action). Material attachments hinder the journey to liberation, while the divine bond with God inspires one to act selflessly, thus leading to spiritual freedom.

The Hrishikesh Gita: Unveiling the Eternal Path to Moral Responsibility offers a profound explanation of the Srimad Bhagavad Gita, making the essence of Sanatan Dharma accessible to all. This book, focused on human welfare, is a treasure trove of Sanatan Dharma's wisdom. It is my sincere wish that, by deepening their divine connection with God through the teachings of the Gita, everyone may achieve the ultimate goal of life: liberation.

Jayamanti Devi

Congratulations

Shrimad Bhagavad Gita is a book of eternal knowledge in the form of verses. It can be called the "Holy Ganga of Knowledge." By drinking its nectar, a person attains enlightenment.Initially, the knowledge of the Gita is compared with the knowledge of the **Upanishads**. In the second stage, it is identified as **Brahma Vidya** (knowledge of the ultimate reality). In the third stage, its essence is compared with the **Yoga Sutras**. In the fourth stage, it is described as the **Shri Krishna-Arjuna Samvad** (dialogue between Krishna and Arjuna). Finally, in the fifth stage, the Gita is divided into 18 chapters, each named according to its contents.In this way, we can say that the holy book **Shrimad Bhagavad Gita** is a combination of all five streams of knowledge: the eternal knowledge of the **Upanishads**, **Brahma Vidya**, **Yoga Vidya**, **Sri Krishna Consciousness**, and the summary of the elimination of doubt in daily life.

The **Shrimad Bhagavad Gita** is the only book in world literature that has been translated into many languages. This work has been carried out extensively in Indian languages and continues to this day. **"Hrishikesh Gita: Unveiling the Eternal Path to Moral Responsibility"** is a new flower filled with nectar in this ongoing transformation. It is full of fragrance. It is not merely a collection of words but is enriched with emotional energy. The simple and lyrical translation by Shri Hrishikesh Mishra is infused with life energy.

The uniqueness of this translation lies in its adoption of the **Doha** and **Chaupai** system, which is lyrical and singable. In this book, the main point of each chapter is described briefly, along with a connection to the next chapter, providing a sense of conclusion. The prayer offered by Arjuna after his **Vishwaroopa Darshan** (vision of the universal form) of Lord Shri Krishna, as mentioned in the eleventh chapter, is presented in the form of a prayer, and its recitation is most enjoyable. For this reason, it has become a complete translation.

I congratulate Shri Hrishikesh Mishra for this admirable work and extend my best wishes to him. This is Shri Hrishikesh Mishra's first book, and I pray to the Supreme Lord that his writings may continue to flow.

With heartfelt best wishes,
Girish Kumar Choubey (Govardhan)
(Akshar Research and Brahma Yoga.Sadhana Center)
(Anupam Amrit Vidyapeeth)37A Kshapanak Marg, Dussehra Maidan,
Ujjain (Madhya Pradesh) Pin.45610
Anant Chaturdashi, vikram Samvad 2080,Ujjain, 17th September,2024

Self-submission

I am fortunate to have the opportunity to connect with the profound insights of outstanding scholars on the spiritual treasures of Indian culture. These interactions inspired a series of thoughts in my mind, which have now taken shape in the form of *Hrishikesh Gita: Unveiling the Eternal Path to Moral Responsibility.*

Through the unparalleled efforts of scholars, the *Shrimad Bhagavad Gita* continues to raise the flag of eternal knowledge across the world. However, the blending of various cultures brought about by historical invasions has introduced Which creats confusion about the original form of this timeless wisdom as experienced in India. Today, many young Indians regard *Sanatan Dharma* as mere imagination and find themselves wandering aimlessly in search of peace of mind. This is largely due to a lack of awareness and understanding of our own cultural heritage.

While studying the *Sri Ramcharitmanas* (originally written in Avadhi by Goswami Tulsidas, based on the Sanskrit *Valmiki Ramayana*), I realized that its popularity stemmed from its simplicity, accessibility, and singable format in *Doha* and *Chaupai.* This inspired me to attempt a similar approach for the *Shrimad Bhagavad Gita,* presenting it in *Doha* and *Chaupai* in Hindi, our national language. My aim was to make the Gita's teachings more comprehensible and relatable, much like the *Sri Ramcharitmanas* has been for generations.

By the grace of God, I was able to translate the *Shrimad Bhagavad Gita* into *Doha* and *Chaupai.* Encouraged by friends who do not know Hindi very well, The translation of the prose portion of my book, *Kratvayabodh Hrishikesh Gita,* into English enhanced its accessibility. This English translation is titled *Hrishikesh Gita: Unveiling the Eternal Path to Moral Responsibility.*

I hope this book will serve as an informative and inspiring resource for those curious about practicing the eternal knowledge of Indian culture and seeking peace of mind.

Hrishikesh Mishra
Shree Krishna Janmastami(26.8.2024)

Table of Contents

The Propagation of Srimadbhagawad-Gita

Almost all scholars in India regard the *Shrimad Bhagavad Gita* as the cornerstone of *Sanatan Dharma* (Hinduism). In this chapter, we will explore some historical facts about how the *Shrimad Bhagavad Gita* became accessible to the common people.

The *Shrimad Bhagavad Gita* consists of 700 verses, which are primarily conveyed through the dialogues of four key characters from the *Mahabharata* as follows:

Sl. No	Characters	No. of Verses
1	Lord Sri Krishna	574
2	Arjuna	84
3	Sanjaya	41
4	Dhritarashtra	1
Total		**700**

In Hindu culture, Lord Krishna is regarded as the incarnation of Lord Vishnu. It is believed that during the *Mahabharata* war in *Dwapara Yuga,* Lord Krishna revealed the knowledge of the *Shrimad Bhagavad Gita* to Arjuna on Marga-Shirsha Shukla Ekadashi. As a result, Marga-Shirsha Shukla Ekadashi (the 11th day of the waxing moon in the month of Marga-Shirsha) is celebrated as *Geeta Jayanti.*

Although much time has passed since the *Dwapara Yuga*, the relevance of the *Shrimad Bhagavad Gita* remains undiminished. It is considered a timeless composition. The *Shrimad Bhagavad Gita* is a part of the epic *Mahabharata*, written by Ved Vyasa. Adi Shankaracharya is perhaps the first saint to establish the *Shrimad Bhagavad Gita* as the foundation of *Sanatan Dharma* in the 8th century.

During that time, *Sanatan Dharma* was on the brink of disappearing due to the growing influence of other religions, such as Buddhism, in India. Additionally, Islam was spreading rapidly, and India's first mosque built in Kodungallur, in the Thrissur district of Kerala, in the 7th century. The social and cultural circumstances of the era led many people to reserve themselves from *Sanatan Dharma.*

The famous conversation between Adi Shankaracharya and Mandana Mishra illustrates this fact. It is said that Mandana Mishra initially intended to abandon *Sanatan Dharma* and embrace Buddhism. However, after conversing with Adi Shankaracharya, he changed his mind and reaffirmed his commitment to *Sanatan Dharma.*

In the 11th century, Shri Ramanuja of Tamil Nadu revitalized *Sanatan Dharma* by effectively propagating the eternal knowledge of the *Shrimad Bhagavad Gita* to the public. During this period, Islam was also spreading rapidly, supported by royal patronage in many parts of India.

In the 13th century, Shri Madhvacharya of Karnataka further spread the knowledge of the *Shrimad Bhagavad Gita* and elaborated on *Sanatan Dharma* in the southern states of India. At that time, there was considerable hypocrisy within *Sanatan Dharma* in southern India. Saint Gyaneshwar translated the *Shrimad Bhagavad Gita* into Marathi, making it accessible to the Marathi-speaking people.

In the 14th century, Shri Madhav Panikar worked tirelessly to spread the message of *Sanatan Dharma* to the common people of South India, translating the *Shrimad Bhagavad Gita* into Malayalam.

The 15th century saw further translations of the *Shrimad Bhagavad Gita*—Shri Tirumalacharya translated it into Telugu, while Shri Balaram Das translated it into Oriya, making the teachings accessible to the common people in the Telugu- and Oriya-speaking regions.

In the 16th century, the *Shrimad Bhagavad Gita* was also translated into Assamese, although the Sanskrit version remained popular in many other parts of India. These centuries were marked by rapid religious conversions across India, but the contribution of the *Shrimad Bhagavad Gita* in preserving *Sanatan Dharma* has been invaluable.

The 17th century witnessed the spread of Islam, along with the growth of other religions such as Christianity in India. Despite this, the *Shrimad Bhagavad Gita* continued to have a profound influence on the world. In the 18th century, Charles Wilkins and Edwin Arnold translated it into European languages, introducing Europe to the teachings of the *Shrimad Bhagavad Gita* for the welfare of humanity.

During the Indian freedom movement in the 19th and 20th centuries, freedom fighters such as Sri Aurobindo, Lokmanya Bal Gangadhar Tilak, Mahatma Gandhi, and Acharya Vinoba Bhave , etc. made the teachings of the *Shrimad Bhagavad Gita* accessible to the common people by translating its wisdom into Indian languages like Hindi. Gandhiji, acknowledging the immense influence of the *Shrimad Bhagavad Gita* on India's freedom struggle, referred to it as ***Geeta Mata*** **(Mother Gita)**, recognizing its invaluable role in shaping India's path to independence.

After the Second World War, the *Shrimad Bhagavad Gita* was firmly established as an eternal religious text, advocating the message of peace for the world. Religious intellectuals of *Sanatan Dharma* have embraced the teachings of the *Shrimad Bhagavad Gita* as the timeless path to salvation.

Now a days, most of the scholars are agreed that the *Shrimad Bhagavad Gita* is not just a religious book, but a unique and inexhaustible reservoir of knowledge on effective life management. It serves as a practical guide for success in every aspect of human life. Thanks to the tireless efforts of various publishers, the *Shrimad Bhagavad Gita* is now available in many Indian and international languages. The contributions of organizations such as Gita Press Gorakhpur and ISKCON in promoting the *Shrimad Bhagavad Gita* around the world are truly commendable. At present, many scholars continue to expand its teachings through various global platforms.

Many ordinary people often believe that the *Shrimad Bhagavad Gita* is meant only for hermits or ascetics. As a result, they may try to shield their children from its teachings, fearing that studying it will encourage renunciation. However, this belief is far from the truth. In fact, it was through the wisdom imparted by Lord Krishna in the *Shrimad Bhagavad Gita* that the Arjuna found the courage to participate in the Mahabharata war. Initially, Arjuna sought to renounce the battle, overwhelmed by the horrors of war. But it was the profound knowledge of the Gita that inspired him to rise above his doubts and fulfill his duty as a warrior.

Now a days , nearly all intellectuals agree that the *Shrimad Bhagavad Gita* is not merely a religious text, but also offers solutions to almost all the profound spiritual and material questions that arise in the human mind. In fact, its teachings are essential for the well-being and progress of humanity.

The study and dissemination of the teachings of the *Shrimad Bhagavad Gita* are regarded as the *Gyan Yajna* (the sacrificial fire of knowledge). To understand it easily the 18 chapters of *Shrimad Bhagavad Gita* are divided in three Parts as

1. Swadharma (The selfinduced virtue),
2. Devotion (Divine Attachment)
3. Chintan (The Critical Thinking) .

These are explained in following Chapters.

PART-1

THE SELF-INDUCES VIRTUE

Chapter-1
The Arjuna Vishad Yoga

First chapter of Srimadbhagwat Gita at a glance	
Total Nos of verses	47
Nos of verses by Dritrastra	1
Nos of verses by sanjay	25
Nos of verses by Arjuna	21
Nos of verses by lord Shree Krishna	0
The main theme of the Chapter	Melancholy of Arjuna

श्री गणेशाय नमः

श्लोकः

प्रणमामि नमामि नमामि भवं,
भव जन्म कृति प्राणिषूदनकम्।
गुणहीनं अनन्तमितं शरणं,
जन तारण ताराय तापितकम्।।

दो0– धृतराष्ट्र चिन्तातुर कर धर्मक्षेत्र का ध्यान।
रणक्षेत्र सज गये जहाँ शस्त्र सहित बलवान।1।
दो0– कह कुरुराज संजय कहो कुरुक्षेत्र का हाल।
पाण्डुतनय का कर रहे करत का मोको लाल।2।

कह संजय सुनहूँ कुरूराजा। योद्धा तन मन तेज विराजा।।
देखी सुयोधन पाण्ड़व सेना। द्रोण निकट गये उत्सुक नैना।।
द्रुपदतनय तव शिष्य धीमाना। देखहूँ अरिचमु उदधी समाना।।
पाण्डव सैन्य सजी व्यूहकारा। धृष्टदूम्न वीर जाको सवाँरा।।
अरिचमु महूँ शूरवीर अनेका। भीम अर्जुन सम युद्ध विवेका।।
शूर सात्यकि विराट् घृष्टकेतु। तत्पर सकल वीर रण हेतु।।
नृपद्रुपद काशिराज चेकिताना। पराक्रमी मतिधीर बलवाना।।
पुरूजित शैब्य वीर उतमौजा। युधामन्यु शूर कुन्तीभोजा।।
सुभद्रासुमन अभिमन्यु रणधीरा। महाबली जिमी तीव्र समीरा।।

द्रोपदी पंचतनय रण योद्धा। महारथी युद्ध नीति पुरोधा।।

दो0– एही प्रकार अरिचमु महूँ बीर विपुल मतिधीर।
पार्थसारथी हृषीकेश अतिधीर वीर गंभीर।3।
दो0–वीर विशिष्ठ निज चमु महूँ देखहूँ हे द्विजश्रेष्ठ।
युद्धनिपुण मतिधीर अपि चमुनायक सब ज्येष्ठ।4।

आपहुँ गुरुवर निज चमु अंगा। अजेय कृपाचार्य निजसंगा।।
महारथी कर्ण केहरि समाना। रिपु मध्य को अस बलवाना।।
सोमदत्त तनय भूरिश्रवा वीरा। अश्वत्थामा कुशल रणधीरा।।
वीर विकर्ण रिपु मर्दनकारी। अस्त्र–शस्त्र पारंगत भारी।।
गुरुवर विजयविभूति दायक। भीष्म पितामह निजचमूनायक।।
करे प्राण मम हेतु बलिदाना। वीर अनेक निज चमू सयाना।।
युद्ध विशारद शास्त्र प्रवीणा। गुरुवर निजचमू अपि भयहीना।।
अगणीत सैन्य पितामह रक्षित। युद्ध महूँ निजजय परिलक्षित।।
निजअनि छाड़ि प्राणक्षय भीति। निश्चयी दृढ़ अटल पुरप्रीति।।
भीमरक्षित रिपूअनि बल थोरा। गिरि अपार सम निजचमु मोरा।।

दो0–सब प्रकार मम अनि प्रबल देखहूँ गुरु धरी घ्यान।
सुनिश्चत कौरव विजय दृष्ट न कछु व्यवधान।।5।।
दो0–युद्ध नीति निज ध्यान धरी रहहूँ सजग रणक्षेत्र।
चमूपति भीष्म सुरक्षा को रखहूँ चतुर्दिक नेत्र।।6।।
दो0–कौरव दल उर हर्ष बढ़े यतन किये कुरू बृद्ध।
शंखनाद करि सिंहसम युद्धोत्साह किए सिद्ध।।7।।

भीष्म पितामह परम प्रतापी। सुयोधन उर हर्ष अति व्यापि।।
बाजन लगे शंख चहूँ ओरा। राजन युद्ध की बजी ढिढोरा।।
रणभेरी बाजन लगे सारी। ढोल मृदंग शोर अति भारी।।
बजे नरसिघें दीर्घ नगाड़ा। सकलअनि उरहर्ष प्रगाढ़ा।।
रथी अर्जुन सारथी नन्दलाला। उत्साहित चमके दीर्घभाला।।
कपिध्वज स्यन्दन श्वेत पताका। अलौकिक शोभा है रणव्यापा।।
पाँन्चजन्य श्री कृष्ण बजाये। ध्वनि सकल ज्ञानेन्द्रीय भाये।।
अनन्तविजय बजाये युधिष्ठिर। धैर्य अनन्त भई मन स्थिर।।
भीम पौण्ड्र महाशंख बजाये। दिग् दिगन्त अरिचमु धबराये।।

पार्थ देवदत् शंख जो फूँका। अरिसैन्य हृदय गति रूका।।

दो0— शुभ घोषणा नकुल की कर रही सुघोष प्रचार।
सहदेव मणिपुष्पक बजा किये वाहित सुविचार।।8।।

कॉशीराज द्रुपद विराट् भूपाला। सात्यकि अरू द्रोपदीलाला।।
द्रुपद पुत्र धृष्टदूम्न महाबाहु। सुभद्रासुत अभिमन्यु अरिदाहु।।
परमलक्ष्य शिखण्डी नियराये। वीर सकल निजशंख बजाये।।
गगन महि महुँ शोर भयंकर। कुरूक्षेत्र लक्षित प्रलयंकर।।
कुरूराज भई शंख ध्वनि भारी। कौरव दल के हृदय विदारी।।
युद्धारंभ महूँ काल बस थोरा। राजन रणसाज बजे चहूँओरा।।
देखी रणभुमि चमू व्यवस्था। अर्जुन की भई आद्र अवस्था।।
कुरूपक्ष लखी आत्मिय कुला। मन विषाद उपजा उरशूला।।
छाड़ि पार्थ सायक सन्धाना। कहे सखा सारथी सुजाना।।
द्वौ चमु मध्य हे देवकीनन्दन। करहूँ स्थापित निज स्यंदन।।

दो0—रणक्षेत्र एकत्रित महारथी अपि युद्धसेना भारी।
दुर्बुद्धि दुर्योधन प्रिये कौरव पक्ष हितकारी।9।
दो0—स्थिर रखहूँ स्यंदन करूं अवलोकन चमुवीर।
अरिपक्ष रणभागी सकल महारथी रणधीर।10।

कह संजय अब सुनहूँ महिपा। रथ स्थित भई द्रोण समीपा।।
कह हृषीकेश हे वीर धनुर्धर। दृष्टिपात अब अरिचमु तु कर ।।
भीष्म अपि रण हेतु सब राजा। पार्थ लखे सब अरिसमाजा।।
पार्थ ज्यों देखे कौरव सेना। भाव विह्वल भर आये नैना।।
ताउ पितामह गुरु अरू भ्राता। पुत्र पौत्र सब रिश्ता नाता।।
रथ अश्व अरू गज आरूढ़ा। निज परिजन युवा अरू बुढ़ा।।
करजोरी पार्थ कहे हृषीकेशा। अब न रही मम शक्तिशेषा।।
मम मन भ्रमित कँपे शरीरा। गांड़ीव गिरत उठत नही तीरा।।
रण परिणाम दीखत विपरीता। करे युद्ध कुल सकल अहिता।।
कह अर्जुन प्रभु कृपानिधाना। परिजन मारी कवन कल्याणा।।

दो0—सुखभोग विजय की ईच्छा अब न रही कछु शेष।
स्वजनहीन संसार में मनशान्ति कहाँ हृषीकेश।11
दो0—चाहत जिन परिजन हेतु राज सकल सुख भोग।

छाड़ी सकल निज जीवनआशा रणभागी वही लोग।12।

पाँउ अगर त्रिलोक के राजा। तो नही मारूं स्वजनसमाजा।।
धरा हेतु परिजन नही मारूं। गुरुहत्या का पाप क्यों धारूं।।
मारू जो रिपुअनि संग कौरव। तो नही बढ़े मित जग गौरव।।
हत्या माधव जग पाप कहलाता। गैर सुजान या रिश्तानाता।।
परिजनमारी करूं सुखआशा। जहाँ सखा कुलधरम हो नाशा।।
भ्रष्टचित लोभी कुरूसेना। पाप–पुण्य इन्हें नही लेना।।
युद्ध उपरांत न शांति आशा। युद्धपरिणाम क्षत्रिय कुलनाशा।।
कुल नाश करे धरम के हानि। बाढ़े पाप धरा कहे ज्ञानी।।
कुलपाप सखा बढ़े जो भारी। दूषित हो जग कुलिन नारी।।
दुषित नारी कुलपाप भयंकर। उत्पन्न संतान करे वर्णशंकर।।
वर्णशंकर करे कुलधर्म नाशा। पितर को नही तर्पण आशा।।

दो0–वर्णशंकर हो कुलघाती चले जाति धरम विपरीत।
कुलधर्म का नाश करे रखे न निजकुल प्रीत।13।
दो0–पितर पाये अधोगति न होय जो तर्पण श्राद्ध।
युद्ध कदापि धर्म नही यह जग में बड़ा अपराध।14।

माधव जानी अस युद्ध परिणामा। न धर्मसम्मत न पुरनकामा।।
जाकर हो कुल धर्म के नाशा। काल अनन्त नरक करे बासा।।
सहस्त्र बार पुराण श्रुति गाये। पापी अधम नरक गति पाये।।
युद्ध सकल करें बुद्धिनाशा। यह शोकविषय कहॉ उल्लासा।।
स्वजन मारी कवन कल्याणा। उद्दत रणक्षेत्र लिये शस्त्रनाना।।
निजसुख राज हेतु युद्ध भारी। अति अधर्म यह पाप तैयारी।।
युद्ध शुभ नही कहे धीमाना। जामें जाये निर्दोष के प्राणा।।
अस जीवन ते मरण ही अच्छा। जामें हो जगधरम की रक्षा।।
शस्त्र सहित कौरव रण माही। हने मोको शोक कछु नाहीं।।
त्यागी शस्त्र न करूं प्रहारा। युद्ध परिणाम परिजनु संहारा।।

दो0–संजय बोले हे महिपति अर्जुन भये अधीर।
धनुष बाण तजि जा बैठे स्यंदन पीछे रणवीर।15।

।। इति प्रथम अध्याय।।

The first chapter of Srimadbhagwat Gita

The Essence

The first chapter of the *Shrimad Bhagavad-Gita* introduces the psychological and emotional crisis faced by Arjuna, a heroic figure caught in the midst of the great Mahabharata war. This chapter, known as *Arjuna Vishada Yoga* (The Yoga of Arjuna's Dejection), serves as an introduction, It can be divided into four distinct sections, each depicting a different aspect of the battle and Arjuna's inner turmoil.

1. Description of military strength by Duryodhan (Shloka 01-11):- Maharaja Dhritarashtra was eager to know about the war preparations of the Kaurava and Pandava armies, which were assembled on the battlefield of Kurukshetra, ready for battle. Since Sanjaya possessed divine vision, Dhritarashtra asked him to inform him about the activities of both his sons and the sons of Pandu.

Sanjaya began to describe that after observing the Pandava army,Duryodhana, went to Guru Dronacharya and compare both armies. Duryodhana told Guru Dronacharya that the Pandava army had numerous renowned warriors, such as Dhrishtadyumna, Drupada, Dhrishtaketu, Chekitana, Kashiraj, Purujit, Kuntibhoja, Shaivya, Yudhmanyu, Uttamauja, Abhimanyu, and the five sons of Draupadi, among others. However, Duryodhana emphasized that their side also had no shortage of great warriors. Grandfather Bhishma, Karna, Vikarna, Kripacharya, Bhurishrava, and, of course, Dronacharya himself. Additionally, there were many other skilled warriors ready to risk their lives in battle.Duryodhana concluded that, when comparing both armies, their own army, protected by Grandfather Bhishma, was more capable of defeating the Pandava army, which was led by Bhima. He then instructed that everyone should focus on protecting Grandfather Bhishma from all sides as per the war strategy.

2. **Encouraging both the armies (Shloka 12-19):-** To inspire and rally the spirits of his warriors, Bhishma blew his conch, which emitted a sound like the roar of a lion. Following this, drums, Mridangas, and Narasimhas were played, creating a terrifying cacophony. In response, the warriors of the Pandava side also blew their conches. Krishna blew his Panchjanya, Arjuna his Devadatta, Bhima his Paundra, Yudhishthira his Anantavijaya, Nakula his Sugosha, and Sahadeva his Manipushpak, among others. Each warrior's conch blast signaled their readiness for battle.The deafening sound of the conches marked the official start of the war, and the atmosphere on the battlefield was charged with tension. For the Kaurava army, this sound was heart-wrenching, foreshadowing the imminent conflict.

3. Arjuna's desire to inspect the enemy's army (Shloka 20-27):-

With no further obstacles to the war, Arjuna, feeling a deep sense of urgency, turned to his charioteer and dearest friend, Lord Krishna. He requested to position their chariot,(adorned with a white horse and a flag bearing the image of a monkey) between the two armies. His intention was to see clearly those who would stand against him in battle—specifically, the warriors aligned with Duryodhana.

Responding to Arjuna's plea, Lord Krishna guided the chariot to a vantage point where both sides of the battlefield were visible, including the formidable Kaurava warriors like Bhishma and Dronacharya, as well as the warriors on Arjuna's own side. As Arjuna gazed out over the battlefield, his heart sank. He saw not just enemies, but his own family members—his paternal uncle, his revered grandfather, his teachers, his maternal uncle, his father-in-law, his brother, his son, his friends, and those who had always shown him love and affection.

Overwhelmed with sorrow and grief, Arjuna's spirit was crushed. His mind became a storm of turmoil, and his courage faltered in the face of such overwhelming emotion.

4. **Arjuna's great sorrow (Shloka 28-47):-**

Arjuna began to speak, saying, "My body is growing weak, my hands are trembling, and the Gandiva is slipping from my grasp. My mind is confused, and I am struggling to even stand. I fear the outcome of this war will be disastrous, as there seems to be no gain in killing my own kin. O Krishna, I do not desire victory or the pleasures of the kingdom anymore. True happiness lies in enjoying the kingdom's pleasures with family and loved ones. Yet here they stand before me on the battlefield, ready to forsake their lives.

Therefore, I feel that if gaining the rule of the threefold world requires me to kill such dear relatives, I will not do so. And what is a mere piece of land on this earth that justifies the killing of my beloved kin? I will not find happiness even after slaying the cruel sons of Dhritarashtra. On the contrary, I feel that I will be committing a sin if I choose to fight in this war. So, tell me, how can we attain true happiness by killing our relatives who stand with Duryodhana? This war will lead to the destruction of our clan. The corrupt and greedy Kauravas do not understand the sins that arise from the destruction of a family. But we understand it very well. Then, why should we not seek to avoid this sin?

The destruction of the clan leads to the destruction of the eternal Kuldharma, and sin spreads throughout the entire family. The women of the family will become tainted due to the increase in such sins, and when women are tainted, Varnsankar (those born from mixed castes) are produced. Varnsankars disrupt the beliefs of the clan, and as a result, the entire family descends into hell after death. They do not perform the necessary rituals like Shraadhas, Pindas, and Tarpans for their ancestors, causing the ancestors to fall into hell as well. The eternal Kuldharma and Jatidharma of the family are destroyed. It is believed that those whose Kuldharma is lost live in hell for an indefinite period. We have heard this from our elders and wise community. After all, if we, despite our wisdom, are ready to commit such a great sin, it is truly shameful. I believe that if I lay down my weapons to avoid this sin and the Kauravas kill me, it would still be more beneficial for us.

Having said this, the troubled Arjuna, overwhelmed with grief, laid down his bow and arrows and sat down at the rear of the chariot.

Note:-1. Arjuna had fought many wars in his life, but he had never considered the sin and destruction of family until this moment. In the war of Mahabharata, he began to reflect on social acceptance. Acharya Vinoba Bhave compares Arjuna's condition to that of a judge who has sentenced many criminals to death, but now faces a close relative whom he must also condemn. In such a situation, it is natural for the mind to be disturbed.

Note:-2. It is important to clarify one important issue,tha the term Varnsankar *is generally understood to refer to children born from parents of different social castes, and such children are often disregarded in Indian society. However, it is worth reflecting on the case of Shantanu (a Kshatriya) who married Satyavati (the daughter of a fisherman). Was their son considered a* Varnsankar *or a Kshatriya? In the Mahabharata, he was considered a Kshatriya. Srila Prabhupada, the founder of ISKCON, explains in his commentary that the true meaning of* Varnsankar *refers to children born as a result of anti-social behavior, who are neglected by society. These children often do not receive the love and support of either parent, leading to a distorted view of society. An example of this is Karna in the Mahabharata.*

The Discussion

The entire essence of the Srimad Bhagavad Gita is introduced in the first chapter. By understanding this chapter, one gains a general understanding of the core concepts of the Gita. Maharishi Ved Vyasa has presented the circumstances of the Mahabharata war to explain the principles of human dharma. Such a clear and precise explanation of human religion, expressed in such simple language, is perhaps unmatched in any other text. That is why it is rightly said

गीता सुगीता कर्तव्या किमन्यैः शास्त्रविस्तरैः

Geeta SuGita Kartavya Kimanyaih Shastra vistraih.

This means that after understanding the Srimad Bhagavad Gita and applying its teachings in practice, there is no need to delve into any other scripture in great detail.

In the first verse of this chapter, two terms—**Dharmakshetra** and **Kurukshetra**—appear, which can be confusing to common readers. While Kurukshetra refers to a specific region in the Indian state of Haryana, where the Mahabharata war was fought at the end of the Dwapara Yuga, the meaning of **Dharmakshetra** (the region of religion) needs further exploration.

To understand this, we must delve into the concepts of **Dharma** (religion or belief) and **Kshetra** (field) as explained in the Srimad Bhagavad Gita.

Dharma (The Religion): Religion is discussed in detail in the later chapters of the Srimad Bhagavad Gita. Its essence is that everything in the world, both animate and inanimate, is influenced by the **Trigunas**—the three natural qualities (Satva, Rajas, and Tamas). The effects of these Trigunas are reflected in human nature as well. According to Sanatan Dharma, only God is unaffected by the influence of these three qualities. Due to the diverse effects of the Trigunas, every individual has unique interests, qualities, and behaviors.

According to the Srimad Bhagavad Gita, **Dharma** or religion is the inherent nature of a person, much like the natural qualities of fire, water, air, and other elements. It is the manifestation of an individual's natural inclination toward specific actions. It is well-known that a person feels happiness when engaged in work that aligns with their natural interests. This form of religion, which is unique to each individual, is eternal and different for every human being. People follow this natural religion spontaneously throughout their lives. This is referred to as Sanatan Dharma or

Shashwat Dharma. True satisfaction or happiness arises when actions are performed in harmony with one's inherent virtues. Therefore, the natural virtues of a person define their personal Dharma.

Kshetra (The Field): Now, we must understand the concept of Kshetra (the field) as explained in the Srimad Bhagavad Gita. It is discussed in detail in the 13th chapter. The second verse of this chapter states:

इदं शरीरं कौन्तेय क्षेत्रमित्यभिधीयते।

Idam Shariram Kaunteya Kshetramityabhidhiyate.

This means that the body is referred to as **Kshetra**, because its nature is like that of a field. Just as seeds are sown in a field, they grow and eventually produce fruit, the outcome of the seed's potential. It is well-known that the quality of the fruit depends not only on the type of seed but also on the quality of the field. Similarly, the seed of **karma** is sown in the body, which eventually yields its outcome over time.

In the 16th chapter of the Srimad Bhagavad Gita, the qualities present within the conscious body are explained in detail. In short, it can be said that when a creature is born, it receives both a body and consciousness. The body is manifest, while consciousness is unmanifest. This consciousness is described as a form of wealth in the Srimad Bhagavad Gita, and it is categorized into two category:

1. The Divine wealth 2. The Demonic wealth

Due to destiny, a human being inherits one of these forms of wealth, or a combination of both, at the time of birth. This wealth influences the individual's actions. Based on this wealth, different people approach the same task in different ways according to their nature.

Therefore, our conscious body is endowed with the wealth determined by destiny, much like fertile land that has a manifest part (the body) and hidden fertility (the consciousness or wealth obtained from destiny). Hence, the meaning of **Dharmakshetra** is deeply profound.

Dharmakshetra is a symbolic term for the conscious body.

In essence, we can say that through the first verses of the first chapter, Shri Veda Vyasa conveys a message that **Dharmakshetra**, our conscious body, is analogous to **Kurukshetra** (the battlefield). The conflict of the mind represents the war between the Pandavas and Kauravas (symbolizing good qualities versus bad qualities).

If we examine Arjuna's situation, we see that, at first glance, his concerns seem like real, human dilemmas. The clear message of the first chapter of the Srimad Bhagavad Gita is that conflict within the mind leads to indecisiveness. This state of indecision creates great confusion, which ultimately results in continuous failure.

The Conclusion

The first chapter of the Srimad Bhagavad Gita highlights the analogy between **Dharmakshetra** (the physical body) and **Kurukshetra** (the battlefield). Just as a war involves two opposing armies, a mental conflict is a battle between two conflicting opinions. In this chapter, it is beautifully described that Arjuna, though standing in the battlefield, is torn by a conflict in his mind—whether the war is about determining what is right or wrong, or whether he should fight or withdraw from the battle.

If a person is not mentally prepared, even the body fails to support them. As a result, Arjuna droped his bow and arrows and sat behind the chariot, overwhelmed by his inner turmoil.

This chapter raises a crucial question for the common people through Arjuna's dilemma: **Is war right or wrong?**

****

Chapter-2
The Sankhya Yoga

The Second chapter of Srimadbhagwat Gita at a glance	
Total Nos of verses	72
Nos of verses by lord Shree Krishna	63
Nos of verses by Arjuna	6
Nos of verses by sanjay	3
Nos of verses by Dritrastra	0
Main theam of the Chapter	The Eternal Knowledge

श्री गणेशाय नमः

श्लोक

आदौ देवकीगर्भजननं गोपीगृहेवर्धनम्।
मायापूतनजीवितापहरणं गोवर्धनोद्धारणम्।।
कंसच्छेदनं कौरवादिहननं कुन्तीसुतापालनम्।
एतद् भागवतं पुराणकथितं श्री कृष्ण लीलामृतम्।।

दो0– संजय विस्मित कह रहे अर्जुन भये युद्ध विरूद्ध।
मन विषाद अश्रुनयन व्याकुल कण्ठ अवरूद्ध।1।
दो0– देखी अर्जुन आर्तदशा सस्मित बोले भगवान।
उठो पार्थ त्यागो विषाद करो गांडीव संधान।2।

असमय पार्थ मोह केही हेतु। न कृतिवर्धक न हीं स्वर्गसेतु।।
श्रेष्ठ पुरुष आचरण न माया। आसक्ती सकल जगत भरमाया।।
करहूँ युद्ध मनमाया त्यागी। क्लिबता छाड़ी बनहूँ रणभागी।।
गुडाकेश कह जोरी युग पाणी। हे सखा मधुसूदन अतिज्ञानी।।
रणभूमि शस्त्र–अस्त्र सब धारे। गुरुद्रोण कृप पुज्य पधारे।।
भीष्म पितामह कुरूकुल नायक। रणभूमि खड़े लिये करसायक।।
गुरुपूजन करूं या रण भारी। निर्णयहीन मति सखा हमारी।।
युद्धकरी पूज्य पितामह मारूं। रूधिर बहा स्वजन संघारू।।
न रक्तपूरित मोको भोग ईच्छा। माधव उचित कही माँगु भिक्षा।।

पुज्य गुरु हति कवन कल्याणा। रिपु कौरव को भ्रात मैं जाना।।

दो0—जय पराजय यही युद्ध में कौन जाने क्या होए।
रूधिर बहे निर्दोष मरे गृह परिजन बच्चे रोए।3।
दो0— शान्ति हेतु रण छोड दूँ या करूं परिजन संहार।
धर्म अधर्म विचारी कहहूँ सखा कल्याणकारी व्यापार।4।

परिणाम ध्यान बिनु रण जड़ता। न धर्मसम्मत् ना हीं शुभकर्ता।।
जगयुद्ध नहीं पौरूष पहचाना। हत्या धरमविरूद्ध जगजाना।।
ज्ञानी कहे धर्म अर्थ अतिगूढ़ा। चित् मम मोहित कर्तव्यविमूढ़ा।।
शुभकर्म जामें सकल कल्याणा। संतापरहित धर्म कहहूँ धीमाना।।
मति मम भ्रमित शुभ्रता इच्छा। शिष्य तुम्हार प्रभु दीजै शिक्षा।।
ममशोक अपार इन्द्रीय सुखाने। कहहुँ उपाय जगधर्म सन्माने।।
भूमि निष्कण्टक देवत्व सुखदाई। तुच्छलगे मोहे कछु न सुहाई।।
हो धनधान्य अरू सम्पदा भारी। युद्ध प्रतीत न कछु उपकारी।।
मम शाँति ईच्छा यदि कायरता। धर्मसम्मत् कर्तव्य कह भर्ता।।
तुम ममसखा गुरु अरू भ्राता। ज्ञान देई भ्रम करहूँ निपाता।।

दो0—संजय आश्चर्यचकित कहा सुनहूँ महिपाल।
युद्ध मुझे करना नही विचलित कुन्तिलाल।5।
दो0—हृषीकेश मुसका रहे सुनी शव्यसाँची अभिलाष।
प्रेम सहित बोले वचन पार्थसारथी लिये विश्वास।6।

तर्क पार्थ तव ज्ञानी समाना। मरण सत्य क्यूं शोक मनाना।।
मृत्युलोक धरम जीवन मरना। मुरख सम क्युं तव आचरणा।।
सत्य स्वीकार सदा सुखकारी। सब्यसाँची तु ज्ञानी अपि भारी।।
अमर न कोई एही मृत्युलोका। करे ज्ञानी जीव हेतु न शोका।।
जीवित प्राणी तो निश्चित मरहीं। कबहू शोक ज्ञानी ना करहीं।।
तुम मैं अपि सब राज भुपाला। वर्तमान प्रकट जो थे भूतकाला।।
भविष्य संभव रहिहें इह लोका। कारण कछु पार्थ नही शोका।।
शिशु बाल युवा जरा अवस्था। पार्थ सकल दृष्ट देह व्यवस्था।।
जीवात्मा धरे जग भिन्न शरीरा। ध्रुव सत्य यही सखा मतिधीरा।।
धरि ध्यान धनंजय करहूँ विचारा।काहू न जन्म मरण अधिकारा।।

दो0– जो आये हैं वे जायेंगे जगसत्य यही क्यूं शोक।
रण छोड़ पार्थ कभी कोई मृत्यु को पाया नहीं रोक।7।

पार्थ न कछु जगत अविनाशी। मतिभ्रम सकल वीर बलराशी।।
ना होय वहीं जो तवमन भावा। पार्थ व्यर्थ अपि तव पछतावा।।
न रहे सदा सुख काहु के संगा। न रहे सदा हीं विपत्तिप्रसंगा।।
जिमिप्रकट ग्रीष्म करे शितनाशा।नहीं अमिट यह निशा प्रकाशा।।
कालचक्र गुण सदा परिवर्तन।निश्चित लोप जो दृश्य यहीक्षण।।
व्यथित न हो जगदूःख पाये। कदापि नही अति सुख हर्षाये।।
रहे सर्वदा अविचल नर नारी। है जीव वही मुक्ति अधिकारी।।
अस्तित्त्व सदा जाकर जगमाहीं। संत विचार सत् विसरे नाहीं।।
अनित्य क्षणिक नश्वर जग जोई। अर्जुन असत् लोक में सोई।।
असत्वस्तु की नहीं जगसत्ता। सत्त् की कबहूँ न घटे महत्ता।।

दो0–सत्त् असत्त् को घ्यान रख सब ज्ञानी करे विचार।
निर्णय स्पष्ट सत्त् करे यही तत्वज्ञानी व्यवहार।8।
दो0–अर्जुन जाके सीमांकन को न कोई शास्त्र प्रर्याप्त।
अविनाशी परमात्मा एक है जो रहे चराचर व्याप्त।9।

यही देह असत् हो निश्चित नाशा।देही सत् मुनि दृढ़विश्वासा।।
उठ करो युद्ध त्यागी मनमाया। भरतवंशी महाबली कुन्तीजाया।।
अनश्वर देही पार्थ है आत्मा। कबहूँ न मरे न मारे महात्मा।।
शरीरान्त आत्मा नही मरता।विश्वव्यापी परमसत्य यही भर्ता।।
शाश्वत अजन्मा नित्य पुरातन। पार्थ है आत्मा सत्य सनातन।।
जीवित प्राणी के निश्चित अन्ता।पार्थ कहे बहु भाँति मुनि संता।।
न जग जाके जन्म अवसाना। आत्मा अमरतत्व ज्ञानी जाना।।
आत्मा निर्लेप्य सर्वदा मृत्युहीना।कोई मार सके कब वीरप्रवीणा।।
जिमि जीर्ण परिधान के डारी। नूतन सुवसन धरत नर नारी।।
आत्मा छाड़ी पुरातन काया। धरे नूतन सकल प्रभु माया।।

दो0–पावक जाको न जला सके गला पाये नही नीर।
जाको पवन न सुखा सके वेध सके नहीं तीर।10।
दो0–जाको बुद्धि न जान सके देख पाये नही दृष्टि।
अचल सनातन आत्मा अद्भुत ईश्वर की सृष्टी।11।

दो0– शोक कबहू नही उचित आत्मा अचिन्त्य अव्यक्त।
कभी विकार इसमें नहीं क्यों होय शोक सन्तप्त।12।

पार्थ शोक का ना कछु कारण। नूतन तन आत्मा करे धारण।।
यदि आत्मा पड़े जन्म अबपाता। तबहूँ शोक से ना कोई नाता।।
जन्म जाके जग ताके अन्ता। जगसत्य यही पार्थ बलबन्ता।।
निश्चित जनम अपि अवपाता। निरूपाय विषय शोक तजभ्राता।।
जन्म पूर्व नही प्रकट शरीरा। जगसत्य यही सुनहूँ मतिधीरा।।
अवसान परे अपि लुप्त हो देहा। पार्थ करे क्यूं असीम सनेहा।।
जन्म मरण बीच प्रकटे काया। फिर केही हेतु शोक औ माया।।
आत्मा जगत अति विस्मयकारी। करे वर्णन ज्ञानी तत्त्व विचारी।।
सुनि अचरज कछु करे विचारा। कहे आत्मा है अगम अपारा।।
यत्नकरी अपि जान नही पाये। आत्मा अतिगूढ़ जग भरमाये।।

दो0–आत्मा सदा अवध्य है बसे सकल जीव देह।
शोक न कर अस देह का तजो सकल संदेह।13।

स्वधर्म स्मरण करो सब्यसाँची। धर्मयुद्ध क्षत्रियकर्म श्रुतिबाँची।।
पार्थ विषाद का ना कोई कारण। तुने किया क्षत्रिय कुलधारण।।
क्षत्रिय पाये जो धर्मयुद्ध अवसर। अति भाग्यवान पुनित धरापर।।
धर्मयुद्ध क्षत्रिय तजे जो देहा। मिले पावन स्वर्ग बिनु संदेहा।।
संशय व्यर्थ सब पार्थ तुम्हारा। धर्मयुद्ध खोलत है स्वर्ग द्वारा।।
यदि मोहित होय धर्मयुद्ध खोये। जगकृति नाशये पाप संजोये।।
कृतिबिसारी अपकृति जग गाये। अपकृति जगत काहु न भाये।।
मरण ते अधिक अपमान दुखदाई। धर्मयुद्ध सखा तुम्हरी भलाई।।
जाने जगत तुम्हरी प्रभुताई। तव वीरता की लोक बड़ाई।।
तजे युद्ध लिए शाँति आशा। भयभीत रणछोड़ कहिहें इतिहासा।।

दो0–स्वधर्म छोड़कर पार्थ कभी भी ना पायेगा चैन।
कृति अपि नष्ट होगी तेरी मोहन बोले मृदु बैन।14।
दो0–धर्मयुद्ध मुख मोड़ना क्षत्रिय हेतु महापाप।
अपकृति मरण ते दुखःदाई बने ये जीवन शाप।15।

रिपु करिहें तव शक्ति उपहासा। निन्दा करी करिहें परिहासा।।
परिहास पार्थ अत्यन्त दुखःदाई। त्यागी मोह करहुँ युद्ध भाई।।

धर्मयुद्धबलिदानी स्वर्ग करे बासा।जीती युद्ध जग आन्नदआशा।।
उभय परिणाम नही चिन्ताकारक।धर्मयुद्ध करहूँ हे धर्मउद्धारक।।
जय पराजय लाभ अपि हानि। सुखदुःख को सम जानेज्ञानी।।
करहूँ युद्ध राखी समभावा। धर्मयुद्ध है पाप अभावा।।
सांख्ययोग अपि ज्ञानयोग कहाये। सिद्ध ऋषि मुनिन के भाये।।
है देहि–देह स्वरूप गूढ़ ज्ञाना। ज्ञानयोग यही कहे धीमाना।।
समबुद्धि सांख्ययोग परिणीति। भ्रम मिटाई जन धारे नीति।।
सांख्य पार्थ अप्रकट वेद भाषा। प्रकट होई करे भ्रम नाशा।।

दो0–सांख्ययोग है पार्थ यही जो किया विषय व्याख्यान।
कर्मयोग विषय को सुनो सखा लगाकर ध्यान।16।

कर्मयोग पार्थ अति उत्तम युक्ति। दे कर्मबन्धन से अपि मुक्ति।।
कर्मयोग नही कर्मबीज नाशक। पार्थ यही फलदोष विनाशक।।
यदि कोई करे कर्मयोग प्रयासा। जनम मरण दुःख भय नाशा।।
कर्मयोगी विवेकी निश्चितबुद्धि। निष्काम कर्मरत विगत अशुद्धि।।
सकाम मनुज बुद्धि अनन्त शाखा।चित अस्थिर विवेकहीन भाषा।।
फल प्रशंसक कछु वेद वाणी। अज्ञानी भ्रमित करे मतिहानि।।
अल्पज्ञानी रखे फल से प्रीति। माने स्वर्ग परमप्राप्य कहे नीति।।
भोग एश्वर्य हेतु करे पाखण्डा। कहे मृदुवचन जोड़े भुजदण्ड़ा।।
मिथ्याभाषी कर्मकाण्ड करे नाना। निज प्रलाप करे वेद बखाना।।
भ्रमित चित्त उत्पन्न आसक्ति। हरे भ्रम निश्चयात्मक शक्ति।।

दो0–वेद धर्म को मानना पार्थ न अंधविश्वास।
मूढ़मति समझे नही करे वेद धर्म उपहास।17।
दो0–फल आसक्ति त्यागकर करे कर्म वेद अनुसार।
सदा समत्व का बोध हो कर्मयोग यही सार।18।

भौतिक जगत की त्रिगुण प्रकृति। सत्व रज तम कहे विभूति।।
त्रिगुण कार्यरूप भोग अरू साधन। वेद करे जिनका प्रतिपादन।
भौतिक आसक्ति त्रिगुण जाया। हर्ष–शोक द्वन्द्व त्रिगुणमाया।।
आसक्ति हो मनद्वन्द्व के कारण। करे मनुज योग–क्षेम धारण।।
अप्राप्त प्राप्ति योग कहे लोगा। भौतिक सकल संचय संयोगा।।
भौतिक संचित रक्षा आसक्ति। क्षेम व्यर्थ व्यतीत जन शक्ति।।

गुड़ाकेश सकल आसक्ति छोड़ो।योग क्षेम से अपि मुख मोड़ो।।
निजमन निर्द्वन्द्व कर प्रभुअधिना। अन्तर्मोह तजि बन स्वाधीना।।
पार्थ कहो कूप का क्या आशय। जब समीप पुर्णशुद्ध जलाशय।।
वेद कूपसम ब्रह्मज्ञान पुस्कर।ज्ञान अविनाशी भौतिकता नश्वर।।

दो0–कर्म क्रिया वर्तमान का इसलिए इसपर अधिकार।
कर्मफल भविष्य गर्भ बसे नहीं जान सके संसार।19।
दो0–कर्म कभी छोड़ो नहीं करी चिन्तन फल आश।
फल आसक्ति को तजो न रखो विशेष अभिलाष।20।
दो0–कर्म सिद्धि की खुशी नहीं न विकल कर्म अवरोध।
समभाव कर्मफल में रहे पार्थ समत्व यही बोध।21।

दीन कृपण फल हेतु विचारे। सकाम कर्म करे भय के मारे।।
क्षणिकयोग यह भौतिक संचय। नित्ययोग समबोध धनंजय।।
कर्मफल में न कबहूँ आसक्ति।समत्व बोध की यही शक्ति।।
दूर रखहूँ सदा अवर जो कर्मा। चैतन्य योग ही पार्थ है धर्मा।।
करहूँ समर्पण चित प्रभुपाही। दुःखसुख कछु उर राखउ नाहीं।।
करहूँ कर्म सम बोध उरधारी।कर्मयोग सकल जगत हितकारी।।
करे कर्म हो समबोध युक्ता। एही लोक में हो पाप मुक्ता।।
कर्मकुशलता पार्थ कर्मयोगा। करे कर्मबन्धन से जो वियोगा।।
आसक्ति पुनर्जन्म का कारण। ईच्छाबस तन करे जीव धारण।।
समत्व बुद्धि रखे यदि जगप्राणी। हो कर्मफल आसक्ति हानि।।
आसक्तिहीन कर्मयोग की युक्ति। पाये जनम मरण से मुक्ति।।

दो0–कर्म तेरा कर्तव्य है वर्तमान हेतु अनिवार्य।
फल चिन्ता छोड़कर करो आवश्यक कार्य।22।
दो0–कर्मफल चिन्तन भविष्य का क्यों बने कर्म आधार।
भविष्य पर ना अधिकार कभी करो सत्य स्वीकार।23।
दो0–समत्वबोध का शरण ले कर्मबन्धन मुक्ति उपाय।
कर्मकुशलता योग परम सत्कर्म सदा करवाय।24।

समबुद्धि पार्थ जब बने सहारा। बुद्धि करे तब मोह पंक पारा।।
भोग कथित इहलोक परलोका। कर्मफल वैराग्य मिटाये शोका।।
तब बदले लौकिक दृष्टिकोणा। पार्थ सुनो जग में जो सलोना।।

भविष्य सुना–जाना जो लौकिक।दृष्टिकोण बनजाये अलौकिक।।
लोक वचन अति भाँति विभाँति। मन विचलित करे दिन राती।।
विचलित मन समबुद्धि स्थिरा। शाँत मनुज ना होय अधीरा।।
धीर मन प्रतिफल है योगा। नित्य आत्म परमात्म संयोगा।।
पार्थ कहे मम् सखा विलक्षण। बतलायें स्थितप्रज्ञ लक्षण।।
कैसे करत स्थितप्रज्ञ संवादा। कैसे करे कर्म निर्बाही मर्यादा।।
कैसे फिरे कैसे हो स्थिरा। समबुद्धि मनुज कैसे सहे पीरा।।

दो0–भौतिक कामना त्याग करे रखे आत्म संतोष।
धनंजय स्थितप्रज्ञ वहीं जा उर भय न रोष।25।

न उद्वेग कभी शूल के पाये। न हर्षित जो सिद्धि मिल जाये।।
भयराग मुक्त जाके व्यवहारा। स्थितप्रज्ञ वहीं कहे मुनि विचारा।।
जाके शुभाशुभ सकल उदासीना। वहीं स्थितप्रज्ञ ज्ञानी प्रवीणा।।
न द्वेष रखे न करे कभी निन्दा।स्थितप्रज्ञ लक्षण कहत् मुनिन्दा।।
जिमी कछुआ निज अंग सिकोड़े। योगी तिमि विषय मुख मोड़े।।
यदि हो इन्द्रिय विषय से मुक्ता। तौ निश्चित चित शाँतियुक्ता।।
इन्द्रिय विषय आसक्ति त्यागा।स्थितप्रज्ञ वहीं पाय सौभागा।।
योगी करे परमात्म साक्षात्कारा।मिटे आसक्ति यही सिद्धविचारा।।
उत्तेजन प्रथमन इन्द्रिय लक्षण। इन्द्रजीत सदा आसक्ति भक्षण।।
नाश न जाके फल आसक्ति। इन्द्रिय बलात् हरे संकल्पशक्ति।।

दो0–इन्द्रिय सकल बस करी परमात्मा का धरी ध्यान।
बुद्धि जब हो स्थिर तो सुख–दुख लगे समान।26।
दो0–यदि चिन्तन हो विषय की उत्पन्न हो आसक्ति।
आसक्ति कामना प्रकट करे हो अधीर तव व्यक्ति।27।
दो0–कामना पूर्ति विघ्न पड़े तो प्रज्जवलित हो क्रोध।
क्रोध भ्रमित करे स्मृति उत्पन्न विचार अवरोध।28।

बुद्धिनाश सकल मनद्वन्द्व करावे।उचित अनुचित विचार भरमावे।।
जाके इन्द्रिय द्वेष राग विमुक्ता। नियंत्रित सर्वदा हो बुद्धियुक्ता।।
करे मनुज प्रकट स्पष्ट विचारा।परमात्मा कृपा अपि अपरंपारा।।
पार्थ सन्तुष्ट यदि अन्तर भावा। हृदय सकल हो शूल अभावा।।
कर्मयोगी सदा रहे प्रसन्नचिता। रहे बुद्धि सदा परमात्म स्थिता।।

जो जन इन्द्रिय मन नही जिता। कैसे करे जग कर्म पुनिता।।
इन्द्रियबस बुद्धि नही निश्चिता। विमुख भाव स्थिर नही चित्ता।।
अस्थिर चित्त जाये उलझन भ्रान्ति।असमानव जग पायेअशान्ति।।
शान्तिरहित जगसुख नही पावे। दुखी मनुज अपि जगभरमावे।।
विषयविचरण बुद्धि हरे कैसे।बुड़त जलयान तुफान में जैसे।।

दो0–सम्पूर्ण कामना त्याग करी रखे आत्म विश्वास।
न हो मृत्युभय विचलित न छोड़े जीवन आश।29।
दो0–कामना ही दुःख मूल है हो जीव इन्द्रिय अधीन।
जाके इन्द्रिय बस नही तो कैसे मनुज स्वाधीन।30।

जाके इन्द्रिय विषय पर निग्रह। पाये वह स्थिरमति अनुग्रह।।
पावन नश्वर लौकिक भोगा। सकल दिवस विचरे जगलोगा।।
चेष्टा करत सकल मुनिवृन्दा। मिले आनन्द मिटे जगद्वन्द्वा।।
परम विज्ञान स्वरूप परमेश्वर। भौतिक जग हर वस्तु नश्वर।।
दिवा करत सब लौकिक संचय। निशा करे योगक्षेम हेतु व्यय।।
संसारिक मनव हेतु जो रात्रि। स्थितप्रज्ञ हेतु निशा योगधात्री।।
वारिधी समात जिमि तारिणीनिरा।जलधी कबहूँ का होयअधिरा।।
वारिधी सरिता मिलन के भाँती। भोग स्थितप्रज्ञ नहीं सताती।।
जाको नही भौतिक भोग सतावे। जग वहीं मनुज मनशाँतिपावे।।
कामना छाड़ी करे जगहिता।मिटे मोहशूल मिली शाँतिपुनिता।।

दो0–स्पृहारहित ममतारहित अहंकार रहित जो लोग।
शान्ति रहे मन में सदा विचलित करे ना भोग।31।
दो0–योगी प्राप्त करे ब्रह्मको यदि मोह दूर हो जाये।
प्रयाणकरी जा ब्रह्ममिले ब्रह्मानन्द सुख पाये।32।

।। इति द्वितीय अध्याय।।

The second chapter of Srimadbhagwat Gita

The Essence

The second chapter of the Bhagavad Gita is known as Sankhya Yoga. Sankhya is the interpretation of Indian esoteric knowledge in symbolic form or language. Many scholars argue that the interpretation of esoteric knowledge through numbers is also referred to as Sankhya. For example, the number 1 represents Brahman, and the number thousand signifies the innumerable. In essence, Sankhya refers to the representation of esoteric knowledge in a simple form, making it easier to understand through contemplation. For the convenience of study, the chapter can be divided into five parts.

1.Arjuna's cowardice (verses 1-10): It is explained in the first chapter that Arjuna did not want to fight, and thus, he seated himself in the rear part of the chariot. Sanjaya narrated to Dhritarashtra that, seeing the tears in the eyes of the distressed Arjuna, Lord Shri Krishna asked him the reason for his confusion. He also explained that such behavior was unworthy of a great man, as it leads neither to success nor to heaven. This kind of behavior could be seen as a form of impotence. It was not the right conduct for Arjuna. Shri Krishna advised him to overcome the weakness of his heart and stand up to fight.

Upon hearing Shri Krishna's advice, Arjuna replied that figures like Guru Drona, Bhishma Pitamah, and others were his revered elders. He felt that it would be better to beg than to kill his respected relatives and inherit a blood-soaked kingdom. He expressed uncertainty about who would win the war. Dhritarashtra's sons were also my brothers, and he could not envision happiness in killing them. Arjuna confessed that he was suffering from indecision because he was not well-versed in matters of religion. He had now taken refuge in Shri Krishna and requested guidance on what was truly good for him. He admitted that he could not fathom a happiness that would outweigh the sorrow caused by the potential destruction, even if he were to gain a kingdom that was free of trouble, filled with wealth, and resembling heaven. Sanjaya told Dhritarashtra that Arjuna fell silent after making it clear that he would not fight.

Lord Veda-Vyas, in order to explain the profound subject of human religion to the common man, compiled the fundamental principles of life through Shri Krishna in a highly captivating way.

2. The first fundamental eternal principle of life – Immortality of the soul (Shloka 11-30):-Shri Krishna started laughing and said to Arjuna, "O Arjuna, you are speaking like a scholar, but you are mourning for those who are not worthy of your grief. There was never a time when I, you, or these kings did not exist, and there will never be a time when we will cease to exist. Just as a living being goes through childhood, youth, and old age, similarly the soul undergoes the experience of different bodies. Just as people endure cold and heat, so should you endure happiness and sorrow, for all these things are temporary; they come and go. Happiness and sorrow arise from the interaction of the senses with their objects. When the body and senses are impermanent, how can happiness and sorrow be permanent? There is no lack of proof for the reality of the soul. Temporary things have no true existence. In the eternal realm, only the soul exists, and it pervades the entire visible world. The entire visible world is the body of the immortal soul. The body is destructible, but the soul is indestructible. Therefore, you should fight."

"The soul neither dies nor kills; it neither takes birth nor dies. It is eternal. Just as a person discards old clothes and puts on new ones, the soul discards the old body and enters a new one. Weapons cannot cut it, fire cannot burn it, water cannot dissolve it, and air cannot dry it. The soul is invincible, eternal, and free from all defects."

(The immortality and integrity of the soul is the first fundamental and eternal principle of life in Indian Sanatan Dharma. Many

religions prevalent on Earth do not accept the existence of the soul within the body, yet they are unable to provide any universally accepted reasoning for the nonexistence of the soul according to their beliefs. This is because the soul is immaterial, and as such, it transcends worldly or physical arguments. Lord Shri Krishna, understanding that a non-physical concept like the soul cannot easily be comprehended by ordinary people, presented a physical perspective to explain it.)

Further Shri Krishna said, "If you believe that the soul takes birth and dies, then there is still no reason for grief, because this body did not exist before birth, and it will not exist after death. Both birth and death are certain and unavoidable, and we have no control over them. In reality, the soul is extraordinary; no one knows its true nature. The soul is a part of the universal God and is present in everyone's body. Therefore, you should not grieve."

(In the mortal, physical world, both birth and death of the body of any living being are certain, and no one has control over them. From this perspective, it is only the body that undergoes change from birth to death. This raises the question: who is it that inhabits the body? The entity that inhabits the body, which is not subject to physical changes, is called the soul. Therefore, no physical principles apply to the soul. The immortality and integrity of the soul is considered the first fundamental and eternal principle of life in Indian Sanatan Dharma.)

3. Second fundamental eternal principle of life – Adoption of own Virtue (Shloka 31-38):- Further, Lord Shri Krishna said, "If you are unable to understand the immortality of the soul, then you should consider your own virtue. You are a Kshatriya, and the virtue of a Kshatriya is to fight against injustice. Therefore, Dharmayuddha (righteous war) is your sacred duty. Only fortunate Kshatriyas gained the opportunity to participate in a war of Dharma. If you fail to fight this war according to your duty, you will lose your glory and commit a sin."

(The second fundamental principle of life is to act according to one's own virtue. Every living being has the ability to adopt virtues based on its nature, which is called Dharma.For example the natural virtue of water is its coolness, while the natural virtue of Fire is its hotness. Ordinary people may consider the path taken to seek the blessings of God as Dharma, but Dharma is not just the path; it is the ability to adopt the qualities of nature. Whenever Dharma is mentioned, thoughts of sin and righteous deeds come to mind. Actions that align with one's natural virtue are considered righteous deeds, while actions that contradict one's inherent nature are viewed as sinful. After explaining the immortality of the soul, Lord Shri Krishna reminds Arjuna of his Kshatriya Dharma. Since Dharma is also immaterial, Shri Krishna further explains Arjuna's duty in the context of worldly circumstances.)

Lord Shri Krishna then told Arjuna, "Leave aside the talk of holy deeds and sins. If you abandon the war, your enemies will ruin your reputation. It is said that dishonor is more painful than death. People will not think that you are leaving the war to establish peace; they will instead believe that you are fleeing out of fear. When your enemies criticize you, you will become distressed. Therefore, you should fight the war; this is in your best interest. If you are killed in a righteous war, you will attain heaven. And if you win, you will enjoy the prosperity of the earth. If you fight the war, considering victory and defeat, profit and loss, happiness and sorrow as equal, you will not commit a sin.

(Worldly matters are empirical, and their effects are easily perceived by a common person. Therefore, while explaining worldly matters to Arjuna, Shri Krishna tries to convince him that one who performs his duties according to his virtue does not commit a sin)

4. The third fundamental eternal principle of life – Selfless Action-Niskam Karma (Verse 39-53):- Lord Shri Krishna said, "The discussions mentioned above are matters of knowledge, which are only perceptible. Now, I will tell you about Karma – action, which is easily understandable. After understanding this, your perspective on sinful and holy deeds will change, and you will be liberated from the bondage of Karma. The concepts of sin and holy deeds are the causes of the bondage created by action. The inspiration behind any action plays a primary role in its performance. This inspiration is considered the seed of the action. According to religious scriptures, after any action, an outcome is always obtained. However, attachment to the outcome is considered the cause of sin. In selfless action, the initial seed of the action – the inspiration – remains undestroyed, while attachment to the result is absent, thus preventing the outcome from binding you. Even a small practice of selfless action protects one from the great fear of sin. In selfless action, the mind becomes self-sufficient.

(If any action is performed according to one's own virtue, extreme joy is experienced during the performance of the work, which leads to a lack of special interest in the joy obtained after the action is completed. Such an action is called Selfless action. For example, a singer experiences great joy while singing, and therefore, has no particular interest in the joy that comes from receiving respect or applause from the audience afterward. In this case, singing is a Selfless action for the singer. The person who performs selfless action is called a Karmayogi, someone who has no attachment to the outcome of the work.)

If the intellect is not determined, it tries to move in countless directions. Many Vedic texts have praised the outcome of actions, which create hallucinations, leading to attachment to the pleasures derived from the results of those actions. These texts often glorify material pleasures, even those found in heaven, making heaven seem like the ultimate goal for a distracted mind. However, a Karmayogi, who is not attached to the outcome of his actions, does not become entangled in these outcome-oriented pursuits and does not let his mind wander in endless directions. As a result, his mind remains focused, and since he is not caught in the cycle of *yoga* (the pursuit of unattained desires) and *kshema* (the protection of what has already been attained), his sense of right and wrong remains crystal clear. This clarity enables him to understand the eternal truth, i.e., Brahma. For one who knows Brahma, the purpose of the Vedas seems as insignificant as a small well in front of a vast ocean.

The ultimate truth is that everyone has authority only over their actions, not over the outcomes of those actions. Actions belong to the present, while the outcomes belong to the future, and no one can control the future. Therefore, performing actions with an equanimous mind, treating success and failure alike, is Karmayoga. The only way to protect everything in the right manner is by performing actions with proper understanding. Only then can one be freed from the bondage of sin and virtue, or the bondage of karma. This practice also leads to liberation from the cycle of birth and death.

When a person's intellect becomes focused with equanimity, they are freed from the swamp of attachment, and their intellect becomes stable. They will never be distracted from performing their duties. It is believed that a Karmayogi always meets God through his duty, which enables him to remain calm in every situation.

(According to Lord Shri Krishna, the person who performs their duty or selfless work with a concentrated mind, in alignment with their own virtue, is always free. Such a person never gets caught in the trap of sin and virtue; they are known as a Karmayogi.

The third fundamental principle of life is that one who performs selfless work is free from sin and virtue. In this way, Lord Shri Krishna, while explaining the three fundamental principles of life to Arjuna, tells him that war is beneficial for him. According to these principles, the body is mortal, one's virtue is the source of inspiration, and duty or selfless work done in accordance with one's virtue transcends the realm of sin and goodness. Therefore, fighting in the war of Mahabharata is beneficial for Arjuna, in accordance with his Kshatriya identity. Arjuna understands this truth, which leads him to express his eagerness to learn about a stable mind and Karmayogi.)

5. The apex of Karmyoga - To have a steady mind (Shloka 54-72):- It seems that Arjuna had begun to understand Karmayoga, so he now sought to understand the highest state of a Karmayogi—namely, a steady mind. He asked Lord Krishna about the characteristics of a steady mind: How does the steady mind speak? How does the steady mind sit? How does the steady mind walk, and so on?

Lord Shri Krishna described the nature of a steady mind in detail. He said that all desires of a person with a steady mind, in the form of bliss derived from the outcomes of their actions, are vanquished. As a result, such a person remains always satisfied, free from fear and anger, and unaffected by sorrow. Similarly, they do not become overexcited in happiness. A person with a steady mind is not involved in the dualities of this world—good and bad. They neither criticize nor praise others. A person of steady intellect is able to separate their senses from the objects of the senses, much like a tortoise withdraws its limbs from the external environment.

Many Yogis control their senses and free themselves from sensory objects, but they often fail to free themselves from attachment. However, a Karmayogi not only becomes free from sensory objects but also from attachment itself. They find greater joy in freedom from attachment than in the pleasures derived from sensory objects, which is why they no longer feel the need for such pleasures.

(Lust, anger, jealousy, hatred, happiness, sadness, etc., are all experiences of the mind resulting from the sensory organs. People with steady intellects are able to control both their mind and sensory organs. Ordinary people can, with some effort, control their senses, but they fail to rid themselves of attachment to the outcome. In contrast, people with steady intellects are also free from attachment to the results of their actions.)

Those who are attached to the outcomes of their actions have their intellect forcibly taken away by the senses. Despite their efforts, they are unable to control their senses. Therefore, when people with steady intellects meditate on God, they not only gain control over their senses but also become free from attachment.

When a person focuses on the senses, they become attached to the subject. This attachment leads to desire or lust. When obstacles arise in the fulfillment of desire, anger follows. Anger clouds the intellect, and when the intellect is clouded, delusions arise. Delusions prevent the intellect from functioning properly, and as a result, intellectual degradation begins. However, the person who is detached and controls their senses does not fall into delusion. Their intellect progresses toward liberation, and in this state, they also receive God's grace. As a result, they remain satisfied in all situations, with their attention fixed on God. Without such focus, however, they often remain restless, unable to experience true happiness. Without peace, happiness cannot even be imagined. A restless mind pulls away the intellect just as a hurricane sweeps a ship off course in the sea. Therefore, when a person's senses are under control, their intellect remains intact.

(Attachment is the desire for previously experienced sensual pleasures. Due to attachment, desire arises in the mind, and when those desires are unfulfilled, anger follows. Anger has the power to overwhelm the intellect, and any decision made in a state of anger is harmful. A person with steady wisdom is free from attachment. Therefore, they perform their duties in accordance with their virtue, with full awareness and without being swayed by emotions.)

Ordinary people wake up to attain material pleasures and sleep to recover from the fatigue of hard work done in pursuit of those pleasures. In contrast, those who have controlled their senses wake up to attain bliss, which comes from detachment from material pleasures. This is why it is said that when ordinary people sleep, Karmayogis are awake, and when ordinary people are awake, Karmayogis are asleep. The reason for this difference is that the goals of ordinary people and Karmayogis are not the same.

(The fundamental difference between Karmayogis and ordinary people is that ordinary people see material happiness as the ultimate result of their actions, while Karmayogis focus on the action itself, without attachment to its outcome. Even when performing the same actions, the intentions behind them differ. This is why their waking and sleeping times are not aligned.)

A person who is not swayed by desires, much like the ocean that remains unmoved despite the constant flow of rivers into it, attains supreme peace and bliss. However, those who constantly struggle to fulfill their desires remain restless and unhappy. Therefore, those who have renounced desires arising from the senses lose their ego and are the ones who can attain true bliss. This is the state of a supreme Yogi. Such Yogis remain undisturbed even at the time of their death, living in freedom throughout their lives and attaining liberation after death.

(Many Vedic texts describe various rituals to attain desired results. Ordinary people, distracted by these, get involved in many rituals hoping for rewards, but some of these rituals have neither a Vedic nor a scientific basis. These practices are often propagated by hypocrites and frauds, leading to no positive outcomes. However, Karmayogis remain unaffected by such false teachings.)

The Discussion

he Vedanta philosophy from the Indian tradition can be referenced. IThe 2nd Chapter of the Srimad Bhagavad Gita is considered to be a summary of the entire Gita. This chapter provides a spiritual analysis of the eternal principles of life. At the same time, most scholars believe that the Gita encapsulates the essence of the Upanishads, and many progressive thinkers seek to understand and analyze the spiritual knowledge contained in the Gita from a scientific erspective.To achieve this understanding, tndian Vedanta serves as a unique source for understanding the spiritual knowledge of India and its culture. It offers a scientific and philosophical analysis of ideas related to life. There is no inherent contradiction between science and spirituality in Vedanta; the only difference lies in the approach. Scientific analysis primarily focuses on the physical aspects, while spiritual analysis takes into account not only the physical but also the emotional dimensions.

Now, let us briefly explore the main topics discussed in Vedanta:

- **The God**
- **The Soul**
- **The Time**
- **The Nature**
- **The Action**

1.God – The Creator

Man has made significant progress in the field of science. In this scientific age, two main theories dominate: the ordinary physical theory and quantum theory. It is said that Max Planck, the originator of quantum theory, discussed in one of his lectures that there is a point in this vast universe where no scientific principles apply, and its properties cannot be tested using logical criteria. From a spiritual perspective, that point is the Supreme Consciousness, which spreads rays of consciousness all around it, much like the Sun. According to Vedanta, this Supreme Consciousness is the main source of life energy in the universe, but it is indescribable. This Supreme Consciousness is referred to as God or Parmatma also.

Indian scriptures tell us that Brahma, the creator, was the first to appear in the universe, at a time when nothing was visible. Brahma is composed of three fundamental spiritual elements:

- **Sat** (the element free from the bondage of eternal time),
- **Chit** (the element containing all knowledge),
- **Anand** (the element free from worries).

Brahma is the fundamental source of all visible and invisible vital energy in the universe. He is the cause of all causes, the main creator, and the controller. Ultimately, Brahma is the supreme consciousness of the universe. While beyond physical knowledge, his influence can be felt. Brahma is referred to as God.

In Indian scriptures, Lord Shiva, Maa Adishakti (Prakriti), and Vishnu are considered to exist before the origination of the universe. They are seen as the intangible forms of **Sat**, **Chit**, and **Anand**.

Based on scientific discoveries, the most widely accepted theory about the beginning of the universe is the Big Bang theory. However, this theory is based solely on physical experiments, whereas in the physical world, there is also life energy.

According to the tenth chapter of the Rigveda, the universe began with the appearance of Brahma after the division of the oval structure of Hiranya (the golden egg) into two parts. From a spiritual perspective, this is called the theory of the appearance of the great consciousness.

After the origination of Brahma, the gods, who possess divine qualities, appeared with different specialized duties. It is said that the number of gods is 33 Koti. In Sanskrit, the word *koti* means both "category" and "crore" (ten million), leading to confusion about whether the number of gods is 33 crores or if they have been divided into 33 categories.

According to a verse in the Atharvaveda (*यस्या त्रयस्त्रिदशम् देवाः अंगे सर्वसमाहिता* -Yasya Trayasyatridasham Devah Ange Sarvasamahita), it means these 33 categories of gods hold the world by the instruction of Brahma. The virtue of each category of gods is different, so they are considered to be 33 categories of gods.

A brief discussion of the categorization of the gods is as follows:

1.Physical Form: To give shape to every physical creation, eight basic divine elements are required. These elements form the eight gods:

1.Earth ,2.Water ,3.Fire ,4. Air ,5.Space or Sky, 6.Splendor (Sun) 7. Emotions (Moon) ,8.Thought (Stars)

These eight deities reside in every living being and are known as the Vasus *(बसु)*.

2.Spiritual Consciousness: In the Upanishads, the eleven Pranas (ten senses and one mind) are called **Ekadasha Rudra**. Every living being requires these eleven Rudras to stay connected with consciousness and remain alive. These Rudras (the ten senses and one mind) represent the active life force.

3.Lifespan: The lifespan of any living being on Earth is determined by the speed of the Earth. Due to this, living beings receive different types of energies at different times, represented by the 12 **Adityas**. These correspond to the twelve months the Earth takes to revolve around the Sun.

4.Sustainable Development: Food is necessary to sustain life, and rain and lightning (thunder) are required for the production of food. The god associated with rain and lightning is **Indra**.

5.Natural Balance: To preserve the creation of the universe and prevent complete destruction, it is necessary to maintain a natural balance. This process of creation and destruction must continue in harmony (like metabolism). The god responsible for this task is **Prajapati**.

Thus, the categories of Sanatan Gods are said to be 33 (8 + 11 + 12 + 1 + 1).

2)The Soul – Aatma

The soul is described in the second chapter of the **Shrimad Bhagavad Gita**, from verses 11 to 30. According to these verses, the soul resides in the body of all living beings. While the soul is immortal, the body is mortal. As long as the soul remains in the body, the body stays alive; when the soul departs, the body dies.

According to Vedanta, the basic spiritual elements of the soul are the same as those of God (**Sat-Chit-Anand**), but while God is infinite, the soul is very subtle. According to the theory of karma, the soul takes different bodies (in different forms of life, or *yonis*) to experience the outcomes of its actions. According to Vedanta, living beings are classified into two categories:

1. **Bhoga yoni** (the category of beings that experience enjoyment)
2. **Mukti yoni** (the category of beings that can attain liberation)

Human birth is considered a special birth, one that provides an opportunity to take steps toward salvation. This is because, in human form, the level of consciousness can be elevated. When the soul leaves the body, it continues its journey with the consciousness acquired during that lifetime. This acquired consciousness is referred to as *acquired wealth* in the **Shrimad Bhagavad Gita**. The qualities and behavior of a living being are based on the consciousness acquired at birth. Since the level of consciousness can only be improved during human life, human beings with high levels of consciousness are often regarded as divine.

From the above discussion, we can understand that the soul is a fundamental energy with the same basic components as God — **Sat**, **Chit**, and **Anand**. It possesses the power to hold consciousness because consciousness arises from the combination of these three elements. The level of consciousness differs in various living beings. According to Vedic theory, as described in the **Padmapurana**, there are 84 lakh (8.4 million) different species *(योनी)* of living beings in the world, which are classified as follows:

- Types of Plants: 2,000,000
- Types of Aquatic Living Beings: 900,000
- Types of Insects, etc.: 1,100,000
- Types of Animals: 3,000,000
- Types of Aerial Living Beings: 1,000,000

- Types of Humans: 400,000

Among these 84 lakh species, humans are considered to have the highest level of consciousness. Humans have the potential to elevate their level of consciousness through their actions and duties. The basic spiritual elements (**Sat**, **Chit**, and **Anand**) of all living beings and God are the same, which is why Lord Shri Krishna describes the soul as eternal, a part of **Parmatma** (the Supreme Soul).

The properties of the soul are described in the second chapter of the **Shrimad Bhagavad Gita**, where it is stated that the soul can neither be burnt by fire, nor melted by water, nor dried by air, nor harmed by any weapon. Just as the gods possess divine powers, other living beings also have certain powers. The soul's embodiment in a body follows the principle of cause and effect.

3)The Time

All bodies in the universe are in motion, and the knowledge of time is essential to measure the speed of any body. Modern science considers the beginning of time to be the moment of the Big Bang, whereas Vedanta views time as eternal. According to Vedanta, the cycle of creation and destruction of the universe continues endlessly, meaning there is no fixed point from which to measure the beginning of the universe.

In Indian spiritual texts, the familiar great unit of time is **Yuga**. According to this system, the one day of the Bramha is of one thousand mahayuga (1000x4320000 earth years), similarly one night of the Bramha is also equal to 1000 Mahayuga (i.e.1000x4320000 earth years) Thus one year of Bramha is equal to 360 bramha's day (i.e.360x2x4320000000 = 31104000000 = $311.04x10^{10}$ earth years) the lifespan of Brahma is considered as 100 Bramha year which is 311.04×10^{12} Earth years. During Brahma's lifespan, the universe remains in a manifested state. Scientific calculations suggest that the Big Bang occurred approximately 13.8 billion (13.8×10^{9}) years ago. However, according to Vedic views, half of Brahma's age has already passed, and we are currently in the seventh Manu period, with approximately 5,000 years having passed in the Kali Yuga. This implies that Brahma appeared approximately 155.522 trillion years ago, meaning the remaining age of the universe is approximately 155.518 trillion years.

4) Nature (Prikriti)

According to Vedanta, the conscious body is formed due to the union of nature and Purusha. The original form of nature is considered to be Adishakti, while the original form of consciousness is called Purushottam. However, according to the Advaita concept, nature and Purusha are not separate entities but are one and the same.

According to the *Shrimad Bhagavad Gita*, nature manifests in two forms:

- **Para Prakriti**: This is the unmanifested form of nature, as in to the wind energy present in the air.
- **Apara Prakriti**: This is the manifested or gross form of nature, like the physical body.

When the spiritual basic elements of the soul—Sat, Chit, and Ananda—are incorporated into these Para and Apara Prakriti, nature becomes conscious.

5) Karma (The Action)

There is a definite reason for the conscious soul to take a body. And when the conscious soul assumes a body, it must perform actions to survive. Indian sages have described human karma (action) as being of three types:

- **Karma for nourishing the body**
- **Karma to increase the level of consciousness**
- **Karma as the prime duty**: This includes repaying the debt of natural gifts (Marti Rina - Debt to Nature), social gifts

(Pitri Rina Debt to Ancestors), and the attainment of knowledge (Guru Rina - Debt to the Teacher).

According to Vedanta, humans are the only creatures capable of improving the level of their consciousness through their actions. When the level of consciousness increases to a certain extent, the person is considered to have steady wisdom. Upon attaining this state of steady wisdom, the individual becomes free from the bondage of karma.

Now, summarizing the main topics of Vedanta mentioned above, let us try to understand the essence of the second chapter of the *Shrimad Bhagavad Gita*. This chapter is the first to address the profound question of Arjuna: "Is it beneficial for Arjuna to fight or not to fight the war?"

To answer this question, Lord Krishna reveals the fundamental theory of life, because understanding these basic principles allows a person to make decisions independently. The three fundamental principles of life are as follows:

1.Soul is immortal and body is perishable.

After this analysis of the soul and body, many wise individuals argue that if the soul is immortal, then killing someone does not lead to death. Therefore, if Arjuna fights, the life of the person he is concerned about is not a matter of worry. This may seem logical, but it cannot be considered practical. If this argument were accepted, people would not regard killing for personal as murder.

According to Chapter 16 of the *Shrimad Bhagavad Gita*, those endowed with divine qualities follow non-violence. So, how can violence in war be considered dharma? No one benefits from war—neither the winner nor the loser—because war is inherently destructive. So, what is the justification for Lord Shri Krishna repeatedly advising Arjuna to fight by presenting knowledge about the soul in the *Shrimad Bhagavad Gita*?

According to many learned scholars, the knowledge of the soul has nothing to do with war. Lord Shri Krishna spoke to Arjuna about the soul to make him realize that his attachment is not to the eternal soul, but to the perishable body. The knowledge of the soul is never intended to justify the war.

2.Practice of one's own religion is beyond the limits of sin and good virtue: From a practical point of view, a destructive war is not necessary for social gain. However, strength is essential to prevent social disorder. The revered national poet Ramdhari Singh Dinkar has written in his famous poem *Shakti aur Kshama* that:

सहनशीलता, क्षमा, दया को तभी पूजता जग है।
बल का दर्प चमकता उसके पीछे जब जगमग है।।
सच पूछो, तो शर में ही बसती है दीप्ती विनय की ।
सन्धि वचन सम्पूज्य उसी का जिसमें शक्ति विजय की ।।

It means the world respects tolerance, forgiveness, and kindness only when the power of a person shines behind them. In fact, it is the power that enables humility to emerge (i.e., everyone respects a person who has the capacity to win).

Maintaining social order is the Kshatriya Dharma. Therefore, Lord Krishna reminded Arjuna of his Kshatriya Dharma, so that Arjuna could decide for himself whether to fight or not, based on the present situation.

3.Those who perform nishkam karma are not attached to the outcome of their actions:-

Lord Shri Krishna told Arjuna that it is necessary to perform one's duty according to their own virtue, with full concentration, which leads to selfless action. Selfless action removes attachment to the outcome. A person who is able to perform selfless action is called Sthitapragya or Karmayogi.

The teachings of the second chapter of the Shrimad Bhagwat Gita are capable of guiding a common person today to control mental conflicts by understanding the fundamental principles of life. Those who have not read the Shrimad Bhagwat Gita often believe it only addresses the soul. However, the truth is that the Shrimad Bhagwat Gita enhances a person's ability to make the right decisions in adverse circumstances.

The Conclusion

In the first chapter of the Srimad Bhagavad Gita, we saw that a dilemma arose in Arjuna's mind about whether it was right to fight in the war. The basic reason for his dilemma was his concern over the consequences of the war, especially the impact it would have on innocent women and children. From this perspective, war could never be seen as advantageous; it is also considered a sin from a religious point of view. Arjuna was confused, and after some deliberation, he asked his charioteer and friend, Shri Krishna, for advice on whether it was right or wrong for him to fight.

To answer Arjuna's question, Lord Krishna first described the three fundamental principles of life. These principles, which form the foundation of Sanatan Dharma, can be summarized as:

1. Immortality of the soul
2. Triguna-borne Swadharma (the inherent nature of a person's duty based on their qualities)
3. Selfless action

At the end of this chapter, Lord Krishna explains the characteristics of a Karmayogi, or a person of steady wisdom.

Through this explanation, Arjuna understood the three fundamental life principles of Sanatan Dharma. He also realized that the ultimate goal of religious life is to become a person of steady wisdom.

However, Arjuna was still confused about Lord Krishna's motivation for encouraging him to fight in the war. He wondered if the attainment of steady wisdom could be achieved through knowledge alone, then what was the need for a destructive war?

The clarification of this confusion in Arjuna's mind is presented in the next chapter.

-: Om Tat Sat:-

****

मति मम भ्रमित शुभ्रता इच्छा। शिष्य तुम्हार प्रभु दीजै शिक्षा।।

Chapter-3
The Karmayoga

The Third chapter of Srimadbhagwat Gita at a glance	
Total Nos of verses	43
Nos of verses by lord Shree Krishna	40
Nos of verses by Arjuna	3
Nos of verses by sanjay	0
Nos of verses by Dritrastra	0
Main theam of the Chapter	Philosophy of actions

श्री गणेशाय नमः

श्लोकः

पितासि लोकस्य चराचरस्य,
त्वमस्य पूज्यश्च गुरुर्गरीयान्।
न त्वत्समो सत्यभ्यमधिकः
कुतोन्योलोक त्रयेप्यप्रतिमप्रभाव।।

दो0–अतिभ्रमित अर्जुन भये सुनी ज्ञान कर्म की रीत।
ज्ञान कर्म से श्रेष्ठ तो क्यूं करूं युद्ध विपरीत।1।
दो0– योगेश्वर युक्ति बता हो जामे सकल कल्याण।
शस्त्र उठाकर युद्ध करूं या धरूं प्रभु का ध्यान।।2।।

कह हृषीकेशहे वीर धनुर्धर। ज्ञान कर्म द्वो साधन सुन्दर।।
सांख्ययोगी निज ज्ञान अपनाये। ज्ञान सकल जीव मोक्षउपाय।।
कर्मयोगी करे कर्म व्यवहारा। कर्म स्थितप्रज्ञ साधन न्यारा।।
प्राणी जो कोई कर्म न करता। कैसे पाये वह निष्कर्मता।।
कर्मत्यागी कभी पाये न सिद्धि। बिना कर्म न अपि ज्ञानबृद्धि।।
परवश जीव प्रकृति के कारण। देह करे प्राकृत गुणधारण।।
रहे नहीं जीव क्षण बिन कर्मा। प्रकृति जनित कर्म जग धर्मा।।
हठीइन्द्रियरोधी विषय मनभारी। वह ढोंगी मूढ़मति मिथ्याचारी।।
मन रखे यदि इन्द्रिय नियंत्रण। है योगी कर्म सदा शुभमंत्रण।।

कर्म करे निजज्ञान की वृद्धि। बिना कर्म न हो कर्मसिद्धि।।

दो0–कर्म हेतु है तन मिला कर शास्त्र विहित सतकर्म।
कर्म छाड़ी कल्याण कहाँ ना निर्बहे अपि देहधर्म।4।
दो0–बिना कर्म जग में कोई नहीं हुआ कभी प्रसिद्ध।
कर्म पहचान है जिवन का देव दानव मुनिसिद्ध।5।
दो0–कर्तव्यकर्म है यज्ञसम जो करे आसक्ति विहीन।
कर्तव्यकर्म जो मनुज करे हो कर्मबन्धन क्षीण।6।

कर्तव्यकर्म जाको नही भावा। कर्मबन्धन पड़ी वह पछतावा।।
कहे प्रजापति अतिहित बचना। सयज्ञ किये जबही जगरचना।।
यज्ञ है जगत उन्नति प्रदाता। यज्ञ सदा वांक्षित फल दाता।।
यज्ञ उन्नत करे देव संवृद्धि। देवन्ह करे मनोकामना सिद्धि।।
परस्पर देव मनुज करे वृद्धि। मंगलकारी यज्ञ देत प्रसिद्धि।।
संवृद्धि देव कृपा बिनु अन्तर। पाये जीव सदा वांक्षित वर।।
प्राकृतिकभोग बिनयज्ञ जो पाये।अस मानव हीं चोर कहलाये।।
यज्ञ अवशिष्ट भोग जाको भाये।सब पापन्ह ते मुक्त हो जाये।।
स्वार्थ हेतु बिनयज्ञ जो खाता।जग में वहीं पापी कहलाये।।
सकल प्राणी के अन्न आधारा। अन्न निमित जल वर्षा धारा।।
जगयज्ञ अपि मेघवर्षा कारण। बिना यज्ञ नहीं पाप निवारण।।

दो0–अन्न न उपजे मेघ बिना मेघ हेतु कर यज्ञ।
बिना यज्ञ बस चोर जिये कहे ऋषि मुनि सर्वज्ञ।7।
दो0–ब्रह्म बसतें यज्ञ में रचते विपुल सृष्टी का चक्र।
मूढ़ प्राणि बिन यज्ञ जिये रहे पूर्ण जीवन सुखवक्र।8।

है वेद अविनाशी ब्रह्म संतति। कर्म समुदाय है वेद व्युत्पति।।
व्याप्त सकल जगत सुखराशि। यज्ञ प्रतिष्ठित ब्रह्म अविनाशी।।
यज्ञ करे सृष्टीचक्र अनुकूला। रहे आत्मतृप्त जीवन बिनशूला।।
आत्मरमण संतुष्ट जग जोई। अस मनुज हेतु कर्तव्य न कोई।।
असमनुज हेतु न कर्म अभिप्राया।असकर्म देखी जगतभरमाया।।
निःस्वार्थ माने कुटुम्ब वसुधैवा। हो कर्तव्यकर्म परमात्मासेवा।।
गुडाकेश एही सत्य अभ्यंतर। निरासक्त करे जगकर्म निरंतर।।
कर्म अनासक्त की करे बृद्धि।जनकादिक कर्म से पाये सिद्धि।।

कर्तव्यकर्म के लोक गुण गाये। सब शुभअशुभ की शिक्षापाये।।
कर्तव्यकर्म सदा हो भक्तिमय। करो कर्म छाड़ि जग विनिमय।।

दो0—श्रेष्ठ पुरुष का आचरण अरू उत्तम व्यवहार।
श्रेष्ठ पुरुष कर्तव्यकर्म अनुसरण करे संसार।9।

पार्थ प्राप्य मोहे सकल संसारा। तौ जग मैं प्रकटूँ बारम्बारा।।
मम अनुसरण करे जग प्राणि। छोडूँ कर्म तो हो बड़ हानी।।
त्याग जो मैं करूं कर्म व्यापारा। हो नष्टभ्रष्ट जगजीवनसारा।।
कहलाऊँ मैं अपि धर्म विनाशक। सकल जीवसंकरता भाषक।।
आसक्त होई कर्म करे जो कोई।आसक्तिरहित ज्ञानी करेसोई।।
शास्त्रविहित अपि संग्रह कर्मा। करे अज्ञानी आसक्ति उरमर्मा।।
अनासक्त निजधर्म बस पाले। ज्ञानी कबहूँ न कछु भ्रम डाले।।
ज्ञानी कर्तव्यकर्म ज्यों करहीं। अज्ञानी सकल ताके अनुसरहीं।।
सम्पूर्णकर्म प्रकृतिगुण जनिता। त्रिगुण मायाबस है जगभ्रमिता।।
पंचभूत पार्थ अपि त्रिगुणमाया।त्रिगुणप्रेरित हीं कर्म करे काया।।

दो0—पंचभूत मन बुद्धि अपि अहंकार ज्ञानेन्द्रि पाँच।
पाँच कमेन्द्रिय तत्त्व सकल गुण विभाग के साँच।10।
दो0—माया गुणविभाग प्रेरित करे जग कर्म अनन्त।
कर्म चेष्टा ही कर्म विभाग जाने ज्ञानी मुनि संत।11।
दो0—सत् रज् तम है त्रिगुण जो करे प्रभावित कर्म।
ज्ञानी जाने गुढ़ता अनासक्त निर्बाहे निजधर्म।12।

कर्म करे मूढ़ धरि निजहिता। ज्ञानी कबहूँ ना करे विचलिता।।
प्रकृतिगुण मोहित होए अज्ञानी।करे कर्म स्वयं को कर्ताजानी।।
आत्मा पर हो न त्रिगुण प्रभावा।तत्त्वज्ञान यही श्रुति सबगावा।।
यह क्षणिक देह पावे अमरात्मा।संसय तज युद्ध करो महात्मा।।
करो कर्म त्यागी फल आशा। तज मायाबन्धन जनित निराशा।।
तन मन कर कर्तव्य समर्पण। कर्मफल कर सदा प्रभु अर्पण।।
सतकर्म रखी चित्त अन्तर्यामी। फल निश्चित करे जगस्वामी।।
सत्कर्म जग पुनित है युक्ति। कर्मबन्धनसे रहे चिन्तामुक्ति।।
फलत्याग विचारी कर्म नर करहीं।कर्मबन्धन में कबहूं नपरहीं।।
हो जाके नहीं निजकर्म भरोसा।वही अज्ञानी चिन्तनयुक्तदोषा।।

दो0—जो माने निज को कर्ता समझ उसे चितभ्रष्ट।
अज्ञानी मोहित अति व्यथित वही चेतना नष्ट।13।
दो0—पार्थ ध्यान करो प्रभु का उर चित करके शुद्ध।
मोह शोक को त्यागकर सव्यसाँची कर युद्ध।14।

प्रकृतिवश कर्म करे सब कोई। सब ज्ञानी मूढ़ प्रकृतिवश होई।।
हठ प्रकृति कोई बदल न पाये। हठी मूढ़ विनष्ट हो जाये।।
इन्द्रिय करे निजविषय के गोचर।रागद्वेष बसे इन्द्रिय अगोचर।।
जाकर मन इन्द्रियवश होई। निजहित अपि कर सके न सोई।।
रागद्वेष मनु शत्रु प्रचण्डा। हितपथ यही हैं विघ्न अखण्डा।।
परधर्म प्रतीत जो हो गुणवाना। परधर्म धारी न हो कल्याणा।।
निज धर्मोचित मरण हितकारी। परधर्म पार्थ सदा भयकारी।।
पार्थ चकित कहे सखा मुरारी। मोको होत संशय अतिभारी।।
प्रकृतिवश कर्म करे सबकोई। सकल कल्याणकारी जग होई।।
मनुज पाप हैं किससे प्रेरित। न कबहूँ करे जो जग का हित।।

दो0—किससे प्रेरित हो करके मनुज करत जग पाप।
कहे अर्जुन ह्रषीकेशसे प्रभु भ्रम दूर करें आप।15।
दो0—कह भगवन हे पार्थ सुनो रजस उत्पन्न हैं काम।
काम विघ्नजनित संवेग क्रोध सकल पाप मूलधाम।16।

क्रोध सकल मानव सुख खाता। वैरी कदापि तृप्ती नही पाता।।
जिमि दपर्ण हो रेणु अच्छादित्।तिमि काम ढके ज्ञान मर्यादित।।
कामातुर ज्ञान करे जीव मोहिता।करे कर्म हो जामें निजहिता।।
इन्द्रिय मन काम वास स्थाना। करे भ्रमित बुद्धि विधि नाना।।
भ्रमित बुद्धि विफलता कारण। विफलता क्रोधरूप करे धारण।।
काम जगत में अत्यन्त पापी। विज्ञान विनाशक हैं सर्वव्यापी।।
धरे काम मोहिनी रूप अनेका।हरे ज्ञान बुद्धि अरू कर्मविवेका।।
जग पापी दुष्ट कामना सारी। ज्ञान सशंकित भ्रमित मनभारी।।
कामदमन पार्थ सच्चीवीरता। कर्मयोगीकभी न छोडे धीरता।।
करे पाप मनुज काम के कारण। कामत्याग अपि पापनिवारण।।

दो0— देहस्थूल इन्द्रिय सूक्ष्म हे पार्थ विशिष्ठ विज्ञान।
है मन इन्द्रियों से परे अति सूक्ष्म महाँबलवान।17।

दो0– बुद्धि मन से बलशाली मन का करता है नियंत्रण।
आत्मा बुद्धि से है अपर दे दिग्दर्शक शुभमंत्रण।18।
दो0–अति श्रेष्ठ हैं आत्मा अतिसूक्ष्म सबसे बलवान।
आत्मबल प्रयोग से हो सकल जगत कल्याण।19।
दो0–आत्मबल करे बुद्धि नियंत्रण बुद्धि मन अधिकार।
मन इन्द्रिय वश में कर करो दुर्जय काम संहार।20।

।। इति तृतीय अध्याय।।

The Third chapter of SrimadbhagvatGita

The Essence

The third chapter of the Srimad Bhagavad Gita, which contains 43 verses, is known as Karmayoga. For the convenience of study, it can be divided into five parts..

1. Anasakta Bhaav- Emotional Detachment (Verse 1-8)

In the second chapter, Shri Krishna described the three fundamental principles of life: first, knowledge; second, self-religion (one's own virtues); and finally, karma. He advised Arjuna to become a Sthitapragya or Karmayogi. However, Arjuna was confused about action and renunciation. Therefore, he requested Shri Krishna to clarify the relationship between renunciation and action, and to tell him which one is more advantageous.

Lord Shri Krishna explained that both renunciation and action are equally valuable; it depends on the devotion. A Sankhya Yogi uses knowledge as a means of salvation but does not cease from performing action. On the other hand, a Karmayogi uses selfless action as a means of salvation, and through action, his knowledge also increases, leading to the attainment of the state of non-action. Therefore, the state of non-action cannot be achieved without first engaging in action. The truth is that, due to natural reasons, man cannot remain without performing karma, even for a moment.

(Karma (The action with trouble) and akarma (The action with joy) may appear to be the same on the surface, but there is a significant difference between the two. In the state of karma, the doer remains troubled due to worries about the outcome of the action. However, in the state of akarma, the doer is not concerned with the result of the action and thus experiences immense joy while performing the action itself.To better understand the difference between karma and akarma, consider an illustrative example: If a child does not know how to swim, he will fear drowning and will be reluctant to swim. But if the same child learns how to swim, he will experience joy while swimming. Before learning how to swim, swimming was an a karma for the child, but after learning, swimming it becomes akarma for him.This example illustrates that by performing karma, knowledge increases, which transforms the action into akarma. As a result, one experiences pleasure even while engaged in action.)

Lord Krishna further explained that each of the senses in the body has its specific subject. Some hypocrites restrain their senses by force but continue to think about their objects of desire. However, the best Karmayogi is the one who controls their senses with their mind and remains detached from their objects. Therefore, if one seeks true welfare, it is not achieved by renouncing work but by performing one's duty with detachment (i.e., selfless action). Without work, even the survival of the body is not possible.

(Practically, our body consists of 11 senses, each with distinct subjects:

- Five sense organs:
    - Eyes – Seeing
    - Tongue – Tasting
    - Ears – Hearing
    - Skin – Touching
    - Nose – Smelling

- Five action organs:
    - Speech organ – The mouth
    - Action organ – The hands
    - Feet – The legs
    - Anus – Excretion
    - Sub-sensory organ – The penis
- One mind

Each of these organs has its specific function, and the role of the mind is to control the sensations received from the sense organs and direct them to the action organs for execution. The mind itself, however, is governed by the intellect, which is responsible for its control. Many people use their intellect to control the mind, thereby managing the impulses of their sense organs. Yet, even with this control, they may remain attached to the objects of desire.

A question naturally arises: How attachment is different from the senses . And how it can be controlled by the mind? To understand this, consider the following example: Suppose you are standing in a flower garden, admiring a beautiful bunch of flowers. The sight of the flowers gives you joy. You can stop yourself from seeing the flowers by closing your eyes or leaving the garden, but you cannot erase the memory of the joy you experienced. This lingering joy, derived from the earlier experience of the flowers, falls under the category of attachment.

3. **Selfless Duty** (Shloka 9-16)

Lord Shri Krishna explains that all actions, except those performed for the sake of Yajna (selfless duty or sacrifice), bind a person to the cycle of karma. Therefore, one must perform Yajna without attachment. At the beginning of creation (Kalpa), Prajapati Brahma created humanity along with the concept of Yajna and established a principle: through Yajna, humans strengthen the gods, and in return, the gods provide the desired pleasures and sustenance to the

Yajna performers. This mutual cooperation uplifts both humans and gods.

If someone seeks pleasure without performing Yajna, they are akin to a thief. Those who consume natural resources responsibly, as if partaking in the leftovers of a Yajna (Prasad), are freed from sin. However, those who exploit natural resources for selfish purposes are sinners.

For the nourishment of living beings, food is essential, and food depends on rain. Rain, in turn, is sustained by the balance of natural resources, which requires Yajna or sustainable development practices. Yajna itself is rooted in knowledge, and knowledge is contained in the Vedas. The Vedas originate from Brahma, indicating that Brahma is established in Yajna (sustainable, selfless action).

Thus, a person who does not perform their duties as a Yajna is considered a sinner, and their life is deemed meaningless. By emphasizing the interdependence between humanity, nature, and divine forces, Lord Krishna highlights the importance of selfless action and sustainable living.

(Yajna and Selfless Duty :-Lord Shri Krishna clearly explained to Arjuna that Prajapati Brahma created humanity along with Yajna. Here, Yajna signifies good deeds—sustainable development work. Sustainable development work refers to actions undertaken for the welfare of all, ensuring no harm to anyone. Yajna holds immense significance in Sanatan Dharma, encompassing many forms, which Shri Krishna elaborates upon in detail in the subsequent chapters. The actions performed in the spirit of Yajna are known as selfless duties. In other words, human life is enriched by various forms of direct and indirect support, such as knowledge, social connections, and natural resources (like water and air). These elements contribute to a happy and fulfilling life. Therefore, it is every individual's duty to respect these supports and carry out their work in a manner that avoids causing harm to them.

Sanatan Dharma believes that every person receives three essential forms of support—natural support, social support, and knowledge. However, this support is not considered free; it comes with a responsibility to give back, which is understood as a debt. These debts are classified as:

1. *Debt to God (Natural Support)*
2. *Debt to Guru (Knowledge)*
3. *Debt to Ancestors (Social Support)*

Actions undertaken with an awareness of these debts and a commitment to repaying them are considered Yajna. This principle emphasizes the importance of gratitude and responsible living as integral aspects of selfless duty.)

3. The need for work for public welfare (Shloka 17-24) :-In our society, a common belief persists: if life itself is temporary, what is the need for public welfare? Based on this reasoning, some argue there is no necessity to work for the greater good, and that one should focus solely on personal benefit. However, in this chapter, Shri Krishna emphasizes the importance of actions performed for public welfare.

For a person who is self-satisfied with their achievements, Yajna (selfless duty) may not appear necessary. Such a person, being free from attachment, may feel disinterested in selfless work, as actions or their results do not affect them. However, selfless work performed without attachment enhances a person's level of consciousness, ultimately leading to the realization of supreme truth. For instance, wise individuals like Janaka achieved supreme success by performing their duties without attachment.

The ability to act without attachment is not something that develops suddenly. As individuals perform their duties, their understanding and knowledge grow progressively. It is the responsibility of the wise to inspire others to act, as engaging in action is far superior to remaining inactive. Ordinary people tend to emulate the behavior of great individuals.

Explaining this, Lord Shri Krishna stated that although He has everything in this world and needs nothing, He still performs actions. If He refrained from action, ordinary people would follow His example, leading to widespread corruption and the destruction of the human race, ultimately causing immense suffering to the world.

While many people perform actions for the welfare of others, Shri Krishna highlights that performing actions, even in such cases, holds greater significance than refraining from them. This is because engaging in action leads to accomplishment. Moreover, the knowledge acquired through the process of performing actions elevates them to the state of *akarma*, where attachment dissolves naturally, and one experiences liberation from the binding effects of action.

(The work performed for the welfare of others does not fall into the category of sin, as such actions do not cause harm to anyone. Work is simply work, whether it is undertaken with the desire for salvation or as a worldly endeavor aimed at the welfare of society.)

4. **Ignorant and Knowledgeable (Shloka 25 - 35)**

The learned sages of Sanatan Dharma believe that ignorance binds a person to their actions, causing attachment. In contrast, the wise perform their duties without attachment. Lord Shri Krishna explained to Arjuna that the tasks undertaken by the ignorant for the welfare of society should similarly be performed by the wise—yet without attachment. This approach ensures that the ignorant remain free from confusion and continue to have faith in their work.

In reality, people act according to their inherent natural qualities (Sattva, Rajas, and Tamas). The wise understand this truth and recognize that they are not the true doers. However, the ignorant, unaware of this reality, develop attachment to their actions and perceive themselves as the sole agents of their deeds. This distinction is why the wise remain unattached, while the ignorant become entangled in their actions.

Shri Krishna further explained that attachment stems from ignorance. Therefore, Arjuna was advised to act in accordance with his virtues and fight without attachment. The simplest way to achieve this is by surrendering all actions to Krishna and performing one's duties without worry. A person who acts in this manner remains free from the bondage of karma. Conversely, those who perceive themselves as the doer, due to ignorance, fall into delusion and suffer destruction instead of liberation.

Since all beings act according to their innate natural qualities, whether wise or ignorant, stubborn resistance serves no purpose. Every sense organ of the body is drawn to its respective subjects, which are influenced by love and hatred. These two forces (love and hatred) are the greatest obstacles to a person's welfare, as they seek to dominate and distract the mind.

A person's inherent natural qualities define their Dharma. One's own natural Dharma (Svadharma) is always beneficial and aligned with their well-being. Adopting the Dharma of another, even if it appears virtuous, is not truly beneficial and can be perilous. Imitating the Dharma of others leads to confusion and harm. The wise recognize that acting in harmony with their natural Dharma is the path of wisdom, while the ignorant either remain unaware of their Dharma or disregard it as insignificant, attempting instead to adopt the Dharma of others.

4. **Cause of Sin (Shloka 36 - 43) :-**A question arises in Arjuna's mind: if all individuals act according to their Dharma, determined by their inherent qualities (Triguna), then what leads them to commit sin? To this, Lord Shri Krishna explains that people dominated by *Rajo Guna* are often driven by intense desires. These

desires are insatiable, no matter how much enjoyment they receive. When such desires are obstructed, anger arises within them. This anger clouds their judgment and knowledge, just as smoke obscures fire or dust covers a mirror.Desires and anger reside in the mind, senses, and intellect. When these faculties are influenced by anger, they deviate from their natural Dharma. This deviation results in sinful actions, which cause suffering not only to others but also to oneself. Lust is considered the root cause of sin and is described as a formidable adversary, difficult to control. However, Shri Krishna emphasizes that it is not impossible for humans to conquer this enemy.

The conscious human body possesses the capability to control lust, and its components are arranged in an increasing order of strength and control:

The Gross Body<The Sense Organs<The Mind<The Intellect<The Soul

Lust, the invincible foe residing in the senses, mind, and intellect, can be subdued through the superior power of the soul. By realizing the supreme soul and aligning oneself with its higher wisdom, one can effectively control this enemy. Just as the intellect governs the mind, so as well the power of the soul can govern the intellect. Therefore, one who successfully controls their lust will not commit sins, as they will remain in harmony with their natural Dharma.

(The primary cause of sins or wrongful deeds in the world is anger, which arises when a man's desires are obstructed. In this scientific era, anger is often classified as a form of mental instability, leading to a man's own suffering. There is, however, only one effective remedy for such mental instability: meditation. Lord Krishna advised Arjuna that the simplest way to overcome lust is to dedicate all actions to God. By doing so, one eliminates both the sense of guilt and attachment to the outcomes of those actions.)

The Discussion

In this chapter, Arjuna's two crucial questions are discussed:

1. *If knowledge is superior to action, why is Shri Krishna asking him to fight instead of embracing sannyas (renunciation)?*
2. *If man's actions are governed by his nature, why does he commit sin?*

In response to the first question, Lord Krishna clarified that both knowledge and action are equally significant. Their application depends on an individual's devotion and nature. Action performed in alignment with one's devotion is referred to as *Swadharma.* Therefore, to fully understand Shri Krishna's response to Arjuna, it is essential to delve into the concept of *Swadharma.*This explanation emphasizes that knowledge and action complement each other, and one must act according to their inherent nature and abilities while progressing on the path of self-realization.

Swadharma: In common understanding, *Swadharma* refers to one's own religion, which a person inherits from society due to their birth. However, many scholars consider this type of social religion more as a sect rather than a true religion. For instance, if a child is born into a Hindu family, he or she may consider themselves a Hindu by religion. Hence, when a Hindu is asked about their *Swadharma*, they may say it is Hinduism.

In the *Shrimad Bhagavad Gita*, *Swadharma* refers to the natural qualities (Satva, Rajas, and Tamas) inherent in every person. In this chapter, Shri Krishna explains that sometimes other religions may seem more appealing than one's own *Swadharma.* For example, a person with a Tamasic nature might be drawn to a Rajasic nature. However, no matter how attractive another path may seem, it is difficult to adopt it because, according to our own nature, we cannot fully embrace the virtues of another person's way. This is why adopting another's religion or way of life is said to be perilous. The truth is, we often do not fully understand the virtues of other beliefs, as each person's capacity to accept their inherent nature is different. Trying to adopt another's way often brings trouble.

The purpose of following *Swadharma* is to work according to one's inherent abilities and skills. Through practice, a person can improve these abilities. For example, people with Tamasic tendencies can reduce their Tamasic qualities and increase their Rajasic qualities, while those with Rajasic tendencies can elevate their Satvic qualities. However, individuals with a naturally Satvic disposition will always remain Satvic, as each person will always have at least one dominant *Guna* (quality). It is also observed that a Satvic person can become egoistic and develop aversion toward others. Ego is a dangerous obstacle for all, and thus one should strive to avoid it. If a Satvic person fails to control their ego, they cannot attain salvation.

While answering Arjuna's second question, Shri Krishna explains the reason for sin as follows:

Reason for sin: Sin is typically committed by individuals with a Rajas nature, as they are driven by material desires. When these desires are obstructed, anger arises. Anger clouds the intelligence, causing a person to deviate from their natural course of action, leading them to commit sinful acts.

Even in *Shri Ramcharitmanas*, Goswami Tulsidas, in the 277th couplet of *Balakand*, describes through Shri Lakshman the anger of Parashuram Ji:

लखन कहेउ हँसि सुनहु मुनि क्रोधु पाप कर मूल ।
जेहि बस जन अनुचित करहिं चरहिं विश्व प्रतिकूल ।।

Lakhan says, smilingly, "Listen, sage, anger is the root of sins, due to which a person does wrong and acts against the welfare of the world."

According to psychology, anger is a type of emotion. Emotion is the manifestation of a human's inner feelings. When any emotion moves and manifests through the body, it is called an impulse. Emotions are of two types: 1) Positive and 2) Negative. Accordingly, impulses are also of two types. Love, friendship, compassion, etc., are symptoms of a positive impulse, while anger, fear, enmity, hatred, ego, etc., are symptoms of a negative impulse. According to Ayurveda experts like Sage Charaka, Sage Sushruta, and others, negative impulses cause physical diseases, while positive impulses strengthen the body, promoting health.

According to Ayurveda, the main cause of physical disease is the imbalance of Tridosha (phlegm, bile, and air) in the body. Ayurveda experts believe that fear imbalances phlegm, which is why people who are fearful due to some reasons easily fall victim to phlegm-related diseases (such as respiratory diseases). People who get angry often are more likely to develop Pitta-related diseases (such as chronic conditions), while people who are inactive or worry unnecessarily are prone to Vata-related diseases (such as pain). Some doctors also believe that contamination of Kapha in the body causes unnecessary fear and disturbing dreams. The contamination of Pitta results in irritability and anger over trivial matters, and the contamination of Vata leads to laziness and a lack of interest in completing tasks properly.

According to psychology, emotional impulses affect both the body and the mind. The basic reason for emotions is the underlying feelings, and impulses are their outward expression. For example, anger is a symbol of negative feelings, while humility is a symbol of positive feelings. Scholars believe that controlling emotions is essential for controlling the mind. The seeds of emotions do not reside in our gross body but in our subtle body, in the form of vibrations. When these vibrations are affected by waves generated by external stimuli, emotions arise, which are expressed through impulses. Impulses are only generated when emotions are impure, and the only way to purify these emotions is through meditation. Meditation increases self-power, and therefore, without meditation, purifying emotions is not possible with medicine alone.

At the end of this chapter, God advises Arjun that it is difficult to conquer the strong enemy in the form of lust (which acts as a stimulus). Lust can only be defeated with the strength of the soul (i.e., self-power). Therefore, by avoiding the attack of the dangerous enemy in the form of lust, one can naturally be saved from all types of sin.

The Conclusion

In the third chapter of the Gita, Arjuna has a doubt: if the culmination of human life is to be a Sthitaprajna, and knowledge alone can be adequate, then what is the need to perform karma?

In response to Arjuna's question, Lord Shri Krishna explained that both Sanyasis (renunciates) or Gyani (the wise) and Karmayogis perform karma because human life is not possible without karma. However, everyone's karma is influenced by the three Gunas (Satva, Rajas, and Tamas). Arjuna came to understand that Karmayoga and Sanyas are similar in that both involve performing karma, but the difference lies in the nature of the action. In Karmayoga, there is no attachment to the action, while in Sanyas, there is no sense of doership.

However, Arjuna is still puzzled as to why, if all beings perform karma according to their Triguna, some people fail to follow Dharma or commit sins.

To resolve this doubt, Lord Krishna explains that anger is the cause of sin. People who are dominated by Rajoguna have many desires, and when these desires are obstructed, they become victims of anger. It is due to this anger that people commit sinful acts. Lord Krishna advises Arjuna that a person can follow their own Dharma only after overcoming the strong enemy in the form of desire. Arjuna agrees with this reasoning of Shri Krishna.

At this point, it is natural for Arjuna to wonder who the people have defeated such an enemy as desire and act according to their own virtue. The solution to Arjuna's curiosity is explained in the next chapter.

-:Om Tat Sat :-

Chapter-4
The Gyan-karma-sanyas Yoga.

The Fourth Chapter of Srimadbhagwat Gita at a glance	
Total Nos of verses	42
Nos of verses by lord Shree Krishna	41
Nos of verses by Arjuna	1
Nos of verses by sanjay	0
Nos of verses by Dritrastra	0
Main theam of the Chapter	Indian Spritual postulates

श्री गणेशाय नमः

श्लोकः

त्वमादिदेवः पुरूषः पुराण
स्त्वमस्य विश्वस्य परं निधानम्।
वेत्तासि वेद्यं च परं च धाम
त्वया ततं विश्वमनन्तरूप।।

दो0– अविनाशी कर्मयोग का दिया प्रथम भानु को ज्ञान।
अति उत्तम कर्मयोग है कहे आनन्द कन्द भगवान।1।
दो0– आदित्य कहे कर्मयोग वैवस्त से जो हैं मन्वन्तराधिष।
ईक्ष्वाकु पाये ज्ञान विमल अपि जनक मनु आशीष।2।

अतिगोपनीय यह योगविज्ञाना। गुरू–शिष्य ऋषि–मुनि जाना।।
कर्मयोग ज्ञान बहु काल है बीता। लुप्तप्रायः यह योग पुनिता।।
तुम भक्त मेरे अपि प्रिय मिता। हित हेतु कहूं योगसुचिता।।
नतमस्तक पार्थ विनत करजोरी। हरहूँ सखा दीर्धसंशय मोरी।।
रवि प्रकटे हैं सृष्टि कल्पादि। अर्वाचीन आप हैं कैसे आदि।।
रवि सीखे आपसे कर्मयोगा। कालान्तर नहीं संभव संयोगा।।
कह भगवान सुन पार्थ रणधीरा। बहुबार हुये हम प्रकटशरीरा।।
शंकाछाड़ी कर पूर्वजन्म ध्याना।हम सब अपि कल्पादि पुराना।।
अजन्मा मैं त्रिगुणतीत अविनाशी। परमेश्वर अगजग सुखराशि।।

सकल प्रकृति कर निज अधिना। प्रकट हुआ दिव्यदेह प्रवीणा।।

दो0–मैं होऊँ प्रकट योगमाया से कर सकल प्रकृति अधीन।
साकार **होऊँ** सत्कर्म को प्रकट कई जन्म नवीन।3।
दो0–**अधर्म बढ़े जब धरती पर बढ़े अग जग मिथ्याचार।**
मर्यादा धर्म घटने लगे तो प्रकटूँ जग साकार।4।
दो0– **दुर्बुद्धि नाश साधु उद्धार सकल करूं सत्कर्म।**
युग युग प्रकट होता रहा रक्षित करने को धर्म।5।

जन्म कर्म मम दिव्य अलौकिक। माया से धरूँ काया भौतिक।।
प्राणी मोहे जो तत्त्व से जाना। प्राप्त मोहे पुर्नजन्म न पाना।।
राग रोष सब भय विलगावे। अविचलित मोसे नेह लगावे।।
भगवत्स्वरूप ध्यान की युक्ति। ज्ञानी तपस्वी पाये जग मुक्ति।।
सुमिरण मोहे भक्त करे जैसे। मैं अपि सुमिरू भक्त को तैसे।।
अनुसरण सदा मनुज करे मोरा। जगसत्य यही कहे चितचोरा।।
कर्मफल हीं है मनुज वासना। कर्मफल हेतु करे देव उपासना।।
पाये शीघ्र कर्म उत्पन्न सिद्धि। होए मनुज की आत्मबल वृद्धि।।
गुणकर्म सब ध्यान का प्रतिफल।होत विकास कर्म से प्रतिपल।।
चातुर्वर्ण जगत पार्थ मम रचना। विदित भुवन समाज संरचना।।

दो0–**रचनाकार मैं चातुर्वर्ण का पर मुझे अकर्ता जान।**
गुण कर्मानुसार है वर्ण सकल छोड़ जन्म अभिमान।6।
दो0–प्रकट **गुण है कर्मकौशल तमस रजस अरू सत्व।**
कर्म ज्ञान अपि करे प्रकट जो त्रिगुण के तत्व।7।
दो0–**कर्मकौशल अरू प्रकट ज्ञान जग चातुर्वर्ण आधार।**
कर्मकौशल ज्ञान प्रभाव हीं जगत करे स्वीकार।8।
दो0–**उच्च अधम कर्म नही जग गुण अनुसार सम्मान।**
जन्म से अधम उच्च न कोई पापी करे अपमान।9।

कर्मफल में नही मेरी आसक्ति। नही मैं लिप्त रहूँ कर्मशक्ति।।
यह तत्त्व जाने जो कुन्तिनन्दन। पड़े नही कबहूँ कर्मबन्धन।।
तत्त्वज्ञान कर्म मुक्ति हेतु। पूर्वापि रहा कर्म मुक्तिसेतु।।
सत्कर्म यज्ञ पूर्वज सिखलाये। सत्कर्म करने भुवन हम आये।।
वरण करो पूर्वज की युक्ति। नित्य सतकर्म से पाओ मुक्ति।।

कर्म अकर्म भेद अति सूक्ष्मतर। ज्ञानीभ्रमित अपि होवे प्रियवर।।
अब भेद कर्म अकर्म का जानों। अति शुभज्ञान मुक्तिप्रद मानो।।
परतंत्र कर्म करे फल अधीना। फल हेतु कर्म करे मतिहीना।।
विकर्म सदा कर्मयत्न को मानों। कुशलकर्म की पौड़ी जानों।।
अकर्म स्वतंत्र अपि आनन्ददाता। आसक्तिहीन श्रुति अस गाता।।

दो0–कर्म की गति अति गहन अक्सर बदले रूप।
कर्म अकर्म विकर्म का समझो मूल स्वरूप।10।
दो0–निज कर्म से मिले खुशी कर्म से सबका हित।
अकर्म अपि हैं कर्म सुखद पावन अति पुनित।11।
दो0–मनुज धन्य वहीं जगत में जो करे निरंतर कर्म।
करत करत अभ्यास सदा बनता कर्म अकर्म।12।

कर्तव्यकर्म संकल्पहीन अखण्डीत।निष्काम कर्म करे सो पंडित।।
भस्मकरे कर्म ज्ञान अग्निरूपा। पुरूषमुक्त न पड़े भवकूपा।।
पार्थ ना जाको कर्मफल प्रीति। सदा सन्तुष्ट न काहूँ से भीति।।
परमात्मातृप्त करे अनेक जगकर्मा। अनासक्त निर्वाहे निजधर्मा।।
जितेन्द्रिय समस्त भोग त्यागा। शुद्धअन्तःकरण चित् अनुरागा।।
करे कर्म शरीररक्षा मन व्यापी। अस मनुज जग कबहूँ न पापी।।
सदा सन्तुष्ट हर्ष शोक अभावा। ईर्ष्या द्वेष मन कबहू न भावा।।
मननिर्द्वन्द सम सिद्धि–असिद्धि। कर्मबन्धन मुक्त पाये प्रसिद्धि।।
अनासक्त देहाभिमान मुक्ता। अस मनुज परमज्ञान युक्ता।।
सकल कर्म लगे यज्ञ समाना। कर्मयोगी मिलन प्रभु विधि नाना।।

दो0–ब्रह्म ब्रह्म सब ब्रह्म हैं यज्ञ–अग्नि–आहुति–दान।
ब्रह्म कर्म अपि कर्मफल ब्रह्म कर्ता अपि ज्ञान।13।

कछु करे देवपुजन यज्ञ नाना।विधि सम्मत जो वेद बखाना।।
कछु परब्रह्म संग रहे एकीभावा। ज्ञान अग्नि आत्मरूप अभावा।।
कछु संयमानल इन्द्रिय आहुति।ज्ञान प्रज्वलित कर्म बने स्तुति।।
सकल विषय इन्द्रियानल युक्ति। अनासक्त पाये जग मुक्ति।।
इन्द्रिय प्राण क्रिया ज्ञानालोकित।संयम करे जगजीवन हित।।
कछु करे यज्ञ हेतुद्रव्य दाना। तपरूप कछु करे यज्ञ नाना।।

कछु करे योगप्रणायाम अभ्यासा।कछु रखे स्वाध्याय ज्ञानआशा।।
कछु प्रण व्रत तीक्ष्ण अहिंसादि। कछु उपवास करे धीरजसाधी।।
कछु करे अपान में प्राण आहूति। प्राण अपान कर पाये विभूति।।
प्रणायामी करे संयमित अहारा। रोके योगी प्राणापान घारा।।
प्राण में प्राण जो करे विसर्जन। साधक यज्ञ ज्ञान पुण्यअर्जन।।

दो0– **पुण्यात्मा हेतु यज्ञशेष सुधासम अनुग्रह प्रभु विशेष।**
नित्य मिलन परमात्मा भौतिक इच्छा रहे ना शेष।14।
दो0–**बिना यज्ञ मनुज हो भ्रमित पाये न सुख इह लोक।**
कल्याण नही अस प्राणी का जाये जब परलोक।15।

वेदवाणी यज्ञ विस्तार बखाना। अनुष्ठान हेतु इन्द्रिय नाना।।
यज्ञक्रिया सकल इन्द्रियमन युक्ति। तत्व जानी कर्मबंधनमुक्ति।।
ज्ञानयज्ञ द्रव्यमय यज्ञ ते उत्तम।ज्ञानविलीन कर्म सकलनरोत्तम।।
पार्थ तत्वदर्शी शरण तु जाओ। ज्ञानी संग तत्वज्ञान को पायो।।
कपट छाडी कर गुरू के सेवा। गुरू समर्थ यही धरा पर देवा।।
कर जिज्ञासा प्रकट गुरू पाँहीं।मिले तत्वज्ञान कछु संसयनाहीं।।
तत्वज्ञान पाई हो मोह से मुक्ति। तत्वज्ञान उपब्रह्म की युक्ति।।
आत्मसात तत्वज्ञान बढ़ाये विवेका। वसुधैव तत्त्व लागे एका।।
न हो प्रतीत भुत –ईश्वर अन्तर। जो हो तत्वज्ञान अभ्यन्तर।।
तत्वज्ञान जो अतिपापी अपि पाये। भवबन्धन से मुक्त हो जाये।।

दो0–**प्रज्वलित अग्नि करतदहन संमिधा जेही प्रकार।**
ज्ञानाग्नि तिमी दहन करे जग पाप–पुण्य कर्म भार।16।

ज्ञान समान न कछु जग पावन।करे शुद्ध अन्तःकरण मनभावन।।
कर्मयोग करे सकल ज्ञान शुद्धि। कालान्तर अपि निर्मल बुद्धि।।
सिद्धनीति यही सुनो महात्मा।ज्ञान से जाने मनुज निज आत्मा।।
श्रद्धावान जितेन्द्रिय साधनयुक्ता। प्राप्त ज्ञान हो मानुष मुक्ता।।
पाये तत्वज्ञान मिटे जग भ्रान्ति।बिना विलम्ब पाये ब्रह्मशान्ति।।
तत्वज्ञान सकल दे शान्ति अनुपा।जग शान्ति परमात्म स्वरूपा।।
विवेकहीन अपि परमार्थभ्रष्टा।श्रद्धारहित मनुज पाये जगकष्टा।।
संशसयुक्त सुखविहिन अवस्था।लोक परलोक यही व्यवस्था।।
कर्मयोग ईश्वर कर्मफल अर्पण। संशयनाश मिले विवेक दर्पण।।

वशअन्तःकरण बुद्धि विवकेयुक्ता। निश्चित हो कर्मबन्धन मुक्ता।।
दो०—पार्थ छाड़ी के मोह को पकड़ विवेक तलवार।
हृदय जनित अज्ञानमय संशय कर संहार।17।
दो०—समत्वरूप कर्मयोग से पाकर ज्ञान करो चित् शुद्ध।
मोह पंक से पार निकलकर पार्थ करो धर्मयुद्ध।18।

।। इति चतुर्थ अध्याय।।

The Fourth Chapter of Srimadbhagwat Gita

The Essence

The fourth chapter of Shreemad Bhagavad Gita is known as Gyan-Karma-Sanyas Yoga. This chapter contains a total of 42 shlokas. For the convenience of study, it can be divided into four parts.

1. Subject of Karmayoga (Shlokas 1-18) :-In the third chapter, Shri Krishna highlighted the necessity of Karmayoga and explained that the greatest obstacle to Karmayoga is lust. Lust can only be conquered by self-power. To support this, he elaborated on Karmayoga with reference to historical evidences .

Shri Krishna explained that initially, this yoga was taught to the Sun. The Sun then passed it on to Vaivasvat Manu, who in turn taught it to his son Ikshwaku. Through this lineage, this yoga was known to the Rajarshis. However, over time, it gradually disappeared from the earth. Shri Krishna, due to his great love for Arjuna, explained the Karmayoga to him, as this esoteric knowledge is a top secret.

Arjuna, bewildered, thought, how could Shri Krishna have taught this Karmayoga to the Sun? The Sun appeared at the beginning of creation, while Shri Krishna was born much later. So, Arjuna asked Shri Krishna to clear his doubt.

(When Lord Shri Krishna says, "I first told this Yoga to the Sun," it is natural for common people to have doubts about how this is

possible. However, in Sanatan culture, it is believed that Lord Shri Krishna is an incarnation of Vishnu, who is said to have existed even before the creation of the universe).

Shri Krishna further elucidated that we all have taken many births. While I am able to remember those births, you are not able to recall your previous ones. I appear by overcoming nature through my Yogamaya. When most people forget their duty and act against nature, the world is filled with disorder. This causes trouble for those who follow their natural duty. Therefore, I appear to protect the righteous and destroy the evil. My birth and deeds are divine and supernatural. However, if one understands me in essence (Sat, Chit, Anand), he becomes free. Just as the culmination of Karma Yoga is detached action, the culmination of Gyan Yoga is to know the Supreme Being in its true form.Many devotees have already attained my form by purifying themselves through the penance of knowledge. Once they gained knowledge, their attachment, fear, anger, and other negative emotions were destroyed, and they became united with me through exclusive divine love. The way the devotees worship me, I worship them in the same way, because all human beings follow my path in one way or another.

In this world, those who seek the results of their actions worship the gods, as they receive the desired outcomes swiftly. The creation of the four Varnas was done by me based on Guna (quality) and Karma. *(When all four types of people have been created by God, there is no one superior or inferior.)* The Lord is the doer of all the four Varnas, but in truth, the Lord is the non-doer, because He has no desire for the outcome of actions. Those who understand me in this way are not bound by actions. In the past, those who sought salvation followed this very nature of mine (free from the pride of being the doer) and attained liberation.

Lord Krishna told Arjuna that he should understand the nature of action and non-action thoroughly. The knowledge of this will help Arjuna to attain freedom from the bondage of action. The nature of action, endeavor, and non-action must be understood well because all three are forms of action. The secret of action is very deep.

2. **Conduct of a great Person (Shloka 19-23) :-**Wise individuals or great persons observe non-action within their actions, which is why all their actions are carried out without desire and without attachment to the outcome. Their desires are burned in the fire of knowledge, and such individuals are considered the best by the most knowledgeable saints. They perform actions without attachment to the results, rising above the illusions and attachments of the world. In fact, they live under the shelter of God.

Those who keep their senses, mind, and intellect under control, renouncing all pleasures, and perform bodily activities, cannot commit any sin. The best of men remain satisfied by considering whatever they receive in the world as God's will. In this way, they do not feel jealousy, and they are free from the dilemmas of happiness and hatred. They carry out their duties with equanimity, remaining stable in both success and failure. This is the behavior of the best Karmayogis.The work (duty) of the Karmayogi is a form of sacrifice. Without attachment, they focus their minds on God, and as a result, their entire work becomes dissolved in God.

3.Yajana and the results of Yajana (Verse 24-32) :-Lord Shri Krishna further said, "O Arjun, there are many types of Yajnas, or holy duties, and accordingly, the results of these Yajnas vary. For example, in Brahma Yajna, the sacrifice, the fire, the offering—everything appears to be imbued with Brahman (Satchidanandamay). The result of this type of Yajna is also Brahman-like."

Some yogis perform ritual Yajnas to fulfill specific desires, offering special offerings for that purpose. Others sacrifice their own pompous form in the fire of the Supreme God to unite with Him. Some yogis offer all their senses into the fire of self-control, while others offer the objects of the senses into the fire of the senses. Some yogis offer all the actions of the senses and the actions of the breath into the fire of self-restraint, illuminated by knowledge.

Many people perform material Yajnas, while others practice yoga Yajnas. Some perform Yajnas with sharp vows, like non-violence, while many perform Yajnas of knowledge through self-study. Some yogis offer their breath into the apana vayu, while others offer the apana vayu into the prana vayu. Those whose food and lifestyle are health-enhancing and who are devoted to pranayama stop the movement of prana and apana, offering the breath in the breath itself.

All types of practitioners understand that it is the Yajna that can destroy the outcome of sins. After offering sacrifices in any Yajna, the result is the receipt of Amrit (nectar) and the experience of unity with the Supreme Brahman (the Supreme Soul). Those who do not perform Yajna are always in trouble. It is a matter of assumption that if they cannot find peace in this world, how can they expect peace or salvation in the next world?

Many types of Yajnas are described in detail in the Vedas, but all of them are simply actions performed by the mind, senses, and body. By understanding the essence of Yajna and performing it, people become completely free from the bondage of karma.

4. The glory of knowledge (Shloka 33-42) :-The knowledge Yajna is far superior to material Yajna. In truth, all duties dissolve in knowledge. To acquire such knowledge, one should approach a Tattvadarshi (one who knows the truth) instructor, show respect to him, and acquire the knowledge of truth from him. By obtaining such knowledge, delusion is destroyed, as after this Tatvagyan, all beings begin to appear as one. Furthermore, all beings start appearing as Brahman-like. With the help of the knowledge of truth, even a great sinner can cross the ocean of sins. Just as a blazing fire burns fuel to ashes, similarly, the fire of knowledge burns all the accumulated sins.

There is nothing in this world that can purify like knowledge. That is why a Karmayogi, after being purified by knowledge, quickly unites with the Supreme Soul. A person who has controlled his senses, is dedicated to the means, and has faith, attains supreme peace immediately upon attaining knowledge. However, a person who lacks wisdom, faith, and is full of doubts, will definitely be deviated from the path of spirituality, causing him to find neither happiness in this world nor the next.

He who has dedicated all his actions to God through the method of Karmayoga and has cleared all doubts through discrimination, controls his conscience and is not bound by karma.

Therefore, Lord Krishna advised Arjuna to destroy the doubts born of ignorance in his heart with the sword of knowledge. By being established in Karmayoga with equanimity, Arjuna should prepare for the battle.

The Discussion

In this chapter, the foundation of Sanatan Dharma is discussed in a very simple manner, making many concepts related to Sanatan Dharma clear. The Sanatan concepts covered in this chapter include the following:

1.The Concept of Rebirth: The concept of rebirth in Sanatan Dharma teaches that until the soul is liberated, it remains trapped in the cycle of birth and death, being reborn according to its deeds. Lord Krishna reveals this concept after Arjuna raises a doubt. At the beginning of this chapter, Shri Krishna explains that he first imparted the knowledge of Karmayoga to the Sun. Arjuna, however, was confused, as the Sun was born at the beginning of creation, whereas Krishna's birth is more recent. How, then, could Krishna have imparted the teachings of Karmayoga to the Sun? To resolve this doubt, Shri Krishna explains the concept of rebirth, saying that both he and Arjuna have experienced many births.

Krishna remembers them, but Arjuna does not, which is why Arjuna has this doubt.

Further, when explaining the purpose of his birth, Lord Krishna says that whenever there is an increase in sin and false conduct on earth, he appears in various forms to protect righteousness (Dharma) and destroy the wicked, ensuring the integrity of religion remains intact. *(Here, Dharma refers to righteousness according to nature, while Papi refers to one who acts against nature. This concept differs from the popular understanding of Dharma in some contemporary cults, as described in the Shrimad Bhagavad Gita.)*

2.Concept of the Varna System: The real meaning of "Varna" is " color." However, in the case of the Indian social classification, Varna refers to the social identification of a person. It is assumed that color serves as an identifier, allowing something to be recognized at a glance. However, this initial identification may be incorrect when judged according to its inherent properties. Indian society, according to mythological texts, is classified in three ways.

i) Varna System:-In this system, the spiritual classification of society has been outlined. According to this system, Varna is divided into four parts:

1. **Brahmin Varna**: The person who has attained the state of inaction and is full of Satvik Gunas.
2. **Kshatriya Varna**: The person performing natural Karma with a predominance of a mixture of Rajas and Satvik Gunas.
3. **Vaishya Varna**: The person engaging in natural Karma with a mixture of Rajas and Tamas Gunas.
4. **Shudra Varna**: The person performing natural Karma with a predominance of Tamas Gunas only.

In verse 4.13 of the *Shrimad Bhagavad Gita*, Lord Shri Krishna states that He has created all four Varnas based on Guna (virtue) and Karma (action). In this context, the classification of society is spiritual. Guna refers to the three natural qualities: 1. Satvik Guna,

2. Rajasi Guna, and 3. Tamasik Guna. Karma refers to the level of skill in actions, with the culmination of skill being Akarma. A person's dedication is based on the quality and division of their actions, which is also called Varna. This dedication can be uplifted through Karmayoga and knowledge. Thus, a person's Varna is not determined by birth, but by their dedication toward action.

In this chapter, Shri Krishna does not recognize the Varna system as one based on birth. The system prevalent in India based on birth is the caste system, which has led to many disputes within Indian society. In the first chapter of the Gita, Arjuna indeed speaks about caste-dharma and family-dharma, but Shri Krishna emphasizes self-virtue instead. Varna is a qualitative term, and change is possible through knowledge. For example, Maharishi Vishwamitra was originally a Kshatriya king, but due to the elevation of his qualities, he was later considered to belong to the Brahmin Varna. Many such examples can be found in Indian texts, including respected figures like Maharishi Valmiki and Maharishi Veda Vyasa etc.

ii)Ashram System:- The human body is considered the yoni (species) obtained for the purpose of attaining salvation. To achieve salvation, the active lifespan of a human being (generally considered to be 100 years) is divided into four stages, each lasting 25 years:

a) **Brahmacharya Ashram**: This is the first stage of human life, during which an individual acquires knowledge. This stage is generally considered to last until the age of about 25 years.

b) **Grihastha Ashram**: The second stage of life, which begins after the marriage ceremony. In this ashram, a person earns a living by using the knowledge and skills acquired in Brahmacharya Ashram. During this phase, one is expected to fulfill social obligations and responsibilities. It is during this stage that a person has the opportunity to clear the three main debts: the Debt to Nature, the Debt to Society, and the Debt to the Educator. This stage typically spans the ages of 25 to 50 years.

c) **Vanaprastha Ashram**: After fulfilling social duties, individuals who seek salvation transition from material life to a spiritual life. This stage is often considered a period of transition, where one begins to shift from worldly attachments to spiritual pursuits. Many people go to the forest during this phase to maintain a calm mind and distance themselves from negative feelings such as jealousy. This stage is usually considered to last from 50 to 75 years, and it culminates in renunciation.

d) **Sanyas Ashram**: The final stage of life begins when an individual renounces material life. In this stage, a person dedicates their time solely to contemplation and union with God, striving to free themselves from worldly attachments. This is the last phase of life, focused on spiritual liberation.

iii) Caste system:- This system is a socio-political classification of society. It is not the Varna system but rather a class system based on skills. According to this system, caste is divided into two parts based on skill. This system is also referred to as the **Caste system**.

a) **Dwijaati**:-Dwijaati refers to one who is born twice in life—first, after staying in the mother's womb for 9 months, and second, after staying in the Gurukul (traditional school) and receiving **sanskars** (knowledge and skills). Dwijaati is further divided into three classes:

- **Brahmin**: Those Dwijaatis who are proficient in all forms of education, especially the knowledge of the Vedas. This class was known for its research and scholarly pursuits.
- **Kshatriya**: Those Dwijaatis who are skilled in the knowledge of weapons and warfare. This class was responsible for the protection and security of society.

- **Vaishya**: Those Dwijaatis who are proficient in the knowledge of commerce and trade. This class was primarily associated with business and economic activities.

2.Shudra: -People of the Shudra caste are not considered proficient in the skills mentioned above (research, security, and business). Because they donot learn in Gurukul , But they learn their traditional work from his family . Hence, they are very hardworking and adept in the traditional work of their families. Although they may not be skilled in commerce, they often live in difficult conditions. According to scholars, the word *Shudra* means "grief-stricken." Dr. B.R. Ambedkar, the great thinker and one of the principal architects of the Indian Constitution, believed that Shudras were also skillful Aryans who arrived in India earlier as a group and assimilated into Indian culture. Later, when another group of Aryans arrived, they defeated the earlier group and made them prisoners of war or slaves. These defeated people were often grief-stricken, which is why they were called Shudras. They were also humiliated by having many of their basic human rights stripped away. This humiliation of the defeated people eventually became institutionalized in Indian society to gain political advantage. The effects of this can still be seen in many contemporary Indian texts, and the ill effects of such social stratification can be observed in various places in Indian society at present also.It is important to note that the caste system is not a religious system. After India's independence, it became a socio-political issue.

Some people believe that the Vedas, the oldest religious texts in India, support the caste system. Let us take a look at the Purushasuktam of the Rigveda, which is often claimed to be the source of the caste system. Common people interpret the 11th verse of Purushasuktam in the Rigveda as supporting the caste system. But by paying attention to the context of the Purushasuktam, it becomes clear that the 11th verse of Purushasuktam does not support the caste system. In the Purushasuktam, the creator of the world is considered to be the Virat Purusha, who extends infinitely. The tenth verse of the Purushasuktam is as follows:

यत्पुरूषं व्यदघुः कतिधा व्यकल्पयन्।

मुखं किमस्यासीत् किम् बाहूँ किमूरूपादाउच्यते।।

Yatpurusham vyadghuh katidha vyakalpayam.

Mukham kimsyasit kim bahunu kimurupadauchyate.

This means that the wise people describe the Virat Purusha, who appeared through resolution, in various ways. According to their understanding, what constitutes the face of the Virat Purusha? What are the arms of the Virat Purusha? What is the thigh of the Virat Purusha? And what are the feet of the Virat Purusha? The answer to these questions is provided in the 11th verse of the Purushasuktam, which is as follows:

ब्राह्मणोंस्य मुखमासीद् बाहू राजन्यः कृतः ।

ऊरूतदस्ययद्वैश्यः पद्भ्याँ शूद्रोअजायत।।

Brahmanosya mukhamaasid baahu rajanyah kritah.

Urutadasyaadvaishya: padbhyaam shudraoajayat.

In the context of the 10th verse of the Purushasuktam, the meaning of the verse should be understood as follows: the face of the Virat Purusha is like that of a Brahmin (thoughtful and wise), his arms are like those of a valiant Kshatriya (symbolizing strength and bravery), his thighs are like that of a Vaishya (the one who nourishes and sustains society), and the feet are like those of a Shudra (the foundation upon which all these functions are carried out).

Looking at the second part of this verse, it becomes clear that symbolic answers are provided to the questions raised in the 10th verse. For example, the Sandhi Vichchhed (separation of meaningful words) of "Urutadasyaadvaishyah" is "Uru + Tadasya + Yad + Vaishya," which means that the Virat Purusha's thigh is like that of a Vaishya. In the social system, those who work for the sustenance of society are called Vaishyas. The word Vaishya is derived from Vishnu, who nurtures all creation. However, the last part of this verse, "Padbhyaan Shudro Ajaayat," is considered to be the most controversial. Its literal meaning suggests that Shudras are born from the feet (the lower part of the body), but this appears inconsistent with the context of the 10th verse of the Purushasuktam. In the 10th verse, the question is "kimoorupadauchyate," which can be separated into "kim + ooru + pad + uchyate," meaning "what are the thigh and the feet called?" According to the 11th verse, the thigh can be called Vaishya and the foot can be called Shudra. Therefore, it can be said that the verse in the Purushasuktam does not support the caste system, but rather symbolically describes the roles and functions of different groups in society at that time.

Many people with limited knowledge claim that Shri Ramcharit Manas supports the caste system. However, Goswami Tulsidas, while describing the caste system of Ram Rajya in the Uttar Kand, says:

बरनाश्रम निज निज धरम निरत वेद पथ लोग।
चलहिं सदा पावहिं सुख नहिं भय सोक न रोग ।।

It means the people of Ramrajya always follows the discipline of the Vedas, they always get happiness, and they have neither fear nor sorrow nor disease.That is, in Ramrajya, people followed the Varnashram Dharma .

Further, Goswami Tulsidas explained about different sects except Sanatan Dharma in Kaliyug:

कलिमल ग्रसे धर्म सब लुप्त भये सद्ग्रंथ।
दंभिन्ह निज मति कल्पि करि प्रकट किए बहु पंथ।।

All the religious texts were lost due to the influence of Kaliyuga. Hypocrites have created many sects according to their own understanding. This means that the sects propagated today are different from Sanatan Dharma.

3. Concept of Karma, Vikarma, and Akarma :-The action (Karma) has been classified into three categories according to the skill of action: Karma, Vikarma, and Akarma. These are simple classifications of skill. Shri Krishna believes that even the best scholars get confused when differentiating between Karma and Akarma. Hence, he suggested to Arjuna that he must understand this differentiation clearly, because by adopting these, he will be freed from the bondage of karma.Many scholars use various examples to explain Karma, Vikarma, and Akarma. One such example is as follows: Imagine a person goes near a pond with his small child, who does not know how to swim, and asks him to jump into the water. It is possible that the child will try to avoid entering the water, or perhaps he will start crying in an attempt to avoid it. It is also possible that, seeing other children swimming, he may decide to try swimming himself. Though he doesn't know how to swim, his belief in his father's support encourages him to attempt it. He tries to swim by imitating other children and, after many attempts, learns to swim well. Eventually, he enjoys swimming and no longer feels the need for his father's presence. In this example, the child's efforts can be divided into three parts:

1. **Karma**: This is the state before learning to swim when he is uncertain whether he should even go near the pond. In this stage, the person is in a dilemma, facing the conflict of success and failure in his mind.

2. **Vikarma**: At this stage, as the child's self-confidence grows through the presence of his father and the inspiration he gets from seeing other swimmers, he starts developing his swimming skills. This state of endeavor, motivated by both external and internal inspiration, is called Vikarma. It is when Karma turns into a higher form through effort and skill.

3. **Akarma**: When the child becomes skilled in swimming, he begins to enjoy it. His fear of swimming disappears, and he no longer worries about the outcome. He finds joy in swimming and no longer feels nervous or fatigued. This joyful state of action is called Akarma. Akarma is the culmination of action where work no longer feels like work but a natural expression of joy.

In fact, work is the fuel of knowledge. When the fire of self-power is added to it, the light of knowledge radiates. When work reaches the state of Akarma, the doer is identified as the Karmayogi,

4. Concept of Yajana :- Yajana means work for sustainable development—work that does not harm nature or others. People believe that to attain salvation, Yajana should be performed according to prescribed rules. However, to clear this confusion, scholars have explained that the rituals of Yajana are symbolic undertakings. The main objective of Yajana is to conquer the mind and senses, renounce attachment, and refrain from seeking external pleasures. This leads to inner satisfaction, and the mind becomes free from conflict. A person who is able to achieve this never commits sin while performing work and thus attains liberation.

(Yajana is a powerful medium for enlightenment. There are three duties for human liberation: Yajana, Tapa, and Daan. However, these three are generally referred to collectively as Yajana. For any Yajana, the following are required: Yajanakarta (the one who performs the Yajana), Yajanapurohit (the priest conducting the Yajana), Agni (the sacred fire), Samidha (wood offerings), and Adhishthan (the foundation or altar).

When the Samidha burns in the fire, Teja (spiritual energy or radiance) is obtained. Many types of Yajanas are performed, as follows:

No	Yajna name	Form of Fire	form of fuel
1	Dev Anushthan	The fire	Medicine
2	Atma Roop Yajna	Supreme soul	Ego
3	Vishay Yajna	Sense	Subject
4	Dravya Yajna	Charity	Matter
5	Karmayoga	Yajana	Ignorance
6	Gyan yajna	Knowledge	All activities
7	Yoga Yajna	Breath	unstable thought
8	Tatvagyan Yajna	Absolute truth	Maya

Lord Shri Krishna said that after performing any form of Yajna, one attains Amrit (nectar) in the form of Tej (experience), which paves the way to attain the supreme soul. Any kind of attachment ends once the ultimate truth is realized. This state of a person is called the state of Renunciation/Sannyas (Truth of Trust), because through Yajna, he gains the knowledge of the truth. In this way, there is no illusion or attachment in the gained knowledge; instead, faith is cultivated, which brings peace to the individual.

The Yajna in the form of Karmayoga protects even the most sinful people, for the knowledge generated by Karmayoga destroys all types of pride and ego.People without wisdom do not perform Yajna, which results in doubt and a lack of faith. Those who neglect Yajna remain unhappy in this world and fail to attain happiness in the next world as well.

5.Yoga and Pranayama- In this chapter, Shri Krishna explains that before practicing Yoga, pranayama is essential. The breath we inhale is called Prana Vayu, and the breath that leaves the body is called Apana Vayu. The process of inhaling is known as Purak, and the process of exhaling is called Rechak. It is often experienced that when performing tasks requiring deep focus, such as threading a needle, the breath almost stops. The process of halting the breath is called Kumbhaka.

Shri Krishna elaborates on the method of Yoga, stating that many Yogis sacrifice the Prana Vayu into Apana Vayu. Similarly, some Yogis sacrifice Apana Vayu into Prana Vayu. Some even stop the movement of both Prana and Apana Vayu simultaneously, performing the sacrifice of Prana within Prana itself. This concept is profound and has been interpreted in various ways by scholars.

- **Sacrifice of Prana Vayu into Apana Vayu**: This is a form of Vahya Kumbhaka. In this process, the Yogi stops the Prana Vayu outside the body for a time after releasing Apana Vayu.
- **Sacrifice of Apana Vayu into Prana Vayu**: This is a form of Antar Kumbhaka. In this process, the Yogi stops the Apana Vayu inside the body for a time after inhaling Prana Vayu.
- **Sacrifice of Prana Vayu into Prana Vayu**: In this process, the Yogi stops the association of Prana and Apana Vayu for a time, in any position. A great deal of practice is required for this.

In the scriptures, the process of stopping Prana Vayu or Apana Vayu in various ways is known as Pranayama. Maharishi Patanjali defines Yoga as the cessation of the fluctuations of the mind. The thoughts of the mind usually affect the speed of breathing, and in meditation, the thoughts of the mind often cease. In such a state, the speed of breathing also slows down or stops. Thus, Lord Shri Krishna explains that Yogis, who perform Yoga Yajna, attempt to stop Prana or the breath in different ways to more easily attain the state of meditation.

6. Concept of Moksha/Salvation :-It is important to understand the meaning of Moksha. Moksha refers to returning to one's original state. Indian sages have compiled spiritual knowledge in the Vedas and explained that the creation of the universe can only be speculated upon because there was nothing before the creation. However, it is certain that there is some conscious power behind the creation. This conscious power began with the splitting of Hiranya's egg into two pieces due to the big bang, and the great conscious power, Brahma, emerged from that egg. The fundamental conscious particle of this power is the Supreme Soul.

Just as every particle of a magnet has magnetic properties, every particle of this great conscious power has consciousness. That is, there is consciousness in the soul, and due to this consciousness, a desire is awakened in the soul. To fulfill this desire, the soul must take a body. However, when the soul recognizes itself as the fundamental element of God, the desires of the soul vanish, and it becomes free from the cycle of birth and death. In the spiritual world, the state of the soul being free from desires is called salvation.

The connecting link that binds the soul to the Supreme Soul is known as devotion. The spiritual theory of the creation of the universe described in the Vedas fully aligns with the concept of salvation as outlined in Shrimad Bhagwat.

The Conclusion

Until the third chapter of the *Srimad Bhagavad Gita*, Shri Krishna presents himself as Arjuna's friend. However, in the fourth chapter, he suddenly reveals himself as a divine power. From a spiritual perspective, according to the Upanishadic statement "Tat Tvam Asi," which means "You are That," a simple living being is essentially the form of Brahman. Therefore, why can't Krishna be God? He mentions a condition for being God: He is beyond the influence of the Triguna Prakriti. Being beyond the influence of the Triguna means being free. Both Karmayogis and Sannyasis are free because Karmayogis perform selfless work without attachment, while Sannyasis do not identify themselves as the doers of work; they feel that they are not doing anything. This state is known as *Akarma*, where one experiences joy in the work itself. Both Karmayogis and Sannyasis are free from the worry of the consequences of their actions.In this chapter, Lord Shri Krishna explains both Karmayog and Sannyas-yog, describing both as equally beneficial and as means of attaining salvation. According to the third chapter, Karmayog is the best means of salvation, while in the fourth chapter, the Lord presents renunciation (Sannyas) as equally good as Karmayog.

In this context, a natural question arises: If both Karmayog and Sannyas-yog are equally beneficial, why is Shri Krishna advising Arjuna to fight and not renounce? Arjuna's question about whether it is right to fight or to take renunciation remains unanswered, even after Shri Krishna's explanations. In the next chapter, Shri Krishna addresses this very question of Arjuna.

-:Om Tat Sat:-

Chapter-5

The Karma-sanyasa Yoga.

The Fifth Chapter of SrimadbhagvatGita at a glance	
Total Nos of verses	29
Nos of verses by lord Shree Krishna	28
Nos of verses by Arjuna	1
Nos of verses by sanjay	0
Nos of verses by Dritrastra	0
Main theam of the Chapter	Action and Salvation

श्री गणेशाय नमः

श्लोकः

वेदेषु धर्मवचनेषु तथागमेषु
रामायणेपि च पुराणकदम्बके वा।
सर्वत्र सर्वविधिना गदितस्त्वमेव
तस्मात्वमेव शरणं मम दीनबन्धो।।

दो0–पार्थ भ्रमित कहने लगे प्रभु करो भ्रम मेरा नाश।
कर्म कभी उतम कहते कभी उत्तम कर्म सन्यास।1।
दो0–स्पष्ट करें प्रभु साधन कौन सा देता जग निर्वाण।
समूल तथ्य विचार के निश्चित कर कहे भगवान।2।

संप्रति सस्मित वोले भगवाना। मार्ग उभय करे जग कल्याणा।।
अतिसुगम पार्थ कर्मयोग साधन। कर्म सन्यास दूष्कर आराधन।।
करे कर्म विगत द्वेष–आशा। यही कर्मयोग अपि कर्मसन्यासा।।
दोनों योग अति सुन्दर युक्ति। योगी सुखपूर्वक पाये मुक्ति।।
द्वौयोग कबहूँ न पृथक फलदाई। व्यर्थ बतकहि अज्ञान है भाई।।
कर्मयोगी अपि कर्म सन्यासी। नित्य योग साकार अविनाशी।।
दोनों पथ भवसागर करे पारा।गुडाकेश यही पाण्ड़ीत्य विचारा।।
यथार्थ यही द्वौयोगफल एका। कर्मयोगी प्राप्य वही कर्मविवेका।।
अति कठिन सन्यास बिनु कर्मा। निर्बाहे मन इन्द्रिय कस धर्मा।।

करे योगी मनन भगवतरूपा। शीघ्र करे प्राप्त वह ब्रह्मअनुपा।।

दो0–जाके हो इन्द्रिय नियंत्रित अंतःकरण अपि शुद्ध।
परमात्मा उर में वसे कभी करे न कर्म विरुद्ध।3।
दो0–सचेत रहे निज कर्म में विगत फल असक्ति।
निर्लिप्त कर्म योगी करे पार्थ अपि यही भक्ति।4।
दो0– कर्म सकल भोजन गमन श्वसन बात व्यवहार।
जगृत रहे या करे शयन सकल इन्द्रिय विकार।5।

करे निजकर्म विगत आसक्ति। अर्पित कर्तापन करे भक्ति।।
पाप योगी को छू नही पाता। जिमी सरोवर जल पंकज नाता।।
निरासक्त कर्म परमात्मा हेतु। बुद्धि इन्द्रिय अपि मुक्ति सेतु।।
कर्मयोगी कर्म फल विलगाई। परमात्म स्वरूप वह शान्तिपाई।।
प्रेरित वांछित कर्मफल अभिलाषा।बन्धे सकाम भौतिककर्मपाशा।।
रहे सन्यासी अन्तःकरण नियंत्रित।न करे कर्म ना करेआमंत्रित।।
रहे नवद्वार गृह देहि पुनिता। शान्त परमात्म अतिसुखीविनीता।।
कर्तापन कबहूँ नहीं रचे विधाता। न रचे कर्म न कर्मफलनाता।।
भौतिक जीवन कर्म स्वाभाविक। जिमि मंझधार मेंनैया–नाविक।।
स्वीकार करे नही पुण्य पातक। परमात्मा निर्लेप्य सर्वव्यापक।।
मनुज ज्ञान–जड़ता आवृति। अज्ञानी पाये न मोह निवृति।।

दो0–कर्तापन कर्म न कर्मफल रचना किये भगवान।
प्रकृति प्रेरित संयोग सब काम क्रोध अभिमान।6।
दो0–मोहित जग में हो रहा ज्ञानी मूढ़ सब आप।
ईश्वर ग्रहण न कछु करे कर्म पुण्य औ पाप।7।
दो0–अज्ञानता नाश जाके भया जानी परम तत्वज्ञान।
जो दिखा सके परमात्मा तत्वज्ञान रवि समान।8।

मन बुद्धि ईश्वर में एकीभावा। करे ज्ञान निरंतर पाप अभावा।।
तत्परायण मनुज परमगति पावे। जन्म अवसान चक्रछूट जावे।।
पापमुक्त जोज्ञान के कारण। न करे जीव पुनः तनधारण।।
विद्या विनय गुण सम्पन्न ज्ञानी। समदर्शी हेतु सकल समप्राणी।।
समदर्शी रहे समभाव सबकाला। सम विप्र गज अरू चाण्डाला।।
निर्दोष सच्चिदानन्द भगवाना। सम मनोभाव वही देवसमाना।।

छूटे जगत्त जन्म–मरण आवृति। जाको ज्ञान समदर्शी धृति।।
जो रहे सदा सम हर्ष विषादा। न करे कवहुँ निज परअपवादा।।
स्थिरचित् संशयहीन ब्रह्मवेता। रहे एकीभाव नित्य आत्मसचेता।।
भौतिकसुख त्यागे संन्यासी। भगवत्भाव पाये सुखराशि।।

दो0–**इन्द्रिय विषय संयोग से उपजे ईच्छा भौतिक भोग।**
विषयी को सुखरूप लगे जग अनित्य दुःखयोग।9।

ज्ञानी नही भौतिक सुख रमता।जाने सकल वह बिषय विषमता।।
काम क्रोध का वेग नियंत्रण। साधक समर्थ है योगी सुमंत्रण।।
अन्तः रमण करे सुख अनुभूति। है आत्मज्ञानी ब्रह्मयोग विभूति।।
है भूत सकल हित योगी प्रवृति।करे ज्ञान सकल संशयनिवृति।।
जाके सकल हो पाप के नाशा। निश्चल मन वह प्रभु निवासा।।
काम विगत हो बुद्धि सचेतन। नित्य घ्यान करे मन अवचेतन।।
ईश्वर संगत नित्य संन्यासी। ज्ञानी प्रतीत सकल ब्रह्म राशि।।
मुनि मनन हरि रूप निरन्तर। निश्चय सच्चिदानन्द अभ्यन्तर।।
सम प्राण–अपान भृकुटि मध्य दृष्टि। बिषयातीत अनुरागीसृष्टि।।
इन्द्रियजीत मुनि मोक्षपरायण। भय रोष मुक्त करे सुख गाायन।।

दो0– मैं हीं सकल लोक का **ईश्वर जाने यह मम् भक्त।**
तप यज्ञ दान सकल मम हेतु करे प्रेम अनुरक्त।10।
दो0– **मूलतत्त्व मैं शान्तिब्रह्म का दयालु स्वार्थ रहित।**
दया प्रेम तत्त्व जान मुझे का तु सत्कर्म पुनित।11।

।।इति पंचम अध्याय।।

Fifth Chapter of Srimadbhagavad Gita

The Essence

The fifth chapter of the *Srimad Bhagavad Gita* is known as *Karma Sannyasa Yoga*. This chapter consists of 29 verses and can be divided into four sections for ease of study:

1.Decision on Sankhya Yoga and Karma Yoga (Verses 1-6):- Arjuna asks Lord Krishna, "Sometimes you praise Karma Yoga, and at other times you praise Karma Sannyasa (Renunciation). Please clarify which of these two paths is more beneficial for me."

Lord Krishna explains that both paths are highly beneficial, but Karma Yoga is superior because it is easier than Karma Sannyasa. A Karmayogi, who is free from attachment, accepts the outcome of his actions like a Sannyasi or monk. Such a person, detached from the dualities of attachment, becomes free from the bondage of the world and experiences happiness. It is not the work of wise people to see Sannyas and Karma Yoga as separate paths with distinct results. Those who excel in either of the two paths attain the Supreme Soul. Karmayogis attain the same result as Gyana Yogis. However, without Karma Yoga, it is difficult to attain the renunciation of doership in all actions. The Karmayogi, who meditates on the form of God, reaches the Supreme Soul quickly.

2. The Virtue of Sankhya Yogi and Karmayogi (Verses 7-12):- A self-controlled person with a pure soul, whose mind is under control, considers all beings as the self. Such a person is a Sankhya Yogi who remains uninvolved even while performing actions. A Sankhya Yogi understands that all the senses perform their duties, while the Karmayogi feels that he himself is not doing anything. Both the Sankhya Yogi and the Karmayogi dedicate the outcome of their actions to the Almighty and renounce attachment. They are untouched by sin, just as the lotus leaf remains above the water. The Karmayogi purifies his inner self by renouncing attachment through the senses, mind, intellect, and body, without possessiveness. By renouncing the results of actions, the Karmayogi attains peace in the form of union with the Supreme Soul, while the selfish person, driven by desire, becomes bound by attachment to the outcomes.

3. Subject of Jnana Yoga (Verses 13-26) :- Those who practice Sankhya Yoga have their inner conscience under control. They neither do any work nor get any work done. Abandoning the desire for results, they live happily in the form of the Supreme Soul, the

Sachchidanandaghan, within their body-like house with nine doors. God neither creates the doership of humans nor the works, nor the conjunction of the results. However, He accepts the nature of humans as it is. The omnipresent God neither accepts anyone's sinful deeds nor anyone's good deeds. But due to ignorance, human intellect becomes deluded, and all ignorant people are misled. The knowledge of *Tatvagyan*—the ultimate knowledge of God (the Supreme Soul)—destroys ignorance and illuminates the soul. Those whose mind and intellect are united with God and devoted to the truth become free from sins through knowledge and attain *Mukti* (salvation).The wise, endowed with knowledge and humility, treat cows, elephants, dogs, and even Chandalas equally. Those whose minds are established in equanimity can conquer the world in this life. This is because God is blameless and equal in all. Those who do not rejoice when they get what they desire, nor become distressed by the unpleasant, have steady intellects, free of doubts, and are always united with the Supreme Brahman, the knower of Brahman. These individuals, who are free from attachment to external objects, experience Satvik bliss through meditation in the soul. Once situated in oneness with God, they experience eternal bliss.

Although materialistic people consider the pleasures derived from the union of senses and their objects to be happiness, these pleasures are temporary and ultimately lead to suffering. Wise individuals do not indulge in such pleasures. A person who, through meditation, is able to control the forces of lust and anger within the body, remains happy. Such a person, who is happy within the soul, attains the state of a Sankhya Yogi or *Shanta-Brahma*. For a Sankhya Yogi, all sins are destroyed, doubts are dispelled by knowledge, and they are always engaged in the welfare of all beings. Their mind is unwavering in devotion to God, and they attain *Brahmaveta Shanta-Brahma*. The wise person who has realized God, keeps their mind under control, and remains free from lust and anger, remains always united with God or the Supreme Brahman.

4. Description of Dhyana Yoga with Devotion (Verses 27-29):- The person who is not distracted by external pleasures and meditates with focused attention, fixing their sight between the eyebrows and equalizing the Prana and Apana Vayu (breaths) in the nose, whose senses, mind, and intellect are conquered, is a sage devoted to salvation. Such a person, free from desire, fear, and anger, remains always liberated. The devotee understands that the Supreme Soul is the enjoyer of all sacrifices and austerities, and that the Supreme Soul is the God of all gods and all worlds. This devotee also recognizes the Supreme Soul as the friend, protector, and lover of all beings. Such a devotee attains peace and salvation.

The Discussion

Karmayoga and Sanyasa (Action and Renunciation)

The fifth chapter of the *Srimad Bhagavad Gita* is significant both from a spiritual and practical perspective. In this chapter, the identity of a Karmayogi is defined as a person who performs selfless work, doing everything without attachment to the outcomes of their actions. But every action produces some result—how is it possible to renounce attachment to the outcome? Similarly, the identity of a Sanyasi is defined as one who has renounced doership. This too seems practically impossible.

According to these definitions, both Karmayoga and Sanyasa may seem impractical. To explain this, scholars often use examples, like those from geometry: a point has no length, breadth, or thickness. Practically, it is impossible to have something without length, breadth, and thickness. Similarly, a line has only length, but no width or thickness, which is also not practical. However, in geometry, these concepts of points and lines are symbolized in a way that is very close to their theoretical definitions.

In spirituality, when defining Karmayogi, it is said that the Karmayogi does nothing while doing everything. Likewise, the Sanyasi is said to do everything while doing nothing. According to these definitions, both Karmayogi and Sanyasi may appear to be abstract concepts, similar to points and lines in geometry. Just as mathematicians use specific symbols to represent points and lines, spiritual practitioners understand Karmayogi and Sanyasi in accordance with their definitions.

In fact, when a person is engaged in work but feels as if they are not the doer, they are in the state of *Karma Sanyasa* (renunciation of action). That is, when a knowledgeable person reaches the state of non-action, they are in a state of Sanyasa. Complete Karmayoga or complete Sanyasa might seem beyond the capabilities of the human body, but their conceptual understanding is possible within the confines of the mind.

In Indian scriptures, Muni Yajnavalkya and Muni Shukdev are considered Sanyasis, while King Janak is regarded as a Karmayogi. According to the scriptures, King Janak was a disciple of Muni Yajnavalkya, and Muni Shukdev was a disciple of King Janak. This shows that the disciple of a Sanyasi (Muni Yajnavalkya) was a Karmayogi (King Janak), and the disciple of a Karmayogi (King Janak) was a Sanyasi (Muni Shukdev). Hence, both Karmayoga and Sanyasa belong to the same tradition.

Until the fourth chapter, Arjuna had doubts about which path, Karmayoga or Karma Sanyasa, is superior. But in this chapter, Shri Krishna clarifies that for a *sadhak* (spiritual practitioner), Karmayoga is better than Karma Sanyasa. This is because even while performing actions, one can imitate the state of doing nothing. However, imitating doing everything by doing absolutely nothing is possible only for a *siddha sadhak* (an enlightened practitioner). In other words, Karmayoga is both a means and a goal, while Sanyasa is only a goal, not a means.

To further explain the superiority of Karmayoga, Acharya Vinoba Bhave provides a practical example in his Geeta discourse. He uses the following analogy:

Suppose the price of gold in the market is Rs. 60,000 per gram. That is, the value of Rs. 60,000 in paper currency and one gram of gold are equal. If the government cancels the validation of paper currency, the value of paper currency becomes zero, while the value of gold never diminishes. Acharya Vinoba presented this idea mathematically:

Karmayog (gold) = Karma (action) + Gyan (knowledge)
Sanyas (paper currency) = Gyan (knowledge)

If the government cancels the validation of paper currency (i.e., if knowledge is removed from both), then Karma remains in Karmayog, but nothing remains in Sanyas. Thus, we can conclude that Karmayoga is the best path for ordinary sadhaks, while Sanyasa is the best for enlightened souls (siddhas).

The Goal of a Man :-The goal of every person in the world is to attain peace. As in the case of Arjuna, two methods are suggested for this:

1. To keep oneself engaged in action.
2. To withdraw from social life.

However, complete peace might not be possible in either case. Lord Shri Krishna explains that a person attains peace when they conquer their senses, mind, and intellect and become free from fear and sorrow. In this material world, this is possible only through Karmayoga. Karmayoga, when used as a means, prevents the senses, mind, and intellect from wandering. As a goal, it leads one to freedom from fear and sorrow. Karma Sanyasa does not mean abandoning action. A Sanyasi is free and performs work with a witness attitude, so it appears that they are not performing any action. In fact, this attitude is what makes it seem as though a Sanyasi does not need to do anything.

The Conclusion

In the fourth chapter of the *Srimad Bhagavad Gita*, Lord Shri Krishna, declaring Himself as God, addresses Arjuna's doubts after explaining various concepts of *Sanatan Dharma*. Shri Krishna clarifies that the root cause of Arjuna's confusion is his ignorance, which is the result of attachment. At the same time, Lord Krishna emphasizes that both Karmayog and Sannyas are paths to salvation. Through a logical analysis of both, Shri Krishna resolves Arjuna's doubts, highlighting the following points:

- *Karma Sannyas* is not possible without *Karmayog*, because both the Karmayogi and the Sannyasi perform actions. The difference lies in the approach: the Karmayogi renounces attachment to the outcomes of his actions, while the Sannyasi renounces the doership of those actions.
- Sannyasis maintain a witness attitude, recognizing that they are not the doers; rather, all the senses perform their functions. On the other hand, Karmayogis engage in work without any desire for personal gain or attachment.
- God is blameless and unique; He does not accept any sin or virtue. Additionally, God neither creates the doership of humans, nor the actions, nor the results of those actions.
- The pleasures arising from the association of the senses with objects may appear to be happiness to those attached to them, but they are ultimately the cause of sorrow. This is because desires such as lust and anger arise from such attachments.
- Doubts can only be dispelled through knowledge. The wise, who possess this knowledge, treat all creatures equally, and by realizing the Supreme Lord in essence, they attain peace.

In this chapter, Shri Krishna makes it clear that, in reality, a Karmayogi (one who performs selfless action) and a Sannyasi are not different. A Karmayogi is, in essence, also a Sannyasi. After understanding the fifth chapter, Arjuna's confusion about Karmayog and Sannyas becomes clear.

An essential condition for both Karmayog and Sannyas is control over the mind. Consequently, Arjuna now has a natural desire to understand how to gain control over his mind. In the next chapter, Lord Shri Krishna explains to Arjuna the methods to achieve mastery over the mind.

-:Om Tat Sat:-

Chapter-6
The Atma-sanyam-yoga

The Sixth Chapter of SrimadbhagvatGita at a glance	
Total Nos of verses	47
Nos of verses by lord Shree Krishna	42
Nos of verses by Arjuna	5
Nos of verses by sanjay	0
Nos of verses by Dritrastra	0
Main theam of the Chapter	**Self Control**

श्री गणेशाय नमः

श्लोक

भजे व्रजैकमण्डनं समस्त पाप खण्डन।
स्व भक्तचितरंजनं सदैव नन्द नन्दनम्।
सुपिच्छ गुच्छ मस्तकं सुनाद वेणु हस्तकं।
अनंग रंगसागरं नमामि कृष्ण नागरम्।।

दो0—हृषीकेशकहे पार्थ सुनो रख निज मन विश्वास।
क्रिया त्याग है योग नही न ताप त्याग सन्यास।1।
दो0—कर्तापन त्यागे संन्यासी योगी त्यागे फल आसक्ति।
दोनो त्यागे संकल्प को बहु भाँती करे प्रभु भक्ति।2।

जो योगारूढ़ होवन मन ईच्छा। निष्काम कर्म ही योगसमीक्षा।।
मोक्षपथ महूँ विघ्न रहे नाना।निष्कामकर्म करे जग कल्याणा।।
पार्थ जगत जो योग आरूढ़ा। संकल्प अभाव राज अतिगूढ़ा।।
संकल्प अभाव है मुक्ति साधन। करे योगारूढ़ प्रभु आराधन।।
अनासक्त नही संकल्प नाना। श्रुति कहे योगारूढ़ पहचाना।।
भवसागर महूँ मनुज तन कैसे। वारिधी महूँ जलयान हो जैसे।।
करे कर्तव्य कर्म मनुज उद्धारा। कर्मयोग करे भवसागर पारा।।
मनुज निज मन अरि अरू मिता।हो भवपार जो निजमन जीता।।
निष्कामकर्म मन इन्द्रिय जीता। जीव वही जग में निज मिता।।

निजअरि मोह बहे भव धारा। नही जाके मन इन्द्रि अधिकारा।।

दो0– शत्रु मित्र बाहर नही करे अन्तर उर में बास।
सदुगुण सखा दुर्गुण रिपु मोह करे मतिनाश।3।

मनोजित चित्तशान्त जीवात्मा। स्वाधीन अपि सम्यक परमात्मा।।
अन्तःवृति की भई जब शान्ति। मिटे जग माया मन भ्रान्ति।।
आत्मतृप्त पाई सम्यकज्ञाना। प्रतीत स्वर्ण–मणि मृदासमाना।।
शीत–उष्ण मान–अपमाना। सुख–दूःख मित–अरि लगे समाना।।
अस प्राणी चित्त् माया मुक्ता।योगारूढ़ हीं भगवत् युक्ता।।
समभाव बिचार करे जग हिता। धर्मात्मा पापी रिपु अरू मिता।।
योगारूढ़ हित यही उपदेशा। एकान्तबासी रहे सजग विशेषा।।
न काहुँ से आशा नहीं परिग्रह। रखे मन इन्द्रियबुद्धि परनिग्रह।।
ईश्वर सदैव रहे आत्मास्थिरा।जगमुक्ति उपाय यही मतिधीरा।।
मन करे इन्द्रिय अनुकूल निर्देशा।योगाभ्यास चित शुद्धविशेषा।।

दो0– करे अभ्यासकर्म योग का चुने एकान्त स्थान।
ना अति उच्च न निम्न ही रहे विशुद्ध वितान।4।
दो0–मृगचर्म करे आवरीत अवनी पर कुशा बिछाय।
मन एकाग्र शुद्धचित् के अन्तःकरण प्रभु रमाय।5।

अचल ग्रिवा आनन अरू काया। रखे दूर भय चिन्ता माया।।
नासिकाग्र पर दृष्टि जमाये। ब्रम्हचारी चित्त मुझमें लगाए।।
जो योगी नित करे अभ्यासा। निश्चित परमानन्द प्रकाशा।।
अतिशयन पार्थ योगविरूद्धा।अति जागरण करे योग अवरूद्धा।।
अतिभोजन अरू अति उपवासा। पार्थ करे योग सिद्धि नाशा।।
यथेष्ट आहार बिहार कर्मवृद्धि। दुःखनाशक योग पाए सिद्धि।।
कामरहित मनकर्म अनुशासित। चित्त परमात्मयुक्त हो भाषित।।
निश्चल चित्त ईश्वर से प्रीति। योगयुक्त योगी यही रीति।।
स्थिरचित योगी मनगति कैसे।गतिमुक्त पवन बीच दीपकजैसे।।
योगनिरूद्ध चित् पाए उपरामा।सुक्ष्मबुद्धि घ्यानजनित परिणामा।।

दो0–समाधि योगकी पूर्णता मनाधिकार प्रभावी युक्ति।
समप्रतीत सुख दुःख सकल हो भौतिक जगमुक्ति।6।
दो0–इन्द्रियातीत आनन्द को ग्रहण करे जब साधक।

सुख अलौकिक व्याप्त रहे भौतिकता नही बाधक।7।
दो0–दुःखरूप संयोग रहित जग में मात्र प्रभुयोग।
मानव कर्तव्य अपि योग है करे धैर्य सहयोग।8।

कामजनित सकल संकल्पा। नष्ट करो मूल बचे न अल्पा।।
मन इन्द्रि पर यदि अधिकारा। बने शनैः अभ्यास सहारा।।
अभ्यास मनुज जो करे निरंतर। रखे धैर्य प्राप्त योग अभ्यन्तर।।
परमात्मा छाड़ी ना कछु चिन्तन। करे भक्ति में अर्पित तनमन।।
मनचंचल कई विषय में बिचरे।मनगति रोकी ध्यान प्रभुका करे।।
मन शान्त जीव पाप रहिता। रजोगुण कछु करे न अहिता।।
रजोगुण पार्थ अपि जगफँदा। रजोगुण शान्त तो परमानन्दा।।
योगी जो ब्रह्म संग एकीभावा। अनन्त परमानन्द वहीं पावा।।
एकीभाव आत्मा पाप नही करता। ईश्वर रूप आनन्द सवरता।।
योगी एकीभाव संग सर्वव्यापी। समभाव जीव धर्मी नही पापी।।

दो0– चैतन्य जीव में आत्मा परमात्मा महूँ सब प्राणी।
अस कल्पना समदर्शी करे जग समान बिनु हानि।9।
दो0– मैं सर्वव्यापी सर्वभूत स्थित प्रतीत करे योगदृष्टि।
ओझल नही मैं योगी से कितनी भी बड़ी सृष्टि।10।

सर्वव्यापी जान करे ममपूजा।मुझे भजे सदा नही कछु दूजा।।
सकल जीव निजसम जो माना।सुख दुःख सब लगे समाना।।
समदर्शी योगी जग अतिउतम।सर्वभुत समभाव रखे नरोतम्।।
कह अर्जुन मधुसूदन हे ज्ञानी। चंचलमन रोक सके न प्राणी।।
कृपानिधान समभाव नही संभव। मन अंकुश जग में है असंभव।।
कैसे जगजीव रखे सम दृष्टि। क्या प्रभु जग में सम सृष्टि।।
मनसंयम जग में अति दूष्कर। यह अतिदृढ़ बलवान भयंकर।।
सस्मित बोले श्री भगवाना। दूष्कर मनरोध जगत ये माना।।
पार्थ रखो निज पर हीं आशा। संभव सब कर नित्य अभ्यासा।।
वैराग्य है पार्थ अपि अनिवार्या।मन वश में रख कहे आचार्या।।

दो0–मोहन मन होता चंचल अतिदृढ़ बलवान।
दूष्कर मन गति रोकना पवन रोध समान।11।

पार्थ नियंत्रित मन नही जाके। योग सकल जग दूष्कर ताके।।
मन बश करी यदि करे प्रयत्ना।पाये सहज योगधन सम रत्ना।।
कह पार्थ योगेश्वर श्री भगवाना। मम मन में है विभ्रम नाना।।
योगश्रद्धा रखे कोई मन माहीं। चाहे प्रभुयोग पर संयम नाहीं।।
अन्तकाल जो योग विचलिता। अस साधक गति कहें मिता।।
योगसिद्धि अप्राप्त जो मूढ़मति। क्या हो अससाधक की गति।।
जीव भगवत् प्राप्ति पथभ्रष्टा।क्या हो मेधसम छिन्नभिन्ननष्टा।।
अस संशय मोहे करे उदासा। भ्रम करहूँ दूर मिटा निराशाा।।
कुन्तिनन्दन से कहे कृपानिधाना। संशय तोर उचित मैं जाना।।
आत्मोद्धार को करे शुभकर्मा। पार्थ र्निवाहे सकल निजधर्मा।।
साधक कदापि जो हो योगभ्रष्टा।न हो इहलोक परलोक नष्टा।।

दो0– भगवत्प्राप्ति को कर्म करे कबहूँ न दूर्गति पाए।
इहलोक परलोक में कर्मफल न कवहूँ नशाए।12।
दो0– योगभ्रष्ट अपि स्वर्ग बसे सखा शुभकर्म अनुसार।
शुद्धचित्त श्रीमन् गृह जन्म हो ले प्रारब्ध उपहार।13।

योगी वैरागी पूर्वजन्म पुण्यकर्मा। जन्में ज्ञानी कुल र्निवहे धर्मा।।
ज्ञानी कुल पार्थ दूष्प्राप्य जन्मा। पाए वहीं जो करे सत्कर्मा।।
कर्मानुसार जीव पावत काया।सकल चराचर हरि की माया।।
पाए शीध्र प्रारब्ध बुद्धि भोगा। भगवत्प्राप्ति को करे कर्मयोगा।।
प्रारब्ध फल मातु पितु भ्राता। सखा समाज सब रिश्ता नाता।।
प्रारब्ध प्रभाव जग संम्पती बृद्धि। सुख दुःख या प्रभुपद सिद्धि।।
योगभ्रष्ट श्रीमनगृह काया पाये। प्रारब्धरूप हरिभक्ति अपनाये।।
समबुद्धि रूप योग प्राप्त जिज्ञासु। कर्म निष्काम प्रारब्ध सुधासु।।
करे कर्मयोगी मुक्ति हेतुप्रयासा।हो ताके पूर्ण मुक्ति अभिलाषा।।
सतं सिद्ध पापरहित जेहीकाला।पाए परमगति जीव निजभाला।।

दो0–तपस्वियों से श्रेष्ठ हैं योगी अपि शास्त्री से उतम्।
सकाम कर्ता से श्रेष्ठ अपि कर्मयोगी बनो नरोतम्।14।
दो0– मोहे परमश्रेष्ठ कर्मयोगी भाए जो हो श्रद्धावान।
अन्तरात्मा से भजन निरंतर सदा करे मम ध्यान।15।

।।इति षष्टम् अध्याय।।

The Sixth Chapter of Srimad Bhagavad Gita

The Essence

The 6th Chapter of the *Bhagavad Gita* is known as *Atmasanyamyoga* (The Art of Self-Control). This chapter consists of a total of 47 shlokas. For the convenience of study, it can be divided into 5 parts.

1.Characteristics of Yogarudha - The Seeker of Salvation (Shloka 1-4):-Lord Krishna further explains that renouncing only fire does not make one a sanyasi, nor does renouncing only actions make one a yogi. The truth is that one who performs actions as part of their duties is both a yogi and a sanyasi. Both yogis and sanyasis renounce attachment to the outcome of their actions because yoga and sanyas are not different. A *Yogarudha* (one who has attained the state of yoga) works without any desire for personal benefit. When there is no attachment to either the pleasures of the senses or the actions themselves, the one who renounces all attachment is called a *Yogarudha.*

2.Signs of Association with the Supersoul (Shloka 5-10):-Man is both his own friend and his own enemy because he is responsible for his own salvation or degradation. One who has conquered the body, mind, and senses is his own friend, while one who has not, is his own enemy. The Supersoul is properly situated in the knowledge of those whose inner thoughts remain peaceful in both happiness and sorrow, in respect and insult. The one who is satisfied in all circumstances due to eternal knowledge, and remains undisturbed by any change, whose senses are well controlled, and for whom soil, stone, and gold hold the same value, that yogi is united with the Supersoul. Such a yogi has similar feelings toward friends, enemies, the indifferent, the moderate, haters, relatives, virtuous, and sinners alike. The yogi who controls the body, mind, and senses, free from desires and attachments, stays alone in a solitary place and continuously focuses his soul on the Supreme Soul.

3.Subject of Dhyana Yoga (Verse 11-32):-In Dhyana Yoga, it is advised that one should establish their seat on pure ground, which is neither too high nor too low, and spread a comfortable *asana* made of kusha grass or cloth on it. After sitting on the *asana*, the practitioner should control their mind and senses, then concentrate their mind. The practice of yoga results in the purity of the soul. The posture should be such that the body, head, and neck are kept straight and steady, with the gaze fixed on the tip of the nose, not looking in other directions. The careful yogi, who observes the vow of celibacy, is fearless, and maintains a peaceful mind, should restrain their mind and focus on the Supersoul. The yogi, with a controlled mind, continuously engages their soul in the Superpower and attains the ultimate peace and bliss that resides in the Supreme Soul.

It is warned that yoga cannot be achieved by one who eats too much or too little, nor by one who sleeps excessively or stays awake continuously. The yoga that destroys sorrow is attained by those who follow a balanced lifestyle, working and sleeping in moderation. The mind, when controlled through proper discipline, becomes established in the Supreme Being. In this state, those who are free from all desires for material pleasures are absorbed in yoga. Just as a lamp does not flicker in a windless place, the mind of a yogi, engaged in meditation on God, remains steady. In this state, the mind, restrained through the practice of yoga, becomes detached. The yogi, realizing God with a subtle intellect purified by meditation, remains satisfied only in God. This state of realization brings infinite bliss, which transcends the senses and can only be grasped by the subtle intellect. In this state, the yogi is never distracted from the form of God. Upon attaining the supreme soul, the yogi considers nothing greater than that realization. A yogi who has attained the Supreme Soul is undisturbed by any sorrow.

Yoga, in its spiritual sense, frees one from the cycle of worldly sorrows. It is our duty to practice this yoga with determination, patience, and enthusiasm. By renouncing everything completely and controlling the senses through the mind, one should practice step by step, keeping the mind focused solely on the Supreme Soul.

The unstable and fickle mind, which wanders in search of worldly pleasures, must be restrained and repeatedly concentrated on God. The yogi whose mind is calm, free from sins, and controlled in *Rajoguna* (the mode of passion), attains supreme bliss by being united with the *Sachchidanandaghan Brahma* (the embodiment of Truth, Consciousness, and Bliss). This sinless yogi experiences the infinite bliss of attaining the Supreme God, able to merge his soul with the Supreme Soul. A yogi who is established in the omnipresent, infinite, conscious oneness, and sees the soul in all beings and all beings in the soul, sees the Lord Vasudeva as the soul of all. They perceive the Lord as pervading all beings, and all beings as contained within the Lord. Such a yogi sees the Lord Vasudeva in all beings, and the Lord sees that yogi, devoted to Him.

The yogi who worships the Lord, understanding that Vasudeva is the soul of all beings, and sees the oneness of all beings in the Lord, is always united with Me. O Arjuna, the yogi who sees all beings as equal to themselves and views happiness and sorrow equally in all beings is considered the best of yogis.

4.Subject of Controlling the Mind (Shloka 33-36):-Arjuna expressed his concern about the mind, stating that it is constantly fluctuating, and he did not see it as being in a permanent state. He wondered how yoga could be possible with such a fickle mind. Lord Krishna acknowledged that the mind is indeed very fickle and restless by nature, powerful and difficult to control. Therefore, controlling the mind is as challenging as stopping the wind.

However, Lord Krishna assured Arjuna that while the mind is difficult to control, it is not impossible. With practice and detachment, the mind can be brought under control. For one whose mind is not under control, yoga is indeed difficult to attain. But for those who put in consistent effort and practice, the mind can be controlled through sadhana, making yoga attainable.

5.The State of a Person Who Has Not Completed His Yoga During His Lifetime (Shloka 37-47):-Arjuna asked what happens to someone who has faith in yoga but is not self-controlled, resulting in a disturbed mind and an inability to attain the perfection of yoga during their lifetime. He questioned whether such a person would be lost, like a scattered cloud, both in this world and in the next. Arjuna turned to Lord Krishna, seeking clarity on this doubt.

Lord Krishna replied that no devotee is ever lost, either in this world or the next. No one who strives for self-liberation, the attainment of the Supersoul, faces destruction. Even if a person does not complete their yoga, they will be rewarded according to their deeds. They will reach heavenly realms or other exalted worlds due to their past actions, where they will reside for a long time. Afterward, they will take birth in the family of noble people with pure conduct. Alternatively, someone detached from the world may be born into a family of yogis. However, such a birth is rare. In this new life, they will easily develop the qualities of right intellect, the spiritual impressions from their previous life, and will continue their efforts to attain God with even greater determination than before.

A person born into a noble family will be naturally inclined toward God due to their previous practices. But a yogi who puts in dedicated effort can perfect their practice in this very birth, using the accumulated spiritual impressions from past lives. This yogi will be free from all sins and attain ultimate salvation immediately. Lord Krishna emphasized that a yogi is superior to ascetics, scholars of the scriptures, and those who perform selfish deeds. He encouraged Arjuna to become a yogi, as the dedicated yogi who constantly worships the Supersoul is the best of all.

The Discussion

After studying the previous five chapters, it is clear that both Karmayoga and Karmasanyas are means of liberation, with Karmayoga being particularly practical for seekers. Karmayoga helps to end attachment to the outcome of karma (action). When the attachment to the result of action is removed, the darkness of ignorance in the intellect fades, and the intellect becomes illuminated by the light of knowledge. However, the intellect of a person functions only when their mind is under control. If the mind is not controlled, all knowledge becomes insignificant.

Therefore, it is natural for Arjuna to doubt how attachment, which is caused by ignorance, can be eliminated by knowledge. Knowledge can only be effective when the intellect can use it, and the intellect can only function properly when the mind is under its control. But the mind is very fickle and strong, making its control as difficult as stopping the wind. This is a very practical doubt of Arjuna. The fickleness of the mind is its inherent nature, and it is almost impossible to predict where the mind will go at any given moment. Because of this instability, our thoughts also become unstable. And if thoughts are not stable, how can the intellect work? Every moment, hundreds of thoughts arise in the mind, and if someone tries to suppress them, they experience mental stress. At present, almost everyone suffers from mental stress, which manifests in abnormal behavior and activities. Various mental and physical diseases arise due to this stress. This issue is also addressed in this chapter of the Srimad Bhagavad Gita.

In other words, we can say that, according to the definition, control over the mind is necessary for both Karmayogi and Sanyasi. Without controlling the mind, both Karmayoga and Karmasanyas are merely abstract concepts.To address Arjuna's doubt, Lord

Krishna explains the practice of Dhyanyoga. Krishna says that the mind can be controlled through Dhyanyoga, which is a sadhana (spiritual practice). For this practice, three essential skills are required:

1. **Concentration of the mind**
2. **Limitation of the needs in life**
3. **Equanimity of vision**

To achieve these three qualities, there are three means:

1. **Exercise**
2. **Renunciation**
3. **Devotion**

Concentration of the mind: Without concentration, it is impossible to achieve success in any field. However, the question arises: how can one concentrate the mind? The problem is that even if external distractions are removed by isolating oneself from external stimuli (such as closing the eyes or ears), the internal thoughts still persist. In other words, the mind cannot be concentrated merely by sitting in a fixed posture. For true concentration, it is essential to have a clear and meaningful goal in front of you. Many people suggest that meditating on God will help concentrate the mind. Regarding God, the great poet Maithilisharangupta explains:

नर हो न निराश करो मन को

कुछ काम करो ,कुछ काम करो,जग में रहकर कुछ नाम करो
यह जन्म हुआ किस अर्थ अहो,समझो जिसमें यह व्यर्थ न हो
कुछ तो उपयुक्त करो तन को,नर हो न निराश करो मन को
संभलो कि सुयोग न जाय चला,कब व्यर्थ हुआ सदुपाय भला
समझो जग को न निरा सपना,पथ आप प्रशस्त करो अपना
अखिलेश्वर है अवलंवन को,नर हो न निराश करो मन को

According to the poet, God, or Akhileshwar (the Supreme Soul), is the ultimate realization. A person must work after determining a meaningful goal. According to the *Shrimad Bhagavad Gita*, when everything is Brahmamay (pervaded by Brahman), the goal itself is also Brahman. Therefore, for concentration of the mind, it is essential to consider our true goal as a task given by the Supreme Soul and continuously strive to achieve it. Only through this process can our mind remain focused.

Limitation of the needs in life: People influenced by the Rajas Guna often have an endless list of desires, but the means to fulfill these desires are limited. In reality, we do not need many things from the list of desires in life. Excessive desires confuse and mislead the mind. Therefore, those who wish to control their minds should categorize their needs and focus only on the most essential ones required to live with dignity in society. Attention should not be given to unnecessary desires. By making such a decision, the chances of the mind becoming confused are reduced.

Samyak Drishti or Shubh Drishti (Right Perspective): There is a famous Sanskrit verse: *विश्वं तद् भद्रं यदवन्ति देवाः* । Vishvam Tad Bhadram Yadavanti Devah.This means that the world is auspicious because God is taking care of it. There is nothing inherently bad in the world. The entire creation reflects our perspective. A negative perspective causes the mind to wander, while a positive perspective keeps the mind focused. The cause of a positive perspective is knowledge, while ignorance leads to a negative perspective. Scholars assert that without cultivating a positive outlook, it is impossible to gain control over the mind.

The above-mentioned skills are crucial for a seeker desiring liberation. A seeker can develop these skills through three types of means:

1.Exercise(Practice): No one gains any skill without effort. To develop any skill, one must practice consistently. Only through persistent practice does a skill strengthen, and eventually, the person masters it. To achieve concentration of the mind, constant practice is also essential.

2.Renunciation (Vairagya): Renunciation does not mean a lack of love. It means not being attached to anything except what is necessary for one's goal. A famous example of Vairagya can be understood from a myth about Hanuman Ji. On one occasion, Mata Sita gifted a pearl necklace to Hanuman Ji. However, Hanuman Ji, instead of wearing the necklace, broke the pearls one by one and threw them away. When asked the reason, he explained that pearls without the presence of Lord Rama held no value for him. From this example, it is clear that Hanuman Ji loved only Rama. Without Rama, the pearls had no significance. Therefore, Vairagya means not loving any person or thing other than what is essential for achieving one's goal. Vairagya is crucial for attaining efficiency in the limited needs of life.

3.Devotion: When a person is determined to achieve something, the reason for this determination can either be divine love or some physical pressure. Determination driven by divine love is called *Shraddha* (Devotion). When someone undertakes any task due to faith or devotion, their vision becomes auspicious and clear.

The Conclusion

It is clear from the dialogue between Shri Krishna and Arjuna up to the fifth chapter that Arjuna has understood *Karmayoga* and *Gnyanayoga* very well. He has also grasped that the ultimate goal of both *Karmayoga* and *Sanyas Yoga* is the same. However, the biggest obstacle in achieving either of these yogas is the wondering mind, as no yoga can be completed without controlling it. The question that arises for Arjuna is: how can the mind be controlled?

To answer this question, Shri Krishna advises Arjuna to practice *Dhyanyoga* and explains that detachment and faith also play an essential role in conquering the mind. However, the method of mind control that Shri Krishna suggests seems difficult and time-consuming to Arjuna. This raises a concern in his mind: the human lifespan is short, and it is possible that he may not be able to attain yoga even after dedicating his life to practicing mind control. According to the eternal principles, if someone does not complete the yoga within their lifetime, they will not achieve liberation from the cycle of birth and death. So, what would be the result of their efforts?

To resolve this doubt, Lord Shri Krishna assures Arjuna that if a person does not attain yoga despite practicing it, then after enjoying the outcome of their good deeds in heaven or other realms, they reborn into a family or situation where they can continue their spiritual journey. The efforts made in previous lives are never wasted. Shri Krishna advises Arjuna to become a yogi—practicing *Karmayoga*—and thus attain liberation.

Though Arjuna is satisfied with this answer, he remains uncertain about the success or failure in *Karmayoga*. This leads him to ask whether there is a specific technique or practice that, when followed, would ensure liberation by being absorbed in yoga within this very lifetime. Lord Shri Krishna answers this question in the next chapter.

-:Om Tat Sat :-

PART-2

THE DEVOTION

Chapter-7
The Gyan -Vigyan Yog

Verses in the Seventh Chapter at a glance	
Total Nos of verses	30
Nos of verses by lord Shree Krishna	30
Nos of verses by Arjuna	0
Nos of verses by sanjay	0
Nos of verses by Dritrastra	0
Main theam of the Chapter	Illusion and the Mind Control

श्री गणेशाय नमः

श्लोकः

जगदीश सुधीश भवेश विभो
परमेश परात्पर पूत पितः।
प्रणतं पतितं हतबुद्धिबल।
जन तारण ताराय तापितकम्।।

दो0– भगवन बोलें पार्थ सुनो चैतन्य योगाभ्यास।
जान इसे भ्रम दूर हो रख मन ध्रुव विश्वास।1।
दो0– तत्वज्ञान मैं बतलाउँ विज्ञान सहित गुडाकेश।
आदर्श ज्ञान तु पायेगा भ्रम न रहें कोई शेष।2।

असंख्य मनुज पार्थ जगमाही।छाड़ि कछुक मोहे जाने नाहीं।।
कछुक कोटि करे पूर्ण प्रयासा। राखी ह्दय तत्वज्ञान आशा।।
सहस्त्र यत्नशील महँ एका। तत्वज्ञान बढ़ाये बुद्धि विवेका।।
जड़ चेतन दो प्रकृति मेरी। अपरा परा कहत जगकेरी।।
जड़ प्रकृति अपि अष्ट रूपा। जो है रचत यह सृष्टि अनुपा।।
गगन पवन जल अवनी अंगारा।अष्टघटक बुद्धि मन अहंकारा।।
परा प्रकृति चैतन्य जग कारण। जासे करूं मैं यही जगधारण।।
जड़चेतन पार्थ सृजन मूला। मैं प्रभव प्रलय धर्म अरू शूला।।

मुझसे परे जगसत्य न कोई। मम् इच्छानुरूप जगत सब होई।।
सकल जगत जुड़ी मुझसे कैसे। मणिगुथित उरमाल में जैसे।।

दो0–वैदिक महाँमंत्र ओंकार मैं पुरुषों का पूरूषत्व।
अवनी गन्ध ताप अगन अरू जीवन मूल तत्त्व।3।
दो0–तपस्वियों की शुद्धतपस्या रवि चन्द्र का तेज।
जल शीतलता गगन ध्वनी मैं अपि रखुं सहेज।4।

सकल सनातन बीज मूलरूपा। मैं तेजस्वी घरूँ तेज अनुपा।।
बुद्धिमान मनुज की निर्मलबुद्धि। करूं सकल विवेक की शुद्धि।।
आसक्तिरहित बलवानो का बल। ज्ञानी ज्ञान बढ़ाऊँ प्रतिपल।।
जीव काम मैं धर्म अनुकूला। जगत हेतु सात्विक सुख मूला।।
मैं स्वतंत्र हर जगह उपस्थित। मुझमें सकल जगत अवस्थित।।
सत्व रज तम है मेरी व्युत्पती। जो करे मोह शोक उत्त्पत्ति।।
मोहित मनुज कहाँ मुझे जाने। त्रिगुणलिप्त मुझे कब पहचाने।।
मैं स्वयंभु जग त्रिगुणातीता। त्रिगुणतत्त्व मोको मोहे न मिता।।
त्रिगुण उलंघन है अति दूस्तर। मोहित करे सकल नारी–नर।।
अहंकार तजि शरण जो आये। त्रिगुणमाया से मुक्त हो जाये।।

दो0–भ्रम सदैव ही बुद्धि हरे कहते है सब ज्ञानी।
नश्वर मुझको जो समझे वहीं जगत्त अज्ञानी।5।
दो0–पार्थ विराट् संसार में मेरे भक्त की श्रेणी चार।
अर्थार्थी आर्त जिज्ञासु अरू ज्ञानी सन्त उदार।6।

जग जीवन में अर्थ की सत्त्ता। अर्थार्थी अर्थ की माने महत्ता।।
अर्थ जग जीवन में सुखदाता। अर्थार्थी अर्थ को भजे विधाता।।
पीड़ा पाए प्रारब्ध के कारण। आर्त इच्छा निज कष्ट निवारण।।
कष्ट निवारण हेतु करे भक्ति। करे कर्मकाण्ड जो श्रुति उक्ति।।
यथार्थ जानी जग भ्रम मिट जाए।जिज्ञासु नित वही करेउपाय।।
यथार्थ ज्ञान हेतु नित्य भक्ति। पाई ज्ञान मिट जाय आसक्ति।।
तत्वतः मोहे जानत जगज्ञानी।चित्त शुद्ध शान्त जस गहरापानी।।
एकीभाव स्थित ज्ञानी है उत्तम।मम प्रियभक्त हो ज्ञानी नरोत्तम्।।
मम भक्त रहे चित्तशुद्ध उदारा। ज्ञानी ज्ञान मोको अतिप्यारा।।
ज्ञान पार्थ मम सुगम स्वरूपा। ज्ञानी मम वाँछित जगरूपा।।

दो0—जन्म जन्म चेष्टा करी जो जाने मम तत्त्व स्वमेव।
सकल तत्त्व है वासुदेव दूर्लभ अस ज्ञानी सदैव।7।
दो0—भोग कामना ज्ञान हरे प्रेरित करे स्वभाव।
अनेक देव अज्ञानी भजे भौतिकता मनभाव।8।

मनुज सकाम करे अर्चन देवा। करे नित्य नियम धरी सेवा।।
भजे मनुज जेही देव आशा। रचूँ साधक उर अस विश्वासा।।
जामें करे वह देव की भक्ति। बुद्धि समझे भक्ति की शक्ति।।
जाके श्रद्धा रहे देव प्रति जैसी। ईच्छित फल साधक की वैसी।।
विधान अनुसार मिले फलनाना। ममरचित जग सकल विधाना।।
कर्मफल क्षणिक अल्पज्ञानी पावे। देव भजे देवलोक ही जावे।।
मम अनन्य भक्त पावे ममलोका। उत्तम अमर कबहूँ न शोका।।
अविनाशी ममरूप मूढ़ न जाने। मुझे अनित्य मानव हीं माने।।
सर्वस्व अप्रकट आवृत माया। अज्ञानी सकल जगत भरमाया।।
ज्ञात मोको है सकल जहाना। काल भूत भविष्य मैं जाना।।

दो0—सृष्टि के सकल भूत को जानु मैं भली प्रकार।
पार्थ अज्ञानी क्या जाने किसने रचा संसार।9।
दो0—इच्छा द्वेष अपि सुख दुःख द्वन्द्व रूप है मोह।
सकल प्राणी मोहित इससे जो अज्ञान आरोह।10।

निष्कामभाव श्रेष्ठकर्म आचरण।निष्पाप करे जग निर्भय विचरण।।
द्वन्द्वमोहमुक्त दृढ़ व्रतधारी। श्रद्धायुक्त करे भजन हमारी।।
शरणागत करे नित्य यत्ना।जरामरण छाड़ी मिले भक्ति रत्ना।।
ब्रह्म समान अध्यात्म जो जाने। करे कर्म अकर्ता मन माने।।
भक्त सचेत वहीं ब्रह्मवेता। अध्यात्मिक कर्म को कर्म प्रणेता।।
नरनारी सकल प्राणी नारायण।कहे ज्ञानीभक्त अध्यात्मपरायण।।
जगमंगल चिंतक पार्थ महात्मा। परमभक्त हो युक्तपरमात्मा।।
अपूर्व साधना परमेश्वर भक्ति। मिले प्राणी जगजीवन मुक्ति।।
भगवत् भक्ति मूलतत्त्व भावना। जस भाव तस मिले पावना।।
जाकर भक्ति ना कोई कारण। मम् भक्त वही है असाधारण।।

दो0–पार्थ भक्त मम अति निकट युक्तचित्त अपि सर्वज्ञ।
प्रयाणकाल मे युक्त सदा अधिदैव अधिभूत अधियज्ञ।11।

।।इति सप्तम् अध्याय।।

Srimad Bhagavad Gita Seventh Chapter

The Essence

The seventh chapter of the Bhagavad Gita is known as *Gyan Vigyan Yog*. This chapter consists of a total of 30 shlokas. For ease of study, it can be divided into five parts.

1.Knowledge (Shloka 1-7):- Lord Krishna said: "Arjuna, you are attached to me with exclusive love and unwavering devotion. Therefore, I shall impart to you the *Tatvgyan* (true knowledge) along with its complete science. By knowing this, nothing in the world will remain unknown to you.

You will come to know me, without any doubt, as the Supreme Soul, adorned with all glory, power, wealth, and other divine qualities. Among thousands of people, only one strives to attain me as a devotee. Out of thousands of such devotees, only one endeavors to know me in essence, that is, in my true form.

My nature is divided into eight forms: earth, water, fire, air, sky, mind, intellect, and ego. These eight constitute my inert or lower nature. Beyond this, there is my conscious or higher nature, by which I sustain the entire universe. All beings are born from these two aspects of my nature, and I am the ultimate root cause of the entire creation. I am both its origin and its dissolution.

There is no other supreme cause apart from me. This entire universe is woven into me, like buds strung on a thread."

2. **Omnipresence of God (Shloka 8-12):-** Lord Krishna further said: "I am the essence in water, the light in the moon and sun, the *Omkar* in all the Vedas, the sound in the sky, and masculinity in

men. I am the fragrance in the earth and the brightness in fire. I am the penance of ascetics and the life force in all beings.I am the eternal seed of all living entities. I am the wisdom of the wise and the brilliance of the brilliant. I am the strength of the strong, free from attachment, and the work that aligns with *Dharma*.The feelings that arise from the *Trigunas* (three modes of material nature) emanate from me, but in truth, I am beyond the influence of the *Trigunas*."

3. **Demonic nature and devotee of God (Shloka 13-19):-** Lord Krishna continued: "The entire world is captivated by the *Trigunas* (three modes of material nature), and because of this, it fails to recognize the *Trigunatita*—the one beyond these modes. This divine *Maya* of mine, filled with the *Trigunas*, is extremely difficult to overcome. However, my devotees, by their devotion, transcend this *Maya* and attain liberation from the material world.Those whose understanding has been clouded by *Maya*, who possess demonic nature, are the lowest among humans, and the foolish ones engaged in impure deeds—such people do not worship me.

Among those who do, there are four types of devotees:

1.Artharthi: One who worships me for material possessions or worldly desires.

2.Aart: One who worships me to find relief from their suffering.

3.Jigyasu: One who worships me out of a desire to know the ultimate truth.

4.Gyani: One who worships me with the true knowledge of my essence.

Among these, the *Gyani* devotee is the best because they truly know me in essence. I am very dear to them, and they are equally dear to me. All four types of devotees are noble, but the *Gyani* is my own embodiment, as they are firmly established in me, the ultimate goal and the highest form of salvation.After many births, the one who attains true knowledge realizes that everything is *Vasudev* (me). Such a sage, who worships me with this realization, is extremely rare."

4. **Worship of Supersoul (Shloka 20-23):-** Lord Krishna said: "people driven by the desire for enjoyment worship many gods. Their understanding is clouded, leading them to follow various rituals and rules. Whatever form of deity a devotee wishes to worship with faith, I make their devotion steadfast toward that deity.

In this way, following the laws established by me, they undoubtedly attain the desired pleasures. However, such results are temporary and perishable. Those who worship the deities reach the realms of those deities, but my devotees ultimately attain me and achieve salvation."

5. **Devotee of God (Shloka 24-30):-** Lord Krishna said: "Those with dull intellect fail to recognize my imperishable supreme nature. They mistake me for a mortal being with a human form, bound by mind and senses, and believe I have attained a personal form. Hidden by my *Yogmaya*, I remain invisible to all, and thus, ignorant people do not perceive me as immortal. Instead, they think of me as being subject to birth and death.I know the past, the present, and the future, but no one without devotion truly knows me. In this world, all beings are overcome by ignorance due to the dualities of happiness and sorrow, born from desire and hatred. However, those who perform noble deeds selflessly, whose sins have been eradicated, and who are steadfast in their devotion, worship me in every way. These devotees, free from the dual attachments of love and hatred, recognize me.

Those who take refuge in me and strive to overcome old age and death gain true knowledge. They come to understand *Brahma* (the eternal essence), complete spirituality, and the totality of actions. At the end of their life, those who know me as *Adhibhuta* (the perishable element), *Adhidaiva* (the divine element), and *Adhiyajna* (the supreme sacrifice), and concentrate their minds on me, are the ones who truly know me in my complete essence."

The Discussion

What is Bhakti?

In the seventh chapter, Lord Shri Krishna explained that if someone seeks *Yog Siddhi* (spiritual perfection) or *Mukti* (liberation), they must come under my protection. This means that, despite countless efforts, no one can free themselves from *Maya* without seeking refuge in the Supreme Soul.As long as ego resides within a person, freedom from *Maya* is impossible. However, one who relinquishes ego and surrenders to the Supreme Soul becomes free from *Maya*. Letting go of ego and taking refuge in the Supreme Soul—becoming one with the Supreme—is known as *Bhakti* (devotion).

In other words, *Bhakti* is the culmination of *Gyanyoga* (the path of knowledge) and *Karmayoga* (the path of action), through which ultimate concentration and spiritual realization can be achieved.

What is Maya?

Maya is a divine power of God, and under its influence, beings remain deluded. This confusion in individuals is also part of the *leela* (divine play) of the Supreme Soul. Deluded individuals become trapped in their own web of attachment.The more they struggle to free themselves from this web, the deeper they become entangled. However, when they exhaust themselves in their attempts and realize the futility of their efforts, their ego begins to dissolve.

In this way, by relinquishing their ego, they attain liberation from its grip and draw closer to God, achieving His proximity.

Types of devotees:- There are two types of devotees of God:

1. **Sakaam Bhakt (Devotee with desire):-** Devotees who have some desire in their hearts are known as *Sakaam Bhakts* (devotees with desires). Such devotees seek something from God, firmly believing that God will fulfill their wishes. Asking something from God is not wrong; in fact, a devotee's unwavering faith that God is with them is significant. A devotee who approaches God with a request is considered extraordinary. That is why God says, "I strengthen the devotion of *Sakaam Bhakts*." In devotion, feelings hold great importance. Regardless of the desire that brings a devotee to seek refuge in God, the essential truth is that they have drawn closer to Him.When a devotee remains close to God, their devotion gradually becomes perfect, leading them to spiritual fulfillment.

2. **Niskaam Bhakt (Devotee witout desire): -** There are two types of Niskaam Bhakt:

A) One-Sided *Nishkaam Bhakt*:A *Nishkaam Bhakt* is a devotee who seeks something from God that cannot be found in physical form. There are three types of one-sided *Nishkaam Bhakts*:

i) Aart:-These devotees are restless to receive God's grace. They perceive the world as full of sorrow and seek liberation from worldly sufferings. To achieve this or to gain God's grace, they engage in various forms of worship, such as *puja*, *bhajan*, or even dancing. An example of such a devotee is Mother Meerabai. These devotees view every action through the lens of God's love, demonstrating unwavering faith in Him. This deep faith fosters a relationship of exclusive love with God.

ii) Curious (*Jigyasu*):-A curious devotee is driven by an insatiable desire to learn and understand. They explore the properties and essence of everything, relying on God, the ultimate source of all knowledge and qualities, for guidance. Such devotees view all actions from the perspective of acquiring knowledge.

iii)Artharthi:-*Artharthi* devotees evaluate their actions based on the welfare of living beings in the world. They seek meaning in their deeds, ensuring their actions align with the principles of welfare and righteousness. These devotees perceive all actions through the lens of intellect and recognize that intellect is a divine gift from God.

B)Gyani (Knowledgeable Devotee):-To a *Gyani* devotee, the entire world appears as a manifestation of God. They firmly believe in the omnipresence of the Supreme Being and, through this realization, merge with God.

In the fourth chapter, Shri Krishna explained that He is *Trigunatita*—beyond the effects of the three *gunas* (qualities) of nature: *Sattva* (goodness), *Rajas* (passion), and *Tamas* (ignorance). Ordinary beings cannot transcend the influence of the *Trigunas*. According to the principles of *Sanatan Dharma*, only the Supreme Soul is *Trigunatita*—free from the effects of the three *gunas*.If someone seeks salvation, they must surrender to the Supreme Soul. The one who surrenders to the Supreme Soul is called a devotee. From a spiritual perspective, the seventh chapter of the *Shrimad Bhagavad Gita* holds great significance. Through this chapter, Shri Ved Vyasa emphasizes that without devotion, neither *Karmayoga* nor *Gyanyoga* can lead to success.

From a practical standpoint, this chapter is equally important. To understand its practical value, it is essential to consider the message of the *Shrimad Bhagavad Gita* up until this chapter.

The *Shrimad Bhagavad Gita* begins with Arjuna's indecision about whether going to war is the right course of action. Shri Krishna first justifies the war by taking into account the practical aspect of society. He then explains *Karmayoga* and *Gyanyoga*, demonstrating that the ultimate goal of both paths is liberation. In essence, *Yogi* and *Sannyasi* are not distinct; both seek the same end. This clarification makes it clear to Arjuna, who was contemplating renouncing the war and adopting the path of *Sannyasa*, that *Karmayoga* is simpler than *Gyanyoga*. Thus, Shri Krishna encourages Arjuna to fight. However, for both *Gyanyoga* and *Karmayoga*, control over the mind is essential. Since controlling the mind is not easy, how, then, can *Karmayoga* or *Sannyasa* be achieved easily?

To address this, Shri Krishna introduces *Dhyanyoga* as a way to control the mind, emphasizing that concentration is key to meditation. Concentration, in turn, can only be attained when the mind is focused on one thing. In the seventh chapter, that one thing to focus on is the Supreme Soul. There is no need for despair.

Many scholars argue that despair is characteristic of an atheist, while hope is the hallmark of a believer. Faith in the Supreme Power supports the belief that we possess immense potential and can accomplish anything. From a practical viewpoint, our motivation for action comes from the joy we anticipate from achieving our goals. Just as devotion is the only means to connect with the Supreme Power, similarly, if we align ourselves with our goals, success is ensured. To achieve a goal, we must first connect ourselves to it.

For instance, if we aspire to become an administrative officer, before taking action, we must envision the joy we will experience upon reaching that position. Once we connect ourselves with that joy, it becomes our motivation, driving us to put forth our best effort and achieve success.

The message of this chapter in practical life is that devotion is the act of connecting oneself with the joy of achieving the goal. Salvation, from a spiritual standpoint, is similar to the achievement of a goal in practical life. The bliss experienced upon attaining salvation mirrors the joy felt when reaching a goal. The effort put into achieving the goal is *Karmayoga* or *Sannyasa Yoga*, while the connection with the joy of achieving the goal is *Bhakti* (devotion).

Conclusion

In the sixth chapter, we learned that Arjuna had a doubt about the shortness of human lifespan and the long time required to practice controlling the mind. He wondered if there was a way to attain salvation with less practice. To resolve this doubt, Shri Krishna advises Arjuna to renounce his ego and practice with devotion. Devotion is the only means that can control the mind and concentrate the intellect. Therefore, at the end of this chapter, Shri Krishna says that at the end of his life, a devotee who knows Him as *Adhibhut* (the perishable world), *Adhidev* (the supreme divine), and *Adhiyajna* (the supreme sacrifice) will attain liberation.

This means that when a person connects with the doer (*Adhibhut*), the inspiration of action (*Adhidev*), and the action itself (*Adhiyajna*), they will undoubtedly succeed in achieving their goal. This is the essence of devotion, through which a devotee sheds their ego and unites with the supreme bliss.

While the earlier chapters of the *Shrimad Bhagavad Gita* discuss practical knowledge, the seventh chapter delves into deep spirituality. It is natural, then, that many spiritual questions would arise in Arjuna's mind. To address these, Shri Krishna provides answers to Arjuna's spiritual queries in the following chapter.

-: Om Tat Sat :-

Chapter-8
TheAkshar-Brahma Yoga

Verses in the Eighth Chapter at a glance	
Total Nos of verses	28
Nos of verses by lord Shree Krishna	26
Nos of verses by Arjuna	2
Nos of verses by sanjay	0
Nos of verses by Dritrastra	0
Main theam of the Chapter	**The Gist of Life**

श्री गणेशाय नमः

श्लोकः

गुणहीन सुदीन मलीन मति।
त्वयि पातरि दातरि चापरतिम्।
तमसा रजसा वृत वृतिमिम।
जन तारण ताराय तापितकम्।।

दो0—विस्मित पार्थ करजोरी कहे पुरूषोतम घनश्याम।
ब्रह्म अध्यात्म अरू कर्म क्या बतलायें सुखधाम।1।
दो0—अधिभूत किसको कहते अधिदैव का कहें स्वरूप।
अधियज्ञ कैसे चित्तबसे प्रयाणकाल तवरूप।2।

गूढ़ रहस्य श्री कृष्ण बखाने। विनाश रहित ब्रह्म जग जाने।।
जो है निजस्वरूप जिवात्मा। अध्यात्म इसे ही कहे महात्मा।।
जग कल्याण हेतु जो सेवा। कर्म वहीं करे संत मुनि देवा।।
जाके होवत जन्म अवसाना। अधिभूत पार्थ कहे वेद पुराणा।।
विश्व विदित प्रकट जो देवा। करे जगपोषण पार्थ अधिदेवा।।
स्वयं परमात्मा अधियज्ञ रूपा। यही बसे देह चैतन्य नरभुपा।।
मम स्मरण करी त्यागे देहा। मम्स्वरूप पाये न कछु संदेहा।।
अन्तकाल जीव भावना जैसी। स्वरूप धरे जीव जग वैसी।।
पूर्वजन्मान्त भावरूप जगदेहा। भावित गुण क्रोध अरू नेहा।।

करो युद्ध उरधरी मम ध्याना। पार्थ अवश्य हो तव कल्याणा।।

दो0—पार्थ अटल नियम यही हरि ध्यान योग अभ्यास।
चिन्तन हरिरूप करे स्थिरचित्त् जाये हरि के पास।3।

जो है सर्वज्ञ अनादि अनन्ता। अर्न्तयामी चर—अचर नियन्ता।।
अति सूक्ष्म अचिन्त्य स्वरूपा। भरण करे अग जग नर भुपा।।
चैतन्य रविसम नित्य प्रकाशा। जो करे तमस अविद्या नाशा।।
शुद्धचित्त अस प्रभु ध्याये ज्ञानी। होय ताके भवबन्धन हानि।।
अस भक्त निज प्रयाणकाला। प्राण स्थापित करे मध्य भाला।।
योगबल मिले योग की सिद्धि। निश्चल मन हो योगबलबृद्धि।।
स्मरण रखे शुद्ध सच्चिदानन्दा।मिले परमगति मिटे जग द्वन्द्वा।।
परमपद प्राप्ती हेतु सब युक्ति। सुनो पार्थ संक्षिप्त पथमुक्ति।।
जाको ज्ञानी कहत अविनाशी। अनासक्त यत्न करे संन्यासी।।
ब्रह्मचर्यकरे धारण ब्रह्मचारी। युक्ति अनेक करे नर नारी।।

दो0—सकल इन्दिय संयम कर मन स्थापित हृदेश।
भृकुटिमध्य में प्राण धरो योगबल से गुड़ाकेश।4।
दो0—अक्षर ब्रह्म निर्गुण स्वरूप कर ओकांर का जाप।
चिन्तन मेरा स्वरूप का समाप्त करे भव ताप।5।
दो0— उच्चारण करे जो ऊँ का तजे पार्थिव देह।
स्मरण ब्रह्मस्वरूप मिले परमगति बिनसंदेह।6।

अनन्यचित्त् रहे नित्य निरंतर। स्मरण करे योगी अभ्यंतर।।
सहज सुलभ दिक् दिगन्तर। योगी मोको भजे निरंतर।।
नहीं शाश्वत क्षणभंगुर काया। दुःखगेह लिप्त रहे जगमाया।।
मम भक्त परमसिद्धि पाये। मरणेपरान्त पुनर्जन्म विसराये।।
ब्रह्मलोक अरू अगजग सारा। सृष्टि लोप प्रकट हो बारंम्बरा।।
ब्रह्मादि लोक कालसीमिता। परमात्मा अनित्य मैं कालातीता।।
मम् भक्त अत्यन्त मोको भाये। यही कारण पुनर्जन्म न पाये।।
ब्रह्म दिवस गुणी कहे बखानी।सहस्त्र चतुर्युग सम जग मानी।।
सहस्त्र चतुर्युग सम ब्रह्म रात्रि। कहे योगी कालतत्त्व धात्रि।।
अहोरात्र ब्रह्म के बीते अनेका। जाने कालगति ज्ञानीविवेका।।

दो0–धरे ब्रह्म दिवस प्रारंभ में चराचर भौतिक देह।
सूक्ष्म ब्रह्म से प्रकट यह चैतन्य जगत आत्मगेह।7।
दो0–सकल चराचर विलिन ब्रह्म जब आए ब्रह्मराती।
कालचक्र जीवजगत में व्यक्ताव्यक्त एही भाँती।8।
दो0– शाश्वत परम दिव्यपुरुष नहीं व्यक्ताव्यक्त आधीन।
निज योगमाया प्रकट अप्रकट रहे सदैव स्वाधीन।9।

अक्षरब्रह्म इति विश्रुत नामा। अव्यक्त भाव भक्ति परिणामा।।
एहीभाव परमगति संचालक। अक्षरब्रह्म अग जग के पालक।।
पार्थ वही परम मम धामा। अव्यक्त भाव जहँ पाए विश्रामा।।
अनश्वर कण कण में स्थित। सर्वभूत है व्याप्त व्यवस्थित।।
शाश्वत ब्रह्म पार्थ सर्वोत्तम। जाको पाये भक्त अतिउत्तम्।।
द्वौमार्ग प्राणी हृषिकेशबखाना। आत्मगति उपरांत अवसाना।।
एकमार्ग जीव परमगति पाये। दूजेपथ प्राणी पुनः जग आए।।
जेहीपथ देवअग्नि अभिमानी। उतरायण शुक्ल दिनकर ज्ञानी।।
वो मार्ग अर्चिमार्ग कहलाए। जेही पथ जीव परमगति पाए।।
रात्रिकृष्णपक्ष दक्षिणायन स्वामी। चन्द्रालोक स्वर्गमारगगामी।।
निशापथ पार्थ धूम्रपथ कहलाये। स्वर्गभोगी जीव बापस आये।।

दो0–सनातन गति द्वौ मार्ग विदित देवयान पितृयान।
देवयान दे परमगति पितृयान फिरी लाये जहान।10।
दो0– तत्वज्ञानी योगी ही जाने सनातन द्विपथ हाल।
योगयुक्त करो साधना समबुद्धि रखों सब काल।11।
दो0– वेद पढ़े ना यज्ञ करे न पुण्य तप दान हजार।
तत्वज्ञानी पाए परमगति जिनका अक्षर आधार।12।

।।इति अष्टम् अध्याय।।

The Eighth Chapter of Srimadbhagavad Gita

The Essence

The eighth chapter of the *Srimad Bhagavad Gita* is known as *Akshar Brahma Yoga*. This chapter consists of 28 shlokas, and for the convenience of study, it can be divided into three parts.

1. **Arjuna's seven queries and Solution (Shloka 1-10):-** At the end of the seventh chapter, Lord Shri Krishna had mentioned *Adhidaiva*, *Adhiyajna*, and other related concepts. In response, Arjuna asks seven questions to Lord Shri Krishna to understand these spiritual topics in more detail:

1. What is Brahma?
2. What is Adhyatma?
3. What is Karma?
4. What is Adhibhuta?
5. Who is called Adhidaiva?
6. Who is Adhigya, and how is He present in this body?
7. How can one know those with a focused mind at the time of death?

Shri Krishna responds to Arjuna's queries as follows:

8. *P*aram Akshar (the Imperishable) is Brahma.
9. Our original form, the soul, is called Adhyatma.
10. The sacrifice that gives rise to the feelings of the elements is called Karma.
11. All things that have the nature of birth and destruction are Adhibhuta.
12. Hiranyagarbha Brahma is known as Adhidaiva.
13. As the inner self, I am the Adhiyajna.
14. The one who remembers Me at the time of death, giving up their ego, attains My form or Salvation.

After answering Arjuna's queries, Lord Krishna further explains that the feeling with which a person leaves their body at the time of death determines their next birth. If a person is immersed in a particular desire at the time of death, they take rebirth to fulfill that desire. Therefore, you must fight to protect Dharma and remember Me, for through this, you will undoubtedly attain Salvation.

The rule is that a divine person, who constantly thinks of the Supreme Lord with concentration, will ultimately attain the

Supreme Lord. Thus, one who remembers the omniscient, eternal, controller of all, the subtlest of all, the inconceivable form, the eternally conscious light like the Sun, and the pure *Sachchidanandaghan* Supreme Lord at the time of death, while properly establishing the life force between the eyebrows with the power of yoga and a steady mind, will attain that divine Supreme Being, the Supreme Soul.

2.Introduction to Bhakti Yoga (Shloka 11-22):- Further, Lord Krishna says that He will briefly describe the supreme position to Arjuna, which is indestructible. Only those devotees who are free from attachment can attain this position. One who utters the Om syllable, which represents Brahma, by closing the doors of all the senses, controlling the mind, and establishing the breath in the supreme, while abandoning the body, attains ultimate salvation.

Lord Krishna reveals that He is easily accessible to the Yogi who is undividedly associated with Him and constantly remembers Him. The great souls (Mahatmas) who have attained the ultimate perfection do not experience a temporary rebirth after reaching Him. All the worlds, up to Brahmalok, are subject to cycles of creation and destruction, but after attaining Him, there is no rebirth. This is because He is beyond time, while all the worlds of Brahma and beyond are temporary, being limited by time.

Those who understand the nature of time know that the duration of one day of Brahma is one thousand Chaturyugas, and similarly, one night of Brahma lasts for one thousand Chaturyugas. At the beginning of Brahma's day, all living and non-living beings are born from the unmanifested, subtle body of Brahma, and at the beginning of his night, they are absorbed back into that unmanifested state. This cycle continues, and the same group of beings, born under the influence of nature, undergoes this process of birth and absorption in the ongoing cycles of day and night.

Beyond all of this, there exists an eternal, unmanifested being that is not destroyed, even when all the elements are destroyed. This unmanifested being, called *Akshar* (the imperishable), and is also known as the ultimate attainment. After attaining this, humans do not return. This is My ultimate abode, which can only be reached through exclusive devotion.

3.Shukla and Krishna Marg (Shloka 23-28):- Lord Krishna further explains the paths by which Yogis who leave their bodies attain either the state that does not lead to rebirth or the state that leads to reincarnation.

The path that leads to the state of no return is associated with the deities of the luminous fire, the day, the Shuklapaksha (bright fortnight), and the six months of Uttarayan (the northern course of the sun). The Brahmavetas (those who know Brahman) who follow this path are taken by these deities in sequence and ultimately attain Brahma.

On the other hand, the path that leads to reincarnation is associated with the deities of smoke, the night, the Krishnapaksha (dark fortnight), and the six months of Dakshinayan (the southern course of the sun). Those who follow this path are taken by these deities in sequence, enjoy the rewards of their good deeds, and then return to the cycle of birth and death.

In this world, these two paths — the Shukla (or Devayana) and the Krishna (or Pitryana) paths — are considered the two eternal paths. One who follows the first path attains the ultimate goal, while the one who follows the second path returns, experiencing rebirth and death.

After understanding these two paths in their true sense, no Yogi will be deluded. Therefore, you should always be endowed with the Yoga of balanced understanding and strive for my attainment.

By understanding this secret fully, the Yogi transcends all the merits earned from reading the Vedas, performing yajnas (sacrificial rites), penance, and charity, and attains the eternal supreme position.

The Discussion

Akshar Brahma:-By the seventh chapter of Srimad Bhagavad Gita, Arjuna has learned that Bhakti (becoming one with the goal) is the only reliable way to achieve success. Without Bhakti, success in all other endeavors, such as Karmayoga, Sanyas, and Dhyan Yoga, is impossible. Bhakti requires the surrender of ego. At the end of the seventh chapter, Lord Krishna says that a devotee, at the time of death, knows God as Adhibhuta, Adhidev, and AdhiYajana. Practically speaking, this means that when someone succeeds in achieving their goal, they see the doer, the inspiration for the action, and the action itself as one. In this way, the one who becomes truly connected with their goal is the one who achieves it.

After understanding these truths, it is natural for Arjuna to wonder what should be the ultimate goal of a being. Lord Krishna provides a very practical answer: the ultimate goal of a living being is Akshar Brahma, the imperishable, which transcends the limitations of time.

How to identify Akshar Brahma?

Man is a statue of his sanskars. He carries all kinds of sanskars—both good and bad—and it is natural for these sanskars to manifest in his actions. In spirituality, death is considered eternal sleep. Just as we sleep every night and wake up in the morning, our eternal sleep happens in a similar way. Before going to bed at night, we often recall some of the main activities of the day. Some of these memories have a strong effect on us, and we fall asleep with them in mind. When we wake up in the morning, these same memories influence our actions and thoughts. The memory with which we fell asleep carries over into the morning, motivating our karma.

Similarly, before entering eternal sleep, we remember the sanskars of our entire life. The sanskars we recall in this state shape our next birth. Our sanskars are always changing in response to our social environment. Some sanskars change quickly, while others have a long-lasting impact. If we have cultivated an abundance of good sanskars, even when facing eternal sleep, we will remember only the good ones, and our next birth will be shaped accordingly.

In this chapter, Lord Krishna explains that even Brahma is born and dies. However, He is beyond the cycle of time. He does not undergo birth and death, which is why He is called Akshar Brahma (the Imperishable). The sanskars of His devotee merge into Him. Since they are egoless, they remember Him before going into eternal sleep, and as a result, they are freed from the cycle of rebirth.

To understand this, consider the following example: Throughout the day, we engage in many activities, but based on our sanskars and ego, we remember only a few of them. In the same way, we perform various activities in life, but at the end of our life, we can remember only a fraction of them based on our sanskars and ego. When we surrender to God, our ego dissolves. Therefore, before entering eternal sleep, we no longer remember what we have done or what we wish to do. By doing so, we are freed from the cycle of birth and death.

Thus, it is essential to recognize our sacred sanskars to remain ego-free. To recognize Akshar Brahma, we must first be free of ego. This means we must recognize and cultivate our own sacred sanskars, which will help us achieve egolessness and ultimately lead to the realization of Akshar Brahma.

How to attain Aksharbrahma?

In some of previous chapters, the focus has been on how to control the mind in order to achieve Karmayoga or Sanyas. However, for our Karmayoga or Sanyas to be successful and timely, it is essential to be aligned with the goal or to be free from ego. Therefore, it becomes necessary to understand the ways to be free from ego. In this chapter, two symbolic paths are described as the solution to this challenge.

Devayana or Shukla Marg:- The path where the luminous fire represents the hardworking deity, the day-owning deity symbolizes light (the light of knowledge), the Shuklapaksha-owning deity refers to the waxing moon (symbolizing a developing intellect), and the six months of Uttarayan signify a generous heart. Brahmavetas who follow this path are guided by these deities in sequence and ultimately reach Brahma.

In this metaphor, the luminous fire represents hard work, the day-owning deity symbolizes the light of knowledge, and the Shuklapaksha-owning deity refers to the waxing moon, representing a developing intellect. When the sun is in Uttarayan, the days are longer and the nights shorter, which scholars interpret as signifying a generous heart. In simple terms, this means that if a person is hardworking, knowledgeable, has a developing intellect, and possesses a generous heart, then the sanskars within them help to free them from ego. This can be described as a person with positive thoughts and a positive attitude.

Pitryaan or Krishna Marg:- The path where the smoke-owning deity, night-owning deity, Krishna fortnight-owning deity, and the six months of Dakshinayan-owning deity are present, is taken by a person who performs selfish deeds. Such a person enjoys the outcomes of their good actions in heaven, as guided by the above-mentioned deities, but eventually returns.

In this metaphor, the smoke-filled fire represents confusion, the night-owning deity symbolizes darkness or ignorance, the Krishna fortnight-owning deity refers to the waning moon, indicating an intellect that lacks development, and the Dakshinayan period represents a narrow heart, as the days become shorter and the nights longer. Scholars interpret Dakshinayan as indicative of a limited, narrow mindset. Simply put, if a person is confused, ignorant, has an underdeveloped intellect, and a narrow heart, their sanskars keep them filled with ego. This is commonly referred to as a person with negative thoughts or a negative attitude.

A person with positive thoughts recognizes Akshar Brahma—his auspicious sanskars—which free him from ego and help him set the right goal. In contrast, a person with negative thoughts fails to recognize Akshar Brahma, and as a result, remains egoistic and lost, unable to set the right goal for themselves.

While this chapter may seem to discuss matters related to death—Shukla Marg and Krishna Marg being the paths taken after leaving the body—it's important to note that those with even a basic knowledge of astronomy understand that there is a day in Krishna Paksha, just as there is night in Shukla Paksha. Similarly, the Sun is in Uttarayan even during Krishna Paksha, and in Dakshinayan during Shukla Paksha. Therefore, the common belief in Indian society that dying during Uttarayan, Shukla Paksha, and daytime leads to salvation, while dying during Dakshinayan, Krishna Paksha, and night does not, seems to be more of a metaphor rather than a literal truth. Practically, it appears to convey a deeper, symbolic message rather than a strict rule about death.

The Conclusion

After learning about devotion in the seventh chapter, Arjuna became curious about whom he should worship. In response, Shri Krishna explains the concept of Akshar Brahma and also outlines the method to attain it. However, Arjuna's curiosity continues, and he now wonders whether Akshar Brahma can be experienced directly. In the next chapter, Lord Shri Krishna addresses this question and provides the answer to Arjuna's curiosity.

-: Om Tat Sat :-

Chapter-9
The Rajvidya Rajguhya yoga

Nineth Chapter of Srimabhagavad Gita at a glance	
Total Nos of verses	34
Nos of verses by lord Shree Krishna	34
Nos of verses by Arjuna	0
Nos of verses by sanjay	0
Nos of verses by Dritrastra	0
Main theam of the Chapter	The practical Devotion

श्री गणेशाय नमः

श्लोक

भव तारण कारण कर्म ततौ ।
भवसिन्धु जले शिव मग्नमतः।।
करूणाश्च समर्प्य तरिं त्वरित।
जन तारण ताराय तापितकम्।।

दो0—कह भगवन हे पार्थ सुनो गोपनीय विज्ञान।
अतुलनीय अतिपावन जो जग में हैं महान।1।
दो0—अतिप्रिय तुभक्त मेंरा निर्दोष तुम्हारी दृष्टि।
इसलिये बतलाता हूँ अद्भुत जग की सृष्टि।2।
दो0—अविनाशी साधन सुगम धर्मयुक्त अति पावन।
यह विज्ञान है फलदाता राजविद्या मनभावन।3।

जाको निजधर्म श्रद्धा नाही । दिशाहीन भटके जग माही।।
श्रद्धाहीन जीवजग संसारा। जन्म अवसान मिले बारंबारा।।
जगत व्याप्त अव्यक्त स्वरूपा। मुझमें सकल चराचर भुपा।।
जिमि हिम महि जल धारा। तिमि अव्यक्त व्याप्त संसारा।।
सकल भूत मुझमें हीं अवस्थित। लेशमात्र नही मैं भूत स्थित।।
दिव्य अलौकिक मम योगशक्ति। पोषित करे भूत अभिव्यक्ति।।
परमतत्त्व सकल भूत महूँ कैसे।गगनोत्पन वायु क्षिति जैसे।।

अवसान जबही कल्प के आये। सकलभूत मम प्रकृति समाये।।
पार्थ दृष्ट अगजग यह सारा। कल्पादि में रचुँ मैं बारम्बारा।।
प्रारब्ध अनुसार करूँ जगरचना। जीव धारण कर्मज संरचना।।

दो0–रचना विनाश कर्मानुसार होवत जग बारंम्बार।
परतंत्र जीव प्रकृतिवश करे जो अंगीकार।4।
दो0– कर्म कभी बन्धन नही जो आसक्ति रहित।
निरासक्त मैं कर्म करूँ जामें हो जग हित।5।
दो0–रचना बिनाश प्रकृति नियम से होता बारंबार।
चराचर जीव है जगत में कालचक्र गतिसार।6।

योगमाया ते धरू निज रूपा। संसार हेतु मम कर्म अनुपा।।
पार्थ मैं विचरू अस संसारा। जामें हो अग जग उद्धारा।।
जाने नही मम मूल स्वभावा। मूढ़मति वहीं ज्ञान अभावा।।
मैं परमेंश्वर सर्वभूत स्वामी। मूढचित कहे संसारी कामी।।
व्यर्थ आशा कर्म अरू ज्ञाना। विक्षिप्त चित मूढ़ कर्म नाना।।
अज्ञानी आसुरी प्रकृति धारे। पड़े शोक ना कोई उवारे।।
जो दैवी प्रकृति युक्त महात्मा। जाने अक्षररूप परमात्मा।।
करे उपासना कीर्तन पूजा। परमभक्त घ्याये नहीं दूजा।।
मम भक्त हो दृढ़ व्रतधारी। ध्यान उपासना करे हमारी।।
जो भक्त ज्ञानयज्ञ उर धरा। भजे मोहे ध्यान निराकारा।।
कछु भक्त मेरे करे उपासना। उर विराट्स्वरूप बिपासना।।

दो0–यज्ञ प्रथा यज्ञ आहुति स्वधा औषधि यज्ञ मंत्र ।
स्वयं यज्ञ मैं यज्ञकर्ता भी धृत अनल वितंत्र।7।
दो0–ब्रह्मरचित संसार का मैं मात पिता परम्ब्रह्म।
मैं पवित्र ओंकार अपि सकल वेद ज्ञान स्तम्भ।8।

साक्ष्य लक्ष्य अपि परमधामा। पोषणकर्ता सर्वस्वामी विश्रामा।।
प्रिय मित्र सकल शुभ कारक। प्रलय प्रभव दिव्य बीजधारक।।
सत् असत् अमृत मृत्यु स्वरूपा। मेधवर्षा अरू शीत रवि धूपा।।
करे सकामकर्म वेदविधाना। सोमरस पिय या करे यज्ञनाना।।
वेद विदित कर्म स्वर्गसाधन। कर्म सकाम जप तप आराधन।।
स्वर्ग इच्छा धरी करे जो पूजा। पूजे मोहें वह देव न दूजा।।

मनुज पुण्यफल स्वर्ग पठाए। पुण्यक्षीण पुनि धरा पे आए।।
कर्तव्यकर्म वेद विदित आधारा। जन्म मृत्यु जग बारंबारा।।
मम परमभक्त पूजे निष्कामा। मम चिन्तन युक्त करे विश्रामा।।
योगक्षेम मैं करूं सब धारण। भक्तचिंता का सकल निवारण।।

दो0—योग क्षेम वहन करूं जो करे कर्म निष्काम।
भक्तों का चिंता हरू अन्त पुनित मम धाम।9।

सकाम मनुज पूजे देव अनेका।अज्ञानी न जाने परमेश्वर एका।।
मैं यज्ञ भोक्ता अपि जग स्वामी। पार्थ हूँ मैं जग अन्तर्यामी।।
अज्ञानी ईश्वर तत्त्व न जाने। देव पूजन वह कामबस माने।।
देवपूजन कहे स्वर्ग की युक्ति। जन्ममरण से पाये न मुक्ति।।
देवों को प्राप्त हो पूजकदेवा। करे मन कर्म देव की सेवा।।
कोई करे निज पितर की पूजा। प्राप्त पितर हो देव न दूजा।।
भूतपूजक पूजे भौतिक कारण। भौतिकदुःख का करे निवारण।।
मम्भक्त पूजे धरी मुक्ति विचारा। जन्म न ले जग बारम्बारा।।
प्रेमसहित जो करे मम भक्ति। अर्पण फल पुष्प जस शक्ति।।
प्रीतिसहित भोग अपि पाउँ। सगुण रूप यही हेतु आउँ।।

दो0—साधु अनन्य भक्त अपि हो जो दुराचारी।
प्रभु भजन सम कर्म नही जाने सत् आधारी।10।

दुराचारी होय शीध्र धर्मात्मा। परमशान्ति वह पाए महात्मा।।
पार्थ परम जगसत्य यही जानो। भक्त अविनष्ट सत्य मानो।।
पार्थ मम शरण जो आए। बिना भेद मुक्ति वह पाए।।
अज्ञानी अरू चान्डाल पापयुक्ता। ममशरण आये होये मुक्ता।।
शूद्रवंचित अपि नारी निःसहाय।पाये मुक्ति मम शरण जो आये।।
वैश्यमुक्त धरी मम् आधारा। जीवन यापन को करे व्यापारा।।
क्षत्रिय अपि परमगति पाता। करी धर्मयुद्ध शरण जो आता।।
ब्राह्मण जाके होय विमलमति। वह निश्चित पाए परमगति।।
राजा ऋषि ममशरण जो आता। वो निश्चित परमगति पाता।।
सुखरहित क्षणभंगुर जग देहा। नित्य परमेश्वर रखो निज नेहा।।

दो0—कर ध्यान पूजन भक्ति अपि मेरा सत्कार।
आत्मा स्थित कर मुझमें करूं तेरा ऊद्धार।11।

।।इति नवम् अध्याय।।

Srimad Bhagavad Gita Ninth Chapter

The Essence

The ninth chapter of Srimad Bhagavad Gita is known as Rajvidya Rajguhya Yoga. This chapter consists of a total of 34 shlokas. For the convenience of study, it can be divided into six parts.

1. **Effect of knowledge (Shloka 1-6):-** Lord Krishna said, "For a faultless devotee like you, I will reveal the most secret knowledge in detail. By understanding this knowledge, you will be freed from the cycle of sorrow. This knowledge is the king of all knowledge, very pure, yields immediate results, is easy to practice in the path of Dharma, and is indestructible.

Those without faith do not attain me and continue wandering in the cycle of birth and death. The entire world is filled with my presence, just as ice is filled with water. All beings are situated in me due to my will, but in reality, I am not confined to them. My soul sustains and nourishes all beings, witness my divine yogic power. Just as the great air, born from the sky, moves freely in the sky, know that all beings are situated in me because they are born through my will."

2. **Subject of the creation of the world (Shloka 7-10):-** At the end of each kalpa, all beings merge into My nature, that is, they are absorbed back into the cosmic essence. And at the beginning of the next kalpa, I create them again by accepting my nature, I recreate the entire group of beings, who are dependent on the forces of nature, again and again according to their deeds. These actions do not bind Me, the Supreme Soul, who remains detached and indifferent, even though I am present in these actions. Nature

creates the entire universe—both animate and inanimate—by my will, and for this very reason, this world continues to revolve.

3. **The type of prayers (Verse 11-15):-** The foolish people fail to recognize My supreme nature. They view Me, the God of all beings, as insignificant, merely assuming the form of a human. While I roam the earth in a human form to guide the world toward salvation through My Yogmaya, they mistakenly perceive Me, the Supreme Lord, as an ordinary human being. These ignorant individuals, filled with futile hopes, actions, and knowledge, adopt demoniac and deceptive natures. In contrast, the great souls, dependent on the divine nature, recognize Me as the eternal cause of all beings and the indestructible form. With this understanding, they worship Me with exclusive devotion.

Those devotees, with firm determination, constantly chant My name and qualities, striving to attain Me. They bow to Me repeatedly, always absorbed in My meditation, and worship Me with love. The Gyan Yogis also worship Me, the formless and attributeless Brahman, through Gyan Yajna, with a deep sense of oneness. Meanwhile, others worship Me, the Supreme Being, manifested in many forms, with distinct and separate feelings.

4. **Form of super power (Verse 16-19):-** Further, Lord Krishna said that He is the action, the yajna, the Swadha, the medicine, the mantra, the ghee, the fire, and He is also the action in the form of havan. He is the one who holds the entire universe, the one who gives the results of actions, the father, the mother, the grandfather, and the sacred Omkar to be known. He is the Rigveda, Samveda, and Yajurveda. He is the supreme abode that can be attained, the provider and nourisher, the master of all, the observer of good and bad, the abode of all, the one in whom all should take refuge. He is the one who performs good without expecting anything in return, the cause of everyone's creation and destruction, the foundation of existence, the repository (the place where all elements merge in

their subtle form during destruction), and He is the indestructible cause.

He shines in the form of the sun, attracts rain, and makes it fall. He is both nectar and death, and He embodies both the true and the false.

5. **Sakaam and Nishkam Upasana (Verse 20-25):-** Those who perform the Sakaam Karmas prescribed in the three Vedas and drink the Som Rasa, and those sinless individuals who worship me through sacrifices with the desire to attain heaven, reach heaven as a result of their good deeds. There, they enjoy the pleasures of the divine gods. However, once their good deeds are exhausted, they return to the mortal world. In this way, those who resort to Sakaam Karmas as a means to reach heaven and seek pleasures are subjected to repeated cycles of birth and death. They go to heaven due to the merit of their good deeds and return to the mortal world when those deeds are exhausted.

On the other hand, those exclusive devotees who constantly meditate on me, the Supreme Lord, and worship me without any desire—those who seek no reward other than me—are ensured of my protection and welfare. Although self-interested devotees who worship other gods with faith also worship me, their worship is done in ignorance. They do not know me as the Supreme Lord, and therefore, they are subject to rebirth.

Those who worship gods attain the gods, those who worship ancestors attain ancestors, those who worship ghosts attain ghosts, but those who worship me attain me alone. Therefore, my devotee does not undergo rebirth.

6. **Disinterested Devotion to God (Verse 26-34):** Whichever devotee offers me flowers, fruits, water, etc., I, appearing in My Saguna form, accept and lovingly partake in those offerings made by a pure-hearted, selfless devotee. O Arjuna, whatever you do, whatever you eat, whatever you offer as oblations, whatever you

give as charity, and whatever penance you perform—offer it all to Me. In this way, all the actions of one who is dedicated to Me, with a mind filled with the yoga of renunciation, will be freed from the bondage of karma, in the form of both good and bad results. After being freed from these, they will attain Me.

I am present equally in all the elements, with neither anyone being disliked by Me nor anyone being dear to Me. However, those devotees who worship Me with love are in Me, and I am also manifested in them. If even a wicked person worships Me with exclusive devotion, then he is worthy of being considered a saint, because he has true determination. That is, he has firmly decided that there is nothing greater than the worship of God. Due to this determination, he soon becomes virtuous and attains eternal peace.

O Arjuna, know for certain that My devotee does not perish. Anyone who takes refuge in Me, whether a woman, a Vaishya, a Shudra, or even a sinner—such as a Chandal—will attain salvation. Likewise, virtuous Brahmins and royal devotees also attain salvation by taking refuge in Me. Therefore, being in this transient human body, which is devoid of lasting happiness, you should constantly worship Me, be devoted to Me, become My devotee, worship Me, and surrender to Me. In doing so, by dedicating your soul to Me and surrendering to Me, you will attain Me.

The Discussion

When Arjuna learned about Akshar Brahma, his curiosity arose regarding the direct experience of Akshar Brahma. Akshar Brahma refers to the truth that can never be destroyed or eroded. However, its direct experience is not possible in this life. This is similar to how it is impossible to experience the happiness of success before actually achieving success. We can only imagine it by hearing the experiences of those who have succeeded. In reality, the experiences of successful people serve as inspiration for us to work, and this inspiration itself is a form of Brahma. Therefore, there is only one way to directly experience Akshar Brahma: by surrendering ourselves in accordance with this inspiration to work. By doing so, we will continue to experience Akshar Brahma directly, even while engaged in our work. Saint Tulsidas has expressed this concept concisely in the following manner:

को जाने को जैहैं जमपुर, को सुरपुर परमधाम को ।

तुलसिहि बहुत भलो लागत जग जीवन रामगुलाम को।।

Who will go to heaven, and who will reach the supreme abode? Tulsidas expresses the view that the life of this world seems most fulfilling when spent in the service of Lord Ram. This means that no one truly knows what will happen after death; therefore, one should engage in deeds during their lifetime that make the world a better place.

Sanatan Dharma is the Vedic religion, and Shri Krishna upholds the worship system of the Vedic tradition, including the symbolic path of salvation through Yajna (sacrificial rites). While describing surrender to Akhileshwar (the Supreme Lord), the essence of Vedic religion as the ultimate means of salvation, he declares: "I am Akhileshwar, and I am Akshar Brahma." Shri Krishna emphasizes that if you understand this and surrender all the Yajnas, actions, and duties described in the Vedas to me, you will be freed from all bondage.

The path of surrender is often called the highway of life. It is firm and secure; even if one were to walk it with closed eyes, there would be no danger of falling. This is why Shri Krishna assures that anyone who comes to his refuge has no need to worry, for he takes care of their spiritual progress and welfare:*"Yogakshema vahamyaham(योगक्षेमं वहाम्यहम्)* "., meaning, "I carry the burden of their welfare."

The ninth chapter of Shrimad Bhagavad Gita is titled *Rajvidya Rajguhya Yog*. It is natural for an ordinary person to wonder about the secret of Raj Vidya (the royal knowledge) and the kingdom.

Many scholars consider this chapter's combined teachings to form what is known as *Rajyog*. Rajyog is believed to be a blend of *Karmayog* and *Bhaktiyog*. According to Karmayog, the practitioner performs work without attachment to the results, while a devotee surrenders everything to God through love and devotion, connecting with the divine.

The truth is, every action will yield some result—this is the law of nature. A Karmayogi performs actions without attachment to the outcome, but the ideal of a complete Karmayogi is challenging to attain in the world, especially for householder. Therefore, a method can be devised in which householders can carry out their duties without anxiety, without accumulating the burden of sin from their actions. This path is called *Raja Yoga*. When Karmayoga and Bhaktiyoga are united, this combined path becomes Raja Yoga.

Raja Yoga = Karmayoga + Bhakti Yoga

In simple terms, we can say that when a person surrenders the results of their actions to God, they free themselves from attachment to the outcome. By surrendering the results of their actions, they are also free from the sin that might come from those actions. This way, they can continue their work without worry. In essence, the core feeling of Raja Yoga is: *"What is mine, when I am offering everything to the Supreme Power?"* This surrender to God forms the foundation of Raja Yoga.

Conclusion

In the previous chapter, the concept of Akshar Brahma was explained. This led Arjuna to become curious about whether Akshar Brahma could be experienced directly. To address this curiosity, Lord Krishna introduces Raja Yoga in the ninth chapter.

Lord Krishna explains that the feeling of surrendering to God is like a highway, smooth and firm, unlike the rough and uneven paths. When a person surrenders their actions to God, God himself ensures their well-being. Through this surrender, one can directly experience God. In India, the method of Yajana, as described in the Vedas, symbolically represents the principle of surrender.

In short, the essence of this chapter is: *तेरा तुझको अर्पण, क्या लागे मोरा ।*

Tera Tujhko Arpan, Kya Lage Mera.

Now a natural question arises: when we are living a household life, we entrust the outcome of our actions to someone who is very trustworthy, with whom we share an unbreakable bond of love. In such a situation, how is it possible to surrender the outcome of our actions to God, whom we do not know well? Therefore, to follow the right path, it is essential to know and recognize God. In the next chapter, Lord Krishna addresses this curiosity of Arjuna.

-:Om Tat Sat :-

Chapter-10
The Vibhuti Yoga

The Tenth Chapter of Srimadbhagwat Gita at a glance	
Total Nos of verses	42
Nos of verses by lord Shree Krishna	35
Nos of verses by Arjuna	7
Nos of verses by sanjay	0
Nos of verses by Dritrastra	0
Main theam of the Chapter	The Glory of the God

श्री गणेशाय नमः

श्लोक

मम जीवन मीन मिमं पतित।
मरू घोर भुवीह सुवीह महो।
करूणाब्धिजलो र्मिजलानयन।
जन तारण ताराय तापितकम्।।

दो0– कृष्ण कहे हे पार्थ सुनो हित बचन मन लाई।
तु मेरा है अति प्रिय भक्त हो जामे सकल भलाई।1।
दो0–यह रहस्य जो कह रहा दिव्य ज्ञान पुनित।
प्रभावी परम बचन से साधक का सब हित।2।

लीला मम् जग कोई न जाना। मनुज देव ज्ञानी न बखाना।।
देव ऋषि मुनि साधु सन्ता। जाने नही मम् आदि अंता।।
आदिकरण मैं देव ऋषिवर का।चराचर जीव धरा अम्बर का।।
मैं हूँ अजन्मा अनन्त अनादि। ईश्वर तत्त्व सब नही इत्यादि।।
परमज्ञान अपि साधक युक्ति। साधक पाये पाप से मुक्ति।।
सकल भाव मेरी दिव्य रचना। जिससे प्रकट सृष्टि संरचना।।
ज्ञान भ्रमशमन दया सत्यबुद्धि। इन्द्रिय नियंत्रण करे मन शुद्धि।।
जन्ममरण चिन्ता दुःखहिंसा। क्षमादया धर्म तुष्टि अहिंसा।।

समता सन्तोष दान तप कीर्ति।उत्पत्ति प्रलय सकल्प अपकीर्ति।।
मम प्रेरणा अरूदिव्य प्रभावा।उत्पन्न करे सकल जगभावा।।

दो0– चतुः सनकादिक सप्तर्षि चौदह मनु का भाव।
संकल्पजात है भावसकल जाके प्रजा प्रभाव।3।
दो0– जो जानत है जगत में हरि योग विभूति शक्ति।
निःसंशय निश्चल साधक हो युक्त सर्वदा भक्ति।4।

मैं बासुदेव जग रचना कारण।मुझसे चराचर चेष्टा धारण।।
तत्त्व जानी करे श्रद्धा अपर्ण। कर्म चित्त प्राणकरे समपर्ण।।
अपर्ण करे कर्म चित्त प्राणा। जगत कहे उसे मद्गत प्राणा।।
करे वासुदेव में रमण निरंतर। श्रद्धा सदा मुझ पर अभ्यन्तर।।
मम चिन्तन चर्चा गुण प्रभावा। नित्य तुष्ट आसक्ति अभावा।।
अस साधक से मम अति प्रीति। तत्वज्ञानी सिद्ध यही रीति।।
पाई तत्वज्ञान मोको वह पावे। अज्ञानजनित भय नही सतावे।।
मैं कृपादृष्टि साधक पर धरता। अन्तःकरण में स्वयंविचरता।।
तत्वज्ञान हरे अज्ञान अन्धकारा। पार्थ अनुग्रह सकल हमारा।।
आलोकित ज्ञान करे हिय कैसे। सूरज हरे निशा तम जैसे।।

दो0–अर्जुन करजोरी कहे परमेश्वर पावन धाम।
शाश्वत पुरुष आप ही सर्वव्यापी पुरणकाम।5।
दो0– अजन्मा कहते ऋषि मुनि आप देवों के देव।
देवर्षि नारद भजें निरंतर आपको आदिदेव।6।

ऋषि देवल अपि महर्षि व्यासा। कहते तव गुण वेद प्रकाशा।।
ऋषि असित गुण आपके गाए। आप स्वयं मोही कहासुनाए।।
प्रभु आप स्वयं दिये संदेशा। अक्षरशः सत्य न कछु अंदेशा।।
लीलाधर आप हैं शाश्वतरूपा। जाने न जग देव मुनि भुपा।।
जगत स्वामी है देव पुरूषोत्तम। आप ही जाने आपको ऊत्तम।।
सकल व्याप्त तव दिव्यविभूति। सुर नर मुनि तव करे स्तुति।।
आप ही जाने आपकी माया। सकल असमर्थ ब्रम्हाण्ड निकाया।।
तव चिन्तन कैसे करूँ निरंतर।कैसे बसे हृदयाकाश अभयन्तर।।
किस भाव करूँचिन्तन योगेश्वर। समझ न पाऊँ मैं परमेश्वर।।
ममबुद्धि तव आचरण न समाये। तव दिव्याचरण वेद सबगाए।।

दो0–प्रभु कहे विभूति अपि बिस्तृत योग संदेश।
जिज्ञासा बढ़ी सुनकर अमियबचन ह्रषिकेश।7।

तब अमियवचन बोले श्रीकन्ता।मम बिस्तार आदि न अन्ता।।
सम्पूर्णभुत उरस्थित मैं देहि।आदि मध्य अरू अन्त सनेही।।
द्वादश अदिति सुतमहूँ अनुपा। मैं ही पार्थ हरि बिष्णुरूपा।।
रवि अंशुमान नित करूं प्रकाशा। तेज देव मरूत उनचासा।।
मैं व्योम चन्द्र नक्षत्र अधिपति। वायु धरा मैं वारि तीव्र गति।।
मैं इन्द्र सकल देवों के राजा। मैं सामवेद हूँ वेद सरताजा।।
इन्द्रिय मन रूद्र महूँ शंकर। अष्टबसु मध्य अनल भयंकर।।
गिरी सुमेरू अपि भौतिकचेतन। वृक्ष पीपल मैं देव निकेतन।।
असुर यक्ष धनस्वामी कुबेरा।जान मोहे अपि दिवस सबेरा।।

दो0– देवगुरु मैं ही वृहस्पति अपि चमुपति स्कन्द।
जलाशय महूँ वारिधी भावना महूँ आनन्द।8।

मैं ऋषि भृगु अक्षर ओमकारा। अचल हिमाचल गंगाधारा।।
जप तप यज्ञ देवर्षि नारद। मुनि कपिल मैं सिद्ध विशारद।।
अश्व उच्चेश्रवा गजराज एरावत्। गन्धर्व चित्ररथ मैं यज्ञउन्नत।।
युद्धास्त्र वज्र मैं बासुकि व्याला।पार्थ समझ मुझे सकलभुपाला।।
मैं कामदेव पुष्पधनु निशाना।शस्त्रोक्तरीति प्राप्ती सन्ताना।।
जलदेव वरूण अरू पितर अर्यमा। सुशासन हेतु मैं नीतिधर्मा।।
पवन गरूड मैं काल यमराजा। कामधेनु शेषनाग मृगराजा।।
निमिष घडी दिवा पक्ष मासा। ब्रह्मविद्या अरू ज्ञान पिपासा।।
भक्त प्रहलाद की मैं भक्ती। शस्त्रधारी श्रीराम की शक्ती।।
मीन महूँ मकर वायु पावन कर्ता। सर्वोतम औषधि दुःखहर्ता।।

दो0–गुडाकेश सृष्टि है मुझसे आदि मध्य अरू अन्त।
उत्पत्ति पालन विनाशकर्ता जाने मोहे योगी संत।9।

तत्त्वनिर्णय अरू वाद विवादा।पार्थ नही कछु मुझसेज्यादा।।
द्वन्द्व समास मैं सत्कृति धारा। अक्षर महुँ मैं सर्व आकारा।।
छन्द गायत्री जग पालन कर्ता।अक्षय काल मैं ही जगधर्ता।।
श्री वाक् मेधा ज्ञान अरू धृति। क्षमादया तप त्याग स्मृति।।
ऋतुबसन्त मार्गशिर्ष मासा। बृहत्साम श्रुति भक्त औ दासा।।

छलिया चौसर महापुरुष प्रभावा। रणविजय मैं सात्वीक भावा।।
जग शिक्षादान हेतु आचार्या। ऋषि वेदव्यास कवि शुक्राचार्या।।
जग व्यंजन भोजन महुँ मेवा। मैं गोपवंश प्रिय वासुदेवा।।
राजदण्ड दमन अपि संगीता। सुनो कौन्तेय अपि तव मिता।।
मैं गुप्त रहस्य रक्षक मौनभावा। तत्वज्ञान अपि ज्ञान प्रभावा।।

दो0—पार्थ चराचर में नहीं कुछ भी मुझसे रहित।
उत्पत्ति का कारण मैं विमल बुद्धि पुनित।9।
दो0—हैं विभूति अनन्त मेरा इसलिये कहा एकदेश।
एश्वर्य कान्ति शक्तीशान्ति है मेरा ही शेष।10।
दो0—ममविभूति अंशमात्र दृश्य जामें सकल जहान।
सखा पार्थ जग में सबकुछ मेरी हीं विभूति जान।11।

।।इति दशम् अध्याय।।

The Tenth Chapter of Srimadbhagwat Gita

The Essence

The 10th Chapter of Srimad Bhagavad Gita is known as Vibhuti Yoga. It consists of 42 shlokas. For the convenience of study, this chapter can be divided into four parts.

1.Vibhuti / Glory of God (Shloka 1-7):- Lord Krishna said to Arjuna to listen to the most secret knowledge of the Supreme Power, which Krishna wanted to share out of his immense love for Arjuna. Krishna further explained, "Neither the gods nor the great sages know my origin because I am the origin of everything. He who knows me as eternal and unborn is a wise person and becomes free from all sins."

Sri Krishna also said, "The power to decide, correct knowledge, non-confusion, forgiveness, truth, control of senses, control of the mind, happiness-sorrow, birth-destruction, fear-fearlessness, non-violence, equality, contentment, tapasya (the purification of the senses by following one's own religion), charity, fame-disgrace—all these feelings of living beings arise from me alone."

To explain the glory of the Supreme Power, Sri Krishna further said, "The Saptarshi, the four Sanakaadis, and the fourteen Manus, such as Swayambhuva, all of them, who have faith in the Supreme Power, are born due to His will."

Krishna further explained, "There is no doubt that those who know the Supreme Divine Glory through the power of yoga, endowed with unwavering devotion, are truly enlightened."

2.Effect and Result of Bhakti Yoga (Verse 8-11):- Lord Krishna says, "I, Vasudeva, am the cause of the creation of the entire universe. The entire universe functions through me. Understanding this, the intelligent devotees, endowed with faith and devotion, worship me constantly. The devotees who focus their minds on me and surrender their lives to me, knowing my influence through the discussion of my devotion, and speaking about me with my qualities and divine power, are constantly satisfied. They continually experience my glory. To those devotees who are constantly engaged in meditation and worship me with love, I bless them with Tatvagyan (the eternal knowledge), by which even the ignorant can attain me."

The Lord Krishna revealed the secret that He resides in the hearts of the devotees, destroying ignorance-born darkness through Tatvagyan (the eternal knowledge).

3.Arjuna's Praise of the Lord (Verse 12-18): Arjuna said with excitement, "O Lord, you are the Supreme Brahma, the Supreme Abode, and the Most Pure, because all the sages consider you to be eternal, divine, the primal God of gods, unborn, and omnipresent. Similarly, sages like Narada, sage Asita, sage Deval, and sage Vyasa also affirm this, and you yourself have said this to me." Arjuna further said, "O Keshav, whatever you say to me, I consider it to be true. Neither the demons nor the gods know your playful form. You are the creator and lord of all beings; you are Purushottama, and you know yourself by yourself. Therefore, only you are capable of describing your divine powers in full, by which you pervade all these worlds and exist. O Yogeshwara, how can I know you through constant meditation on you? O Lord, in what all forms should I meditate upon you? O Janardan, please tell me in detail about your Yogic power and glory, for I am never satiated by listening to your nectar-like words; my eagerness to listen remains unfulfilled."

4.Description of Yog Shakti by God (Shloka 19-42):- Lord Krishna said, "O Parth, now I will tell you about my divine powers, primarily because there is no end to my expansion. I am the soul of all beings, situated in the heart of all, and I am also the beginning, middle, and end of all beings. I am Vishnu among the twelve sons of Aditi, the sun with rays among the lights, and I am the brilliance of the forty-nine Marutas (wind gods) and the moon, the lord of the stars. I am Samveda among the Vedas, Indra, the king of gods, among the gods, the mind among the senses, and consciousness, the life force among living beings. I am Shankar among the eleven Rudras, Kubera, the lord of wealth, among the Yakshas and demons. I am Agni among the eight Vasus and Sumeru mountain among the high mountains. Brihaspati among the priests, Skanda among the commanders, and the ocean among the reservoirs. I am Bhrigu among the great sages and the single syllabled Omkar among the words. I am the Japa Yajna among the Yajanas, the Himalaya mountain among the stable ones. I am the Peepal tree among the trees, Narad Muni among the Devarshis, Chitrarath among the Gandharvas, and Kapil Muni among the Siddhas.I am the horse named Uchchaisrava among the horses that spring up with nectar, Airavat among the elephants, and the king among humans. I am Vajra among weapons, Kamdhenu among cows, Kamadeva, the reason for procreation as per the Shastras, and Vasuki, the king of snakes among snakes. I am Sheshnaag among snakes, and Varun Devta, the lord of aquatic creatures. I am Aryama among ancestors and Yamraj among rulers. I am Prahalad among demons, time among those who calculate, Garuda among birds, and the lion among animals. I am Air among purifiers, Shri

Ram among weapon holders, Makar among fishes, and Shri Gangaji among rivers.I am the beginning, end, and middle of creation. I am spiritual knowledge among knowledge and the debate conducted for deciding the truth in mutual arguments. I am Om among letters, conflict among the complex, Mahakaal, the time of time, and the one who supports and nourishes everyone with a huge form, having faces in all directions. I am the cause of everyone's birth, and I am the one who destroys everyone—death. Among women, I am the seven women named Kirti, Shri, Vak, Smriti, Medha, Dhutti, and Kshama. I am Brihatsam among the singable Shrutis, Gayatri among the verses, Margashirsha among the months, and Vasant among the seasons. I am gambling among the cheats, the influence of influential men, victory among the winners, determination among the determined, and the sattvic feelings of the sattvic people.I am Vasudev among the Vrishnis, Arjuna among the Pandavas, Vedvyas among the sages, and Shukracharya among the poets. I am the punishment of the suppressors, the power to suppress, the policy of those who wish to win, the silence of the feelings to be kept secret, and the philosophy of the wise. Nothing in the animate and inanimate world is devoid of me. There is no end to my divine powers.

I have told you about myself in brief. Whatever is endowed with glory, splendor, and power, know it to be the manifestation of a part of my brilliance. O Arjuna, what is the use of knowing so much? Just know that I hold and sustain this entire universe with just a part of my yogic power."

The Discussion

In the first half of the Bhagavad Gita, both the theoretical and practical aspects of Vedic religion are explained in a very simple manner. This makes it clear that neither a complete Karmayogi nor a complete Sanyasi is practical in everyday life. The practical path of religion is household life, and one can live a successful and happy life by following the household path through Raja Yoga.

However, there is a challenge in Raja Yoga: the results of one's actions must be dedicated to God. The question then arises, where can God be found? To answer this, the great saint Kabirdas has said:

कस्तुरी कुण्ड़ल बसे मृग ढूंढत बन माही।
वैसे घट घट राम है दुनियाँ देखे नाहीं।।

It means that the deer, who contains the musk, is constantly searching for it in the forest. Similarly, while Rama is present in every heart, the world has not yet recognized Him. The meaning is that God is present everywhere, in some form or another.

The Upanishads reveal the presence of the divine in every person, stating: मातृ देवो भव, पितृ देवो भव, आचार्य देवो भव,अतिथि देवो भव इत्यादि / Matru Devo Bhava, Pitru Devo Bhava, Acharya Devo Bhava, Atithi Devo Bhava etc.

In the ninth chapter, God says that when a person entrusts the outcome of his actions to Me (God), I myself bear the burden of his yoga (the attainment of the unattainable अप्राप्य की प्राप्ती) and kshem (protection of the attained प्राप्त की रक्षा), That is, God takes full care of His devotee, ensuring that the devotee faces no trouble and can perform his work without worry. Therefore, the one who passes this test is like a god. Just as a mother takes full care of her child in such a way that the child faces no difficulty and can carry out his tasks properly, the same applies to the father and Guru. Hence, the statement of the Upanishads is literally true. According to the tenth chapter of the Bhagavad Gita, parents, Gurus, and similar figures are considered manifestations of God.

If we look closely at every object, emotion, and aspect of the world, God's manifestation is clearly visible in it. Therefore, in Vedic religion, God is worshipped in the form of nature, as both animate and inanimate objects are believed to be manifestations of God. For instance, the earth, sky, trees, rivers, mountains, sun, moon, cows, food, water, snakes, lions, mice, and so on—all are considered manifestations of God.

Thus, God's presence is in every particle of the world. According to Vedic religion, we do not need to search for God in a distant place because His manifestation is present everywhere. The message of the Gita, to entrust the outcome of our deeds to God, teaches that we should seek altruism in our actions, not selfishness. For example, no one plants a tree with the sole thought of benefiting from its fruits and shade; the fruits and shade are meant for all. Here, other beings—whether animals, birds, or humans—are like gods in the form of guests. Therefore, when our actions are motivated by altruism, they become akin to worship, and there is no blame for the result.

Now, a natural question arises: are demons also manifestations of God, since they are part of the world? According to Vedic religion, both humans and demons are manifestations of God—that is, both Ram and Ravana, Arjuna and Duryodhana, are all manifestations of God. The question then becomes: if both are manifestations of God, why do their thoughts and actions differ so drastically? Goswami Tulsidas explains this by saying:

एक पिता के बिपुल कुमारा । होहिं पृथक गुन सील अचारा ।।
एहि बिधि जीव चराचर जेते । त्रिजग देव नर असुर समेते ।।
अखिल बिस्व यह मोर उपाया । सब पर मोहि बराबरि दाया ।।

Many sons of the same father have different qualities and behaviors. Similarly, all living beings—animate and inanimate—along with the three worlds, gods, humans, and demons, are all like children of the same father to me. I treat all of them equally because the entire world is my creation.

It is also said, according to Vedic religion, that God is without any defects. However, geographical and social circumstances can affect the expression of God's glory, leading to differences in color, form, behavior, and thoughts among individuals. Therefore, while God's glory is flawless, the circumstances of one's environment can cause these differences to appear as defects.

Vedic religion believes in rebirth, which occurs according to destiny as a result of the deeds performed in previous lives. As described in the Ramayana, there were two devotees of Vishnu, Jai and Vijaya, who were cursed by Maharishi Narada and reborn in Lanka as Ravana and Kumbhakarna. Despite being originally devotees of God, their karma led them to be born into the demon clan. Due to their actions, their conduct became contrary to dharma, even though they were born in a noble sage lineage.

Goswami Tulsidas explains this simply in the following words:

उपजही एक संग जग माही । जलज जोंक जिमि गुन बिलगाही।।
सुधा सुरा सम साधु असाधू । जनक एक जग जलधि अगाधू ।।
भल अनभल निज निज करतूती। लहत सुजस अपलोक बिभूती।।
गुन अवगुन जानत सब कोई । जो जेहि भाव नीक तेहि सोई ।।

The lotus and the leech both arise from the water, but their qualities are different. Similarly, saints and sinners, though they share the same origin, possess different virtues. In fact, good and bad are the result of one's own deeds. People earn good reputations or bad credit based on their actions. Everyone is aware of virtues and vices, and it is those with good feelings who perform good deeds.

Mahatma Gandhi, in one of his articles, said that the main reason for opposing a thought is fear, which is naturally present in living beings. For instance, a dog barks at an unknown person but does not bark at its master. The reason is that the dog is not afraid of its master, so it remains calm. However, the dog fears the unknown person and barks in response. The primary difference in the thoughts of Arjuna and Duryodhana was rooted in fear. Duryodhana feared that if even a small part of the kingdom was given to the Pandavas, they could pose a future threat to Hastinapur.

In conclusion, we can say that all living and non-living things are manifestations of God. Support or contradiction arises from the effects of His Maya (which is explained in the seventh chapter). Goswami Tulsidas expresses this truth simply in the Uttarkand.

सुनहुँ तात मायाकृत गुन अरू दोष अनेक ।
गुन यह उभय न देखिअहिं देखिअ सो अबिबेक ।।

Listen, brother, Maya has created many virtues and faults. You cannot perceive both virtues and faults simultaneously. Therefore, before forming any conclusions, one should think carefully and without prejudice.

Conclusion

The doubt Arjuna discussed was: Where should we look for God after learning about Raj Yoga? This is addressed in the 10th Chapter of the Srimad Bhagavad Gita.

In response to this question, God clarified that there is no need to search extensively for God in order to practice Rajayoga, as the divine power of God is present in every particle of both the animate and inanimate world.

In the first half of the Srimad Bhagavad Gita, Arjuna was given knowledge about the principles and practical aspects of Vedic religion. After that, to satisfy Arjuna's curiosity about knowing God, he was shown the divine power of God present in all animate and inanimate objects, using examples of great things known in Sanatan Dharma.

After learning so much about the glory of the Supreme Power, it is natural for Arjuna to be curious about knowing the complete form of God. This is because knowing only a partial aspect of God cannot give a complete understanding. The confusion that arises from partial knowledge can be compared to the famous story of the four blind men, each imagining different things about an elephant by touching different parts of its body. Similarly, it is impossible to know fully about the God by only understanding one aspect of Him. In the next chapter, we will see the Vishwarupa (Universal Form) of Lord Shri Krishna to resolve Arjuna's curiosity.

-: Om Tat Sat :-

Chapter-11
The Vishvarupadarshan Yoga

The Eleventh Chapter of Srimadbhagwat Gita at a glance	
Total Nos of verses	55
Nos of verses by lord Shree Krishna	14
Nos of verses by Arjuna	33
Nos of verses by sanjay	8
Nos of verses by Dritrastra	0
Main theam of the Chapter	Glimpus of Supreme Power

श्री गणेशाय नमः

श्लोक

अनादि मध्यान्त अनन्त वीर्यः ।
अनन्तबाहुं शशि सूर्य नंत्रम्।।
पश्यामि त्वां दीप्तहुताशवक्त्रं ।
स्वतेजसा विश्वमिदं तपन्तम्।।

दो0–अर्जुन करजोरी कहे प्रभु अनुग्रह आपकी भारी।
गोपनीय अध्यात्म विषय सुन गई मूढ़ता सारी।1।
दो0– प्रभु अविनाशी आपने प्रभव प्रलय बतलाया।
स्वयंसिद्ध यह आत्मज्ञान मेरे मानस आया।2।
दो0– प्रत्यक्ष दर्शन दें मुझको ऐश्वर्य तेजयुक्त रूप।
ज्ञान शक्ति बलयुक्त सकल विश्व रूप अनुप।3।

अमियबचन कहे श्री भगवाना। मम विश्वरूप तु देख धिमाना।।
वर्ण सहस्त्र आकृत संसारा। पार्थ आश्चर्यमय रूप हमारा।।
द्वादश आदित्य अरू बसुअष्टा। पार्थ देख अपूर्व जगस्रष्टा।।
एकादशरूद्र द्वो अश्विनीकुमारा।उनचास मरूदगण जगसंसारा।।
सकल जगत सम्पूर्ण चराचर। स्थित मम तन कहे मुरलीधर।।
पार्थ कभी देखा सुना न पूर्वा। देख उसे निश्चीत सत्य धुर्वा।।
असमर्थ प्राकृतनयन तव पार्था। जो समझे यही दृश्य अर्था।।

देख पार्थ योग शक्ति अलौकिक।नही समर्थ दृश्य चक्षु भौतिक।।
दे रहा तुझे दिव्य दृष्टि अनुपा।जो शक्य दृश्य दिव्यविश्वरूपा।।
प्रकट विश्वरूप प्रभु दिखलाये। विश्वरूपदर्शन पार्थ हैं पाये।।

दो0—संजय कहे हे महीपति पाये अर्जुन दिव्य दृष्टि।
रूप दिखाये महायोगेश्वर निहित जहाँ जगसृष्टी।4।

नाना अयन नयन अपि नाना। अलौकिकरूप को करे बखाना।।
दिव्य भूषण युक्त सब अंगा। हस्त विभुषित शस्त्र के संगा।।
दिव्य वसन उर दिव्य माला।दिव्य गन्ध तन तेज भुआला।।
सीमा रहित आनन चहूँ ओरा। रूप विराट् अति विस्मयधोरा।।
विराट्रूप निहित सब सृष्टि। पार्थ देखे सब अपलक दृष्टि।।
कोटि रवि जो प्रकटे अकाशा। नही सदृश प्रभु तेज प्रकाशा।।
लौकिक जगत में नाना रूपा। विश्वरूप महुँ बिन्दू स्वरूपा।।
आश्चर्यचकित तनतेज स्पन्दन। नमन कीन्ह अब कुन्तीनन्दन।।
कोटी समदसम् विस्तृतनयना। विश्वस्वरूप प्रकाशमय अयना।।
देखी पार्थ प्रभु दिव्य स्वरूपा। करजोरी वचन कहे नरभुपा।।

नयनाभिराम रूप मित तेरा दिव्य ऋषि अहि नमन करे।
जय जगन्नाथ प्रभू हे गिरिधारी हृषीकेशश्री कृष्ण हरे।।

सकल देव ब्रह्म कमलासन अपि महादेव तन बास करे।जय0।
विश्वरूप अनन्ता हे भगवन्ता सब साधु संत के ताप हरे।जय0।
नाना भुजा उदर अरू अयना नयन दृष्टि चहूँ ओर फिरे।जय0।
आदि दृष्टिगोचर नही तेरा मध्य अन्त अपि सबसे परे।जय0।
शीश मुकुट तन तेज विराजे कर शंखचक्र अरू गदा धरे।जय0।
कोटी रवि सम जोत चहूँ ओरा प्रभू दृष्टिगत कौन करे।जय0।
अप्रमेय रूप अविनाशी सनातन कोई ज्ञान न तुझसे परे।जय0।
परम अक्षर परब्रह्म परमात्मा जग धर्म रक्षा तुही करे।जय0।
प्रज्वलित अनलमुख नेत्र शशि—भानु तेज जगत् संतप्त करे।जय0।
अन्नत शक्ती अन्नत बाहु आदि अन्त मध्य भी सबसे परे।जय0।
स्वर्ग धरा अरू गगन है तुझमे विकराल अलौकिक देह धरे।जय0।
व्यथित लोक देखी तव रूप प्रभु करजोरी देव गुणगान करे।जय0।
देव समुह पैठत तन तोरा महर्षि उत्त्म सिद्ध स्तोत्र पढ़े।जय0।

कल्याण करो हे प्रभु जगत् के देव समुह सब तुझसे डरे।जय0।
रूद्र एकादश द्वादश भानु अपि अष्टबसु विस्मित निहरे।जय0।
सकल साध्य पितर मरूदगण अश्विनीकुमार अपि ध्यान धरे।जय0।
यक्ष गर्न्धव सिद्ध अपि असुरा विस्मित हो दृष्टिपात करे।जय0।
नाना मुख अपि नाना नयना भुजा विशाल महि गगन घरे।जय0।
पाद् विशाल उदर बहुतेरे अयन विशाल सब लोक हरे।जय0।
मैं व्यकुल देखी तव रूपा सकल जगत् लिए आप खड़े।जय0।
प्रज्वलित अनलसम नैन प्रचण्डा धैर्य प्रभु कोई कैसे धरे।जय0।
गगनचुम्बी विशाल तव अयना नाना वर्णयुक्त ज्योति करे।जय0।
प्रलयअनल सम् मुख प्रज्वलित देखी दिग् दिगन्त विसरे।जय0।
भयभीत मैं अन्तःकरण से हे विष्णु शान्ती प्रदान करे।जय0।
विकराल दाढ़ भयभीत करे प्रभु जगनिबास दुःख कैसे टरे।जय0।
द्रोण कर्ण कुरू चमु पितामह अपि प्रभु मुख में प्रवेश करे।जय0।
वीर अनेक मम पक्ष अपि प्रभु धावत तव मुख पैसार करे।जय0।
कई चुर हुये चिपके दन्तन में सिर चूर्णसम दिख पडे।जय0।
जिमि समद नदी दौड समाये प्रभु जीव तव मुख जा ठहरे।जय0।
जिमि पतंग नाश होवे दीप महुँ तव प्रताप जग नष्ट करे।जय0।
सम्पूर्ण लोक प्रभू लील रहे प्रज्वलीत मुख जग ग्रास करे।जय0।
तव तेज तपाये सकल जगत् प्रभु उग्र रूप क्यु आप धरे।जय0।
हे देवश्रेष्ठ शत नमन आपको प्रसन्न होई कल्याण करे।जय0।
आदि पुरुष कहे निज प्रवृति प्रभु ज्ञान प्रदीप प्रदान करे।जय0।

दो0—कह भगवन् हे पार्थ सुनो में ही हूँ महाकाल।
न मुझसे बच सका है कोई देवासुर ले ढाल।5।
दो0—तुम युद्ध करो या ना करो निश्चित सबका अन्त।
एही क्षण मैं प्रवृत नाश को हो प्रतिचमु या संत।6।
दो0—सव्यसाँची उठ युद्ध करो धन राज सुख पाओ।
वीर पहले हैं मर चुके तुम निमित् मात्र बन जाओ।7।
दो0—जयद्रथ कर्ण द्रोण भीष्म अरू नानावीर महान।
तु मार उन्हे जो मर चुके विजय सुनिश्चित जान।8।
दो0—भय त्याग पार्थ तुयुद्ध करी निज वैरी को जीत।
यही युद्ध कर्तव्य है तेरा तु बना इसी के निमित्।9।
दो0—संजय बोले हे महिपति जो कहे श्री जगन्नाथ।

अर्जुन करन लगे विनय कर जोरी भय साथ।10।

अन्तर्यामी हे जग स्वामी हर्षित अग जग गुणगान करे।
जय जगन्नाथ प्रभू हे गिरिधारी ह्षीकेशश्री कृष्ण हरे।।

जय चक्रपाणि मुरली मनोहर तु भवसागर पार करे।जय0।
नाम प्रभावा जन सुख पावा तव अनुराग अपि प्राप्त करे।जय0।
हे स्वामी चराचर दूर निशाचर सिद्धयोगी नित नमन करे।जय0।
ब्रह्मादिक कर्ता जग दूःखहर्ता सत् असत् सकलादि परे।जय0।
तु अनन्त तु ही सच्चिदानन्द ब्रह्मा अपि तुझे नमन करे।जय0।
तु देव सनातन अति पूरातन सकल चराचर व्याप्त करे।जय0।
तु जग आश्रय तु जग ज्ञाता सकल जगत परिपूर्ण करे।जय0।
तु वरूण अनल वायु यमराजा रवि शशी महूँ जोत भरे।जय0।
तु ही ब्रह्मा ब्रह्म के कर्ता जग पुनः पुनः नम नयन करे।जय0।
जय चहूँ ओरा बस प्रभु तोरा पराक्रम जग संताप्त करे।जय0।
तु देव महाना सखा न जाना मम अपराध को क्षमा करे।जय0।
प्रेम अधिना सखा प्रविणा अपि मम अपराध तु उर नधरे।जय0।
कभी कृष्ण कभी यादव मैं कहा हठात् बिना विचार करे।जय0।
कभी विनोद कभी अपमानित् अपि ग्वाला काला नाम धरे।जय0।
अपराध मेरा मित सगं तेरे इसका निदान प्रभु आप करे।जय0।
जगत पिता हे गुरु पूजनीय अनुपम प्रभाव जग कौन धरे।जय0।
प्रभु आप समाना कोइ न आना फिर अति कोई कैसे करे।जय0।
तन–मन अर्पित तुझे समर्पित निज शरण प्रभू अब आप धरे।जय0।
जनक पुत्र सखा–सखा पति–प्रिया अपराध को सहन करे।जय0।
हे पूज्य विधाता प्रिये सखा मम् समर्पण अपि स्वीकार करे।जय0।
अश्चर्यमय रूपा हे सुरभुपा चित्त भिति हर्ष दोनो सें परे।जय0।
सिर मोर मुकुट कर चक्रसुदशर्न दृष्टिगत निज सौम्यरूप करे।जय0।
प्रभू सहत्रबाहु हे विश्वरूप निजरूप चर्तुभुज प्रकट करे।जय0।
मेरी यही तृष्णा हे प्रभू कृष्णा दूर करें शंखचक्रधरे।जय0।

दो0–कह भगवन हे मित् मेरे मम रूप विराट अपुर्व।
किसी ने देखा नही यह रूप तुझसे कभी पुर्व।11।

सकलादि तेजमय सीमाभावा। पार्थ सकल मम योगप्रभावा।।
वेद अध्ययन यज्ञ अरू दाना। उग्र तप कोई क्रिया महाना।।
संत योगी पण्डितया भूपा। देखा नहीं यही विश्वरूपा।।
मुझसे व्याप्त सकल जगसृष्टि। पार्थ पास तेरे दिव्यदृष्टि।।
देखी अलौकिक विराट स्वरूपा। व्याकुल क्यों होये नर भुपा।।
तुझको है मुझसे अति प्रीति। भक्त भावनाधिन मम नीति।।
भयरहित होइ मम देख प्रभावा। पार्थ मोको तव भक्ति भावा।।
पार्थ देख हरि विष्णु ममरूपा। ममभक्ति पार करे भवकुपा।।
शंखचक्र गदा पद्मम् विराजा। चारो भुजा यही साज से साजा।।
चित्त अतिशान्त भुजंग है असना। नाभिकमल देह पीत बसना।।

दो0—दिया धैर्य भगवान ने पार्थ तु मम प्रिये भक्त।
रूप चतुर्भुज धर रहा दृष्टिपात करो इस वक्त।12।
दो0—संजय बोले हे कुरूपति देख अर्जुन की भक्ति।
प्रकट किये निजरूप प्रभु पार्थ ने पायी शक्ति।13।
दो0—पार्थ कहे श्री कृष्ण प्रभु दें मुझको निज भक्ति।
पा लिया निज स्थिति छूटी मम् भ्रम आसक्ति।14।
दो0—मम दशर्न है देव दुर्लभ बोले सस्मित भगवान।
यज्ञ ज्ञान तप दान से न सका न इसे जान।15।
दो0—हे परंतप पार्थ सुनो करे निष्काम जो भक्ति।
परमात्मा को जान ले पाये वही अस शक्ति।16।
दो0—जिसे प्रेम हो अग जग से ना कोई गुरु भाव।
प्राप्त करे वही भक्त मुझे जामें अहं अभाव।17।
दो0—सकल कर्म करो तुम होकर मेरा परायण भक्त।
मोक्ष प्राप्त तुझको होगा मत हो फल आसक्त।18।

।।इति एकादश् अध्याय।।

The Eleventh Chapter of Srimadbhagwat Gita

The Essence

The eleventh chapter of the Srimad Bhagavad Gita is known as Vishvarupadarshan Yoga. This chapter consists of a total of 55 shlokas. For the convenience of study, it can be divided into 8 parts.

1. **Arjuna's prayer (Shloka 1-4):-** Arjuna said to Lord Krishna, "My ignorance has been dispelled by the extremely confidential spiritual teachings you have shared with me, which have blessed me. O Krishna, I have heard in detail from you about the creation and destruction of the elements, and I have also learned about your indestructible glory. O Supreme Lord, you are exactly as you describe yourself to be, but now I wish to see your glorious form, filled with knowledge, power, strength, and brilliance. If you believe it is possible for me to witness that form, then please show me your indestructible, divine form."

2. **Description of His universal form by God (Shloka 5-8):-** Lord Krishna said, "O Parth, now behold hundreds and thousands of my supernatural forms, of various types, colors, and shapes. You will see the Adityas (the twelve sons of Aditi), the eight Vasus, the eleven Rudras, the two Ashvinikumars, the forty-nine Maruts, and many other astonishing forms that you have never seen before.

O Arjuna, now witness the entire world, both animate and inanimate, all contained within my body. And whatever else you wish to see, you shall behold that as well.

But you cannot see me with your natural eyes, so I am granting you divine vision, supernatural eyes, with which you will be able to perceive my divine yogic powers."

3. **Description of the Universal Form by Sanjaya (Shloka 9-14):-** Sanjaya said, "O King, after speaking these words, the great yogi and Lord, who has the power to destroy all sins, revealed to Arjuna His divine form, radiant with immense splendour. Arjuna saw the Supreme God, with countless faces, adorned with divine ornaments, holding divine weapons in His hands, boundless and facing in all directions, filled with countless wonders. The light

radiating from the Supreme Form was so intense that it seemed to surpass the brightness of thousands of suns rising together.

Arjuna saw the entire universe, divided into countless parts, all contained within the divine Universal Form of the Supreme Lord. Overwhelmed with astonishment and reverence, Arjuna, with folded hands, praised the Lord."

4. **Arjuna's vision and praise of the cosmic form of the Lord (Shloka 15-31):-** Arjuna said, "O Lord, I see all the gods and countless beings, Brahma seated on a lotus, Mahadev, all the sages, and divine serpents within Your body. O Vishwanath, You have many arms, stomachs, mouths, and eyes, and Your beginning, middle, or end is not visible. You are crowned, armed with the Sudarshan Chakra, and Your body radiates a mass of light from all sides, akin to the infinite light of the sun and fire, which is almost impossible to look at. I only see Your immeasurable form from all directions.I believe You are the eternal, indestructible Param Brahma and the supreme being, beyond time, without beginning, middle, or end. Your eyes shine like the Sun and the Moon. The entire world is overwhelmed by Your radiance. O Lord, You are omnipresent, yet Your terrifying form is disturbing the three worlds. Groups of gods are merging into You, while others are praying with folded hands. The great sages are offering excellent hymns, and the Rudras, Adityas, Vasus, Rakshasas, and others look at You in awe.

Seeing Your dreadful form, everyone is in distress, and I too am troubled. I cannot maintain my patience or peace upon witnessing Your form. Therefore, I humbly pray to You to be merciful. The Kaurava army is also being consumed by Your form. Some of their heads are caught between Your teeth. Just as the waters of rivers naturally flow into the ocean, the warriors of the human world are being drawn into Your blazing mouths.Like insects rushing into a blazing fire, all these people are being drawn to destruction due to their attachment. O Lord, Your fierce light is burning the entire world with its radiance. I am unable to comprehend who You are; therefore, I beg You to explain Your true nature to us."

5. **Description of His power by the Lord (Shloka 32-34):-** Shri Bhagwan said, "I have now come to destroy the worlds. I am Mahakaal. Many warriors will be killed, even against your wishes, because they have already been destined for destruction by me. Therefore, you are merely the instrument in this process—fight without fear. Many of your opponents have already been slain by me, so you will undoubtedly emerge victorious. So, fight."

6. **Praise of God by the frightened Arjun (Shloka 35-46):-** Sanjaya said to Dhritarashtra, "O King, now Arjuna, with folded hands, praised the Lord and said, 'O Lord! The people are rejoicing with your praises, while the wicked are fleeing in fear. The Siddhas are bowing to you. O Dweller of the Universe, you transcend both truth and falsehood. You are the eternal being, the shelter of the world, and the entire universe is pervaded by you. You are the one worthy of being known, and you are also the father of Brahma. I repeatedly offer my salutations to you. You are supremely valiant and omnipresent. I bow to you a million times.Not knowing the full extent of your divine power, I have, in my ignorance, treated you casually, calling you my friend or referring to you by your caste, Yadav. I ask for your forgiveness for this offense. You are the father of both the animate and inanimate worlds, and there is none like you in the three worlds. You are the greatest Guru, the most revered. I pray for your grace. Just as a father forgives his son’s ignorance, and a beloved forgives her husband's faults, please forgive my sins.

I am overjoyed to witness your divine form, but my heart is also troubled with fear. Therefore, I request that you show me your four-armed Vishnu form, holding the Sudarsan Chakra and adorned with your crown. O Dweller of the Universe, please be pleased and grant me this vision.'"

7. **The Lord's coming back in the four-armed form (Shloka 47-50)** Lord Krishna said, "O Arjuna, the form you have witnessed is my colossal, universal form. No one else has seen it, except for you. In the human realm, this form of mine cannot be seen by anyone else—neither through the study of the Vedas, nor by performing sacrifices, charity, rituals, or austerities. Do not be disturbed by what you have seen, nor should you be bewildered. Now, without fear and with love, behold my four-armed form, adorned with the conch and Sudarshan Chakra." After this, Sanjaya narrated to Dhritarashtra, "By saying this, Lord Vasudev revealed his four-armed form and reassured Arjuna."

8. **Statement of the rarity of seeing the four-armed form without exclusive devotion and exclusive devotion with its fruits (Shloka 51-55):-** Arjuna said, "O Lord, after witnessing your divine form, I have now become steadfast in my mind and have returned to my natural state."

The Lord replied, "This form of mine is very rare to behold. Even the gods desire to see it, but it cannot be perceived through sacrifices, charity, or other such means. It can only be known through exclusive devotion.

O Arjuna, those who perform all their duties solely for me, are devoted to me, and are free from attachment and animosity towards other beings—such exclusive devotees attain me alone."

The Discussion

Without complete knowledge of an object, our understanding of it is considered incomplete. The tenth chapter of the Bhagavad Gita describes the divine powers of God, which manifest in all living and non-living things. The aspect of these powers presented in this chapter highlights only the creative aspect of God. However, every object in nature has two aspects. According to the Upanishads, *यथा पिण्ड़म् तथा ब्रम्हाण्ड़म्* 'Yatha Pindam Tatha Brahmandam', The universe is exactly like the smallest particle. Just as we observe, all creation (the divine powers of God) has two aspects: 1) Creative, and 2) Disintegrative or destructive. Therefore, God must also have two forms: 1) Creative and 2) Disintegrative or destructive. In the present world, anything is considered authentic only when both its constructive and destructive aspects are thoroughly examined. For example, before authenticating allopathic medicines, both their positive and negative effects are studied in detail. Therefore, anything should be considered authentic only when both aspects have been studied practically, with scientific explanation.

The complete view of the Supreme power is perhaps not available anywhere except in the Srimad Bhagavad Gita (God's gigantic form is also described in the Purush Suktam of the Rigveda). While dedication, meditation, and worship are discussed in Sanatan Dharma for the Supreme power, Shri Krishna's statement that even sages, saints, deities, etc., are eager to see his cosmic form confirms that learned scientists and researchers are always eager to gain complete knowledge of nature, but they are unable to do so. For complete knowledge, exclusive devotion is necessary. This is practically an unshakable truth. At the same time, Shri Krishna's statement that it is not possible to see him completely with physical eyes, so he grants supernatural eyes to Arjuna to see his supernatural form, confirms that without the knowledge imparted by the Guru, we cannot fully comprehend the essence of anything.

The word "God" is often described as the essence of the Generator, Operator, and Destroyer. This message is conveyed in this chapter, affirming that, according to Sanatan Dharma, God himself is the Creator (Brahma), the Operator/Regulator (Vishnu), and the Destructor (Shiva). The statement in many scriptures that God is omnipotent is absolutely true. Arjuna saw that not only the warriors of the Kaurava side but also those of his own side were absorbed into the universal form of God. This illustrates that it is not necessary for God's will to align with our desires; rather, all occurrences happen according to God's will, for only God has dominion over the future.

This chapter can be regarded as the backbone of Sanatan Dharma, which teaches us not to believe in hearsay before acquiring complete knowledge. The cause of all the troubles in society and the world is the lack of complete knowledge. The Supreme Power is the storehouse of knowledge. Therefore, surrendering to the Supreme Power means acquiring complete knowledge, which is a continuous process.

This is why Shri Krishna concludes by saying that those who perform all their duties solely for Him, who are devoted to Him and free from attachment and hostility towards material beings, are the exclusive devotees who attain Him. The practical message here is that whatever a person desires, they can obtain it, if they have full devotion to it. Goswami Tulsidas expresses this in simple words when he says:

जेहि के जेहि पर सत्य सनेहू , सो तेहि मिलइ न कछु संदेहू।

Jihi ke jihi par satya snehu, so toh milai na kakhu sandehu.

Conclusion

It is generally believed that Lord Shri Krishna showed his Virat Vishwaroop to Arjuna to assure him that his victory in the war was certain, as his opponents had already been defeated by the Lord. Arjuna's role was merely to act as a medium. This interpretation may hold true in the context of the Mahabharata war. However, the Virat Vishwaroop of the Lord conveys a deeper message: devotion is essential to gain a complete understanding of the glory of God, which pervades both the animate and inanimate aspects of the Supreme Power. Without devotion, it is impossible to fully comprehend any being, whether animate or inanimate. The Lord emphasizes this in the last verse of the chapter.

Bhakti (devotion) has been discussed from the sixth to the eleventh chapters of the Srimad Bhagavad Gita. The Vedic scriptures describe two forms of Bhakti: Sagun Bhakti (devotion to the divine with attributes) and Nirgun Bhakti (devotion to the formless divine). It is natural for Arjuna to be curious about which of these two types of Bhakti is superior. Shri Krishna addresses this curiosity of Arjuna in the next chapter.

-:Ohm Tat Sat:-

Chapter-12
The Bhaktiyoga

The Twelfth Chapter of Srimadbhagwat Gita **At a glance**	
Total Nos of verses	20
Nos of verses by lord Krishna	19
Nos of verses by Arjuna	1
Nos of verses by sanjay	0
Nos of verses by Dritrastra	0
Main theam of the Chapter	Types of Devotion

श्री गणेशाय नमः

श्लोक

अप्रमेयो हृषीकेशः पद्मनाभोऽमरप्रभुः ।
विश्वकर्मा मनुस्त्वष्टा स्थविष्ठः स्थविरो ध्रुवः ।।

दो0–अर्जुन बोले हे हृषीकेश भक्त कौन है श्रेष्ठ।
सगुण उपासक आपका अथवा निर्गुण ज्येष्ठ।1।

अमिय बचन बोले गिरिधारी। जो मम ध्यान करे नर नारी।।
श्रद्धायुक्त करे भजन हमारा। सगुण उपासक मोको प्यारा।।
जितेन्द्रिय हो भजे निराकारा। एकीभाव ब्रह्मध्यान की धारा।।
हितरत सकल भुत समभावा। निराकार उपासक मोको भावा।।
परिश्रम साध्य है निर्गुण भक्ति। कठिन देहाभिमान अनासक्ति।।
सकलकर्म मोकों करे अपर्ण। अनन्य भक्त करे सकल समपर्ण।।
पूजन भजन अपि चिन्तन मोरी। बाँधे प्रभू से प्रेम की डोरी।।
अर्जुन सगुण जो भक्त हमारा। हो शीघ्र मुक्त जीवन उद्धारा।।
जाको मनकर्म बुद्धि प्रभुलय। हो निवास ममलोक बिन संशय।।
यदि कठिन मुझमें मननिग्रह। आभ्यासयोग कर पायो अनुग्रह।।

दो0–योग अभ्यास भी दुष्कर करो कर्तव्य कर्म निःस्वार्थ।
सिद्धि सफलता मिले जगत मिल जाये जीवनार्थ।2।
दो0–निःस्वार्थ कर्म भी कठिन तो करो कर्मफल त्याग।
मन बुद्धि पार्थ होगा सजग भक्ति जायेगा जाग।3।

करे अभ्यास जाने बिन मर्मा। अस अभ्यास ते श्रेष्ठ ज्ञानधर्मा।।
ज्ञानापि अतिउत्तम ममध्याना। सर्वोत्तम त्याग कहे धिमाना।।
कर्मफल त्याग शीघ्र दे शान्ति। पार्थ मिटे सकल जगभ्रान्ति।।
जो सन्तुष्ट न करे जगद्वेषा। अहंकारशून्य दूर क्लेशा।।
रहे सब प्रति समभाव दयालु। सुख दुःख में समभाव कृपालु।।
मनइन्द्रिय जीत अपि क्षमावाना। मम अतिप्रिय कहे कृपानिधाना।।
जो रहित हर्ष–अमर्ष भय–उद्वेगा। पाये जगमुक्ति अतिवेगा।।
ईच्छारहित हो शुद्धअभ्यान्तर। आरम्भत्यागी उदासीन निरंतर।।
दूःख–अविचलित करे दक्षकर्मा।मम भक्त सदा निर्बाहे निजधर्मा।।

दो0–न हर्षित हो ना द्वेष करे न ईच्छा करे न शोक।
शुभाशुभ कामना त्यागी मम प्रिय भक्त इहलोक।4।
दो0–सम व्यवहार मित्र शत्रु से अवचलित मान अपमान।
आसक्ति रहित को शीतताप सुखदूःख लगे समान।5।
दो0–निन्दा स्तुति समभाव रहे हो मननशील सन्तुष्ट।
आसक्तिहिन समव्यवहार करे साधु रहे या दुष्ट।6।
दो0–निज निकेत मोह रहित स्थिरबुद्धि भक्तिमान।
अस भक्त दुर्लभ हे पार्थपर मोहे अतिप्रिय जान।7।
दो0–श्रद्धायुक्त भक्त मम आश्रित धर्मामृत अपनाये।
करे प्रेमयुक्त निष्काम कर्म भक्त मोहेवही भाए।8।

।।इति द्वादश् अध्याय।।

The Twelfth Chapter of Srimadbhagwat Gita

The essence

The 12th chapter of the Srimad Bhagavad Gita is known as Bhaktiyoga. This chapter contains a total of 20 shlokas. For the sake of study, it can be divided into two parts.

Saakar and Niraakar Upasak (Verse 1-12):- Arjuna asked Lord Shri Krishna, "Who is the best worshipper: the one who worships the Saguna (with form) or the Nirguna (without form)?"

Lord Krishna replied that the worshippers of the Saguna, who continuously worship me by concentrating their minds, are very dear to me. However, those who worship the eternal, formless Brahman by meditating and controlling their senses also attain me. Worshipping the formless Brahman requires special effort, as it is difficult for body-conscious individuals to attain the state of the unmanifested.

But my devotees surrender all their actions to me and worship the Supreme Being, constantly thinking about me with exclusive devotion. O Arjuna, I quickly deliver those loving devotees who concentrate on me from the cycle of birth and death. Therefore, concentrate your mind on me and use your intellect for me alone, and you will reside in me—there is no doubt about this.

If you cannot fix your mind on me, then try to attain me through yoga practice. If you are unable to practice yoga, then do your work for me alone, and by this, you will attain the perfection of being like me. If you cannot do even that, then become the conqueror of your mind and intellect and renounce the results of all actions. Knowledge is better than mere practice without understanding the essence. Meditation on the Supreme Lord is superior to knowledge, and renunciation of the fruits of action is better than meditation because through renunciation, one attains immediate peace.

2. **Characteristics of God-realized men (Shloka 13-20):-** He who is free from ego, hatred, and selfishness, who remains equanimous in pleasure and pain, who is always satisfied, and who controls the body, mind, and senses, with firm faith in me, that devotee is very dear to me. Similarly, he who is free from joy, anger, fear, and anxiety is also dear to me.

My devotee, who is pure both inside and out, unbiased, and who renounces all desires, is also dear to me. He who is beyond good and bad, who remains steady in the face of respect and insult, and who is free from attachment—such a devotee, with a steady mind, is dear to me.My devoted and selfless devotee, who is full of faith, is truly dear to me.

The Discussion

Saguna and Nirguna Bhakti: In India, when the words Bhakti and Bhakt come to mind, two terms are often highlighted:

1. **Saguna Bhakti**
2. **Nirguna Bhakti**

According to Vedic scriptures, a worshipper of Saguna Brahma is called a Saguna Bhakt (devotee), while a worshipper of Nirguna Brahma is called a Nirguna Bhakt (devotee).

A **Saguna Bhakt** concentrates his mind on the manifest Brahma (Saguna Brahma). For this, the Saguna worshipper uses the direct senses. Senses become the means of worship: the eyes to see God, the ears to hear the glorious stories of God, the tongue to pronounce God's name, the feet for pilgrimages, the hands to offer fruits and flowers to God, etc. Saguna Bhakti is full of love and emotions. The common form of Saguna Bhakti is selfless service, and it is an outward expression. Its Vedic form is **Yajna** (sacrifice).

On the other hand, **Nirguna Bhaktas** worship the formless (Nirakar) Brahma through constant meditation. Nirguna worshippers are immersed in their duties day and night, without any expectation, and it is often not even known whether they are consciously remembering the Supreme Being. Nirguna Bhakti is full of knowledge; it is inward. Its common form is the acquisition of knowledge with concentration and a feeling of benevolence. Its Vedic form is **Tapasya** (austerity).

The differences between Saguna and Nirguna Bhakti can be understood through the characters of **Laxman** and **Bharat** in the Ramayana. Laxman stays with Lord Rama and serves him, making him an example of Saguna Bhakti, as he serves the Lord with his senses. On the other hand, Bharat serves the subjects of Lord Rama in Ayodhya, without any personal gain or expectation, even though Lord Rama is not physically present. This, too, is the service of Lord Rama and an example of Nirguna Bhakti.

Goswami Tulsidas expresses this beautifully in simple words:

अगुन सगुन दुई ब्रह्म सरूपा । अकथ अगाध अनादि अनूपा।।

Agun Sagun Dui Brahma Sarupa. Akath Agadh Anadi Anupa.

The terms **Sagun** (manifest) and **Nirgun** (unmanifest) refer to two different forms of one Brahma, and it is difficult to distinguish between them. Our respected Gurudev Shri Lal Bahadur Singh Ji used to explain that **Sagun** means with qualities, and **Nirgun** refers to that from which qualities emerge. However, if **Nirgun** is understood as **Neer-Gun** (where *Neer* means water), then the specific meaning of Nirgun becomes clearer. According to the Shruti (scriptures), first, water emerged by the will of Hari, and then Brahma was created. Hence, **Nirgun Bhakti** can be understood as meditation on the original form of Brahma.

Sagun devotees worship God by focusing on His form and qualities, such as through the worship of idols of Shri Ram, Shri Krishna, Mata Kali, Mata Durga, etc. On the other hand, **Nirgun devotees** perceive God as the storehouse of all qualities and believe that God cannot be given a form because His qualities are limitless. However, the feelings of the Nirgun devotee give form to the formless Brahma, just as a vessel gives a definite shape to water. In this analogy, the feelings of the devotee act like the vessel, shaping the formless Nirgun Brahma.

Goswami Tulsidas beautifully expresses this concept in simple words:

जाकी रही भावना जैसी । हरि मुरत देखही तिन तैसी।।

Jaaki rahi bhaavna jaisi. Hari murat dekhahi tin taisi.

The worship of Nirgun with a Sagun body also becomes Sagun. Therefore, although the concepts of Sagun and Nirgun Bhakti may appear different, in reality, they are not. Sagun worshippers focus on the worship of idols, while Nirgun worshippers consider selfless action as worship. Despite these differences, God treats both Sagun and Nirgun devotees equally, loves them equally, and provides them with liberation.

Navadha Bhakti: According to Vedic texts, devotion can be expressed in nine ways, which is known as *Navadha Bhakti*. In the *Srimad Bhagavat Mahapuran*, Navadha Bhakti is described, and it is said that the devotee Prahlad taught the nine forms of devotion to his father, Hiranyakashipu. These are as follows:

श्रवणं कीर्तनं विष्णोः स्मरणं पादसेवनं।
अर्चनं वन्दनं दास्यं सख्यम् आत्म निवेदनम्।।

Shravanam Kirtanam Vishnoh Smaranam Padasevanam.

Archanam vandanam daasyam sakhyam atma nivedanam.

The nine forms of devotion, or *Navadha Bhakti*, with examples, are as follows:

1. **Shravan (Listening)** – Parikshit
2. **Kirtan (Chanting/Recitation)** – Shukdev
3. **Remembrance (Smaran)** – Prahlad
4. **Charan Seva (Service to the Lord's Feet)** – Lakshmi
5. **Worship/Archan** – Prithyu
6. **Salutation (Pranam)** – Akrur
7. **Dasya Bhav (Servitude)** – Hanuman
8. **Sakha Bhav (Friendship)** – Arjuna
9. **Self-Surrender (Atma Nivedan)** – King Bali

In the *Ramayana*, Lord Rama also teaches *Navdha Bhakti* to Mata Shabari, which is described in the *Aranya Kanda*. Goswami Tulsidas has also described *Navdha Bhakti* in his works as follows:

कह रघुपति सुनु भामिनि बाता। मानउँ एक भगति कर नाता।।
जाति पाँति कुल धर्म बड़ाई। धन बल परिजन गुन चतुराई।।
भगति हीन नर सोहई कैसा। बिन जल बारिद देखिअ जैसा।।
नवधा भगति कहउँ तोहि पाही। सावधान सुनु धरू मन माहीं।।
प्रथम भगति संतन्ह कर संगा। दूसरी रति मम कथा प्रसंगा।।
दो०—गुर पद पंकज सेवा तीसरि भगति अमान।
चौथिभगति मम गुनगन करई कपट तजि गान।।
मंत्र जाप मम दृढ़ बिस्वासा। पंचम भजन सो वेद प्रकासा।।
छठ दम सील बिरति बहु करमा। निरत निरंतर सज्जन धरमा।।
सातवाँ सम मोहि मय जग देखा।मोतें संत अधिक करि लेखा।।
आठवाँ जथालाभ संतोषा। सपनेहुँ नही देखई परदोषा।।
नवम सरल सब सन छलहीना। मम भरोस हियँ हरष न दीना।।
नव महुँ एकउ जिन्ह के होई। नारी पुरुष सचराचर कोई।।
से अतिसय प्रिय भामिनि मोरे । सकल प्रकार भगति दृढ़ तोरे।।

Lord Rama explained the nine types of devotion to Mata Shabari, as presented in the *Aranya Kanda* of the *Ramayana*. These can be summarized as follows:

1. **Meeting with devoted persons (Sants)**
2. **Listening to and advocating eternal knowledge through stories that explain the glory of the Supreme Power**
3. **Respecting the knowledgeable person**
4. **Singing the glory of the Supreme Power**
5. **Chanting the name of the Supreme Power**
6. **Controlling the sensory organs**
7. **Regarding all beings as manifestations of the Supreme Power**
8. **Remaining always satisfied with one's condition**
9. **Being simple and humble**

Lord Rama said that if a person follows even one of these types of devotion, they are dear to me.

Conclusion

While describing Sagun and Nirgun Bhakti, Lord Krishna made it clear that Sagun Bhakti is easier because the devotee has a definite form of the Supreme Power to focus on. In contrast, the Nirgun devotee serves the creatures, who are manifestations of God, without any expectation. In Nirgun Bhakti, no specific form of God is present before the devotee, making it more challenging. Both Sagun and Nirgun Bhakti are equally important, but the devotee who performs selfless work and remains pure both inside and outside is dearer to me.

For the both Swadharma and Bhakti, a conscious body is essential. Therefore, it is important to have a curiosity to understand the soul, as discussed in the beginning of the second chapter. No creature in the world wishes to die, even for the sake of going to heaven or attaining salvation. The solution to Arjuna's curiosity regarding this has been presented in the next chapter.

-: Om Tat Sat:-

PART-3

THE CONTEMPLATION

Chapter-13
The Kshetra-Kshetragn-Yoga.

The Thirteenth Chapter of srimadbhagwat Gita **At a glance**	
Total Nos of verses	35
Nos of verses by lord Krishna	34
Nos of verses by Arjuna	1
Nos of verses by sanjay	0
Nos of verses by Dritrastra	0
Main theam of the Chapter	The Supremesoul and the Nature

श्री गणेशाय नमः

श्लोकः

किरीटिनं गदिनं चक्रहस्तमिच्छामि त्वां द्रष्टुमहं तथैव।
तेनैव रूपेण चतुर्भुजेन सहस्त्रबाहो भव विश्वमूर्ते।।

दो0–प्रकृति–पुरुष क्षेत्र–क्षेत्रज्ञ क्या बतलाये हृषिकेश।
मेरी इच्छा पूर्ण करे करजोरी विनत् गुड़ाकेश।1।
दो0–यह शरीर एक क्षेत्र है आत्मा क्षेत्रज्ञ तु जान।
तत्वज्ञानी कहते यही बोले श्री भगवान।2।

मैं परमपुरूष क्षेत्रज्ञ समाना। सकल क्षेत्र रहस्य मैं जाना।।
सुनो पार्थ क्षेत्र–क्षेत्रज्ञ समासा।जासे होय सकल भ्रम नाशा।।
क्षेत्र –क्षेत्रज्ञ तत्त्व मुख्य ज्ञाना। गाये ऋषि मुनि बिधि नाना।।
ब्रह्मसूत्र अपि पद यही गाये। विभाग पृथक करी वेद सुनाए।।
शब्दस्पर्श रस गन्ध अरू रूपा। पंचभूत पार्थ है बिषय अनुपा।।
पंचभूत रचित विविध शरीरा। खग मानव अपि वृक्ष जीव नीरा।।
अहंकार बुद्धि संग व्यक्त प्रकृति। रचे दशेन्द्रिय मन आकृति।।
ईच्छा–द्वेष सुख–दूःख मन चेतन।सबही बसत है क्षेत्र निकेतन।।
स्थुलपिण्डध् ृति अपि क्षेत्र विकारा।कहे भगवन् क्षेत्र संक्षेप

सारा।।
निज देह पार्थ है क्षेत्र समतुला। धारण करे सब कर्मफलमूला।।

दो0—क्षेत्र प्रकृति विकार सहित पुरुष ज्ञेत्रज्ञ को जान।
क्षेत्र क्षेत्रज्ञ तत्वज्ञान को श्रुति पुराण कहे सद्ज्ञान।3।

दम्भाचरण अरू हिंसा अभावा।दया सरलचित क्षमा के भावा।।
भक्ति सहित करे गुरुसेवा। शुद्ध अभ्यन्तर स्थिर मन देवा।।
इन्द्रियसहित देह का निग्रह। आसक्तिरहित भोग अनुग्रह।।
जन्म मरण अरू जरा जवानी। करे विचार कभी दोष न हानि।।
गृहधन अरू परिजन सुत दारा। वहे कबहू नहीं मोहधारा।।
प्रिय अप्रिय महु चित्त समाना। जाकर हो शुद्ध देश विताना।।
परमेश्वर से हो अनन्य भक्ति। जगत् श्रद्धामय बिनआसक्ति।।
आत्म–अनात्म विभेद अपि नाना। समझाये वहीं अध्यात्मज्ञाना।।
तत्वज्ञान कर्म परमात्मा ध्याना। पार्थ जगत व्यवहारिक ज्ञाना।।
ज्ञान वीपरीत सकल अज्ञाना।हो उत्पन्न पुनि पुनि भ्रमनाना।।

दो0—सत् असत्हीन है परंब्रह्म अनादि ज्ञानतरू कन्द।
परंब्रह्म हीं ज्ञानयोग्य अनुभव कर ज्ञान आनन्द।4।

सत्असत्रहित परमब्रह्म अनादि। अहंकारहीन भक्ति भक्तादि।।
जाके हस्त पाद चहुँपासा।नेत्र कर्ण मुख व्याप्त अकाशा।।
जाने सकल इन्द्रिय अनुशासन।इन्द्रियहीन परंब्रह्म निरासन।।
आसक्तिरहित करे सबकोधारण।जगपोषणकरे दूःखनिवारण।।
निगुर्ण रही जो गुण अपि पावा।प्रकटअप्रकट हर भाँतीसुहावा।।
प्रभु निर्गुण सगुण सम कीर्ति।पार्थ आश्चर्यमय ब्रह्म रीति।।
ब्रह्म चर अचर सुक्ष्म स्वरूपा। अविज्ञेय अतिनिकट अनुपा।।
ब्रह्म अतिदुरस्थ मेघ जल भाँती। कृपाकरी हरे भक्त आराती।।
गगन समान विस्तृत बस एका। अनेक भूत महुँ दिखे अनेका।।
परमात्मा विष्णु जगपालनहारा। रूद्र रूप धरी करे संहारा।।

दो0—परमब्रह्म सकल ज्योति के ज्योति माया से अतिदूर।
तत्वज्ञानगम्य बोधस्वरूप अपि बसत ज्ञानीजनउर।5।

ब्रह्मरूप परमात्मा सृष्टि रचयिता।परमपुरुष जग जीवन हिता।।
क्षेत्र क्षेत्रय है अतिगूढ़ ज्ञाना। मैं ज्ञेय स्वरूप संक्षिप्त वखाना।।
तत्वज्ञानी भक्त जाने मम रूपा। बास करे मम् सत्य–स्वरूपा।।
प्रकृति पुरुष है दोनो अनादि। प्रकृति जनित ही राग द्वेषादि।।
जग में जो है त्रिगुण विकारा। सत्व रज तम प्राकृत धारा।।
कार्यकरण सब प्रकृतजनिता। सुखदूःख सकल हित औ मिता।।
महि गगन अनल जल वाता। स्पर्श शब्दरूप गन्ध रस पाता।।
यही प्रकृति के कार्य कहे ज्ञानी। तेरह करण पाए जग प्राणी।।
मन कर्ण त्वचा बुद्धि अहंकारा। रसना नेत्र ध्राण जलधारा।।
वाक्पाद गुदा सकल उपस्थि। हस्तादि तेरह करण विभक्ति।।
प्रकृति कार्यकरण की जननी। सुखदूख जग में इनकी करणी।।

दो0–जीवात्मा स्थित प्रकृति में जामें है गुण तीन।
त्रिगुण भोग त्रिगुण कारण पाये जन्म नवीन।6।

पार्थ देह स्थित जो जिवाात्मा। वास्तव में है वहीं परमात्मा।।
जीवात्मा साक्षी सकल जग कर्मा। पाप पुण्य अरू धर्म अधर्मा।।
उपद्रष्टा एही हेतु कहे ज्ञानी।जीवात्मा साक्षी कर्म करे प्राणी।।
यथार्थ सम्मति देत कहे संता। आत्मा पथ प्रदर्शक अनुमन्ता।।
देह पोषक इसलिए है भर्ता। जीवात्मा विष्णु सम पोषणकर्ता।।
भोगे भोग इसलिय है भोक्ता।चैतन्य यही शरीर संग उक्ता।।
ब्रम्हादि स्वामी इसलिय महेश्वर। शुद्ध सच्चिदानन्द परमेश्वर।।
पुरूषतत्त्व अरू त्रिगुण प्रकृति। है सत्यरूप चैतन्य आकृति।।
करे कर्तव्यकर्म यही जगमाही। पुर्नजन्म के भय न सताहि।।
पुर्नजन्म पार्थ अज्ञान के कारण। तत्त्वज्ञान वस करे निवारण।।

दो0–सुक्ष्मबुद्धि ध्यानसे परमात्मा निजउर पावे।।
ज्ञानयोगी तत्वज्ञान पाई चराचर पाप नशावे।7।

दो0–कर्मयोगी कर्म करे कर्मफल आसक्ति त्याग।
कर्मफल परमात्मा अर्पण अगजग से अनुराग।8।

पार्थ जगत में कछु मन्दबुद्धि। चाहे तनमन बचन की शुद्धि।।
ते अनुशरण करत तत्त्व ज्ञानी। प्रभुप्राप्ती की पंथ यही जानी।।
तद्नुसार उपासना श्रुतिपरायण। तरे भवसागर पाए नारायण।।

जग के सकल स्थावर जंगम। फलरूप पुरुष प्रकृति संगम।।
क्षेत्र क्षेत्रज्ञ जनित जग सृष्टि। सब पर है जग प्रभु शुभदृष्टि।।
अविनाशी समभाव जग स्थित। ईश्वर चैतन्य जीव प्रतिष्ठित।।
परमेश्वर सबमें जो जग सृष्टी। यही जग में है यथार्थ दृष्टि।।
कण कण परमेश्वर अपनाये। वह अन्तहीन परमगति पायें।।
सकल कर्म जग प्रकृति कर्ता। आत्मा तो है पार्थ अकर्ता।।
यथार्थ परमात्मतत्त्व सब दृष्टि। अटल ज्ञानमय है जग सृष्टि।।

दो0—सकल सृष्टि विस्तार में है परमात्मा एक।
जबही मनुज यह जान ले पाये ब्रह्म विवेक।9।
दो0—अलिप्त सदा परमात्मा शरीरस्थ करे न कर्म।
अनादि निर्गुण अविनाशी शास्त्रोक्त यही है धर्म।10।
दो0—लिप्त न हो संसार से जैसे व्याप्त आकाश।
आत्मा अलिप्त हो कर्म पर अर्जुन कर विश्वास।11।
दो0—ब्रह्माण्ड प्रकाशित करे रवि चमके जगमग सृष्टि।
आत्मा क्षेत्रज्ञ रूप है रखे क्षेत्र सकल पर दृष्टि।12।
दो0—सकार्य प्रकृति को जाने अपि जाने क्षेत्रज्ञ क्षेत्र।
परमब्रह्म परमात्मा मिले जाके जागृत नेत्र।।13।

।।इति त्रयोदश् अध्याय।।

The Thirteenth Chapter of srimadbhagwat Gita

The Essence

The thirteenth chapter of Srimad Bhagavad Gita is known as *Kshetra-Kshetragnyoga.* This chapter consists of a total of 35 verses. For the convenience of study, the subject matter of this chapter has been divided into two parts.

(It is worth noting that in many editions of the Srimad Bhagavad Gita, only 34 verses are given for this chapter, which leads to the total number of verses in the Gita being counted as 699 instead of 700. However, in some versions of the Srimad Bhagavad Gita, 35 verses are included, bringing the total count to 700 verses.)

The first verse of this chapter is as follows:

प्रकृति पुरूषं चैव क्षेत्रम् क्षेत्रज्ञानं ईवं च
एतद् वेदितुम इच्छामि ज्ञानं ज्ञेयं च केशवः ।।

Arjuna said:

Prakriti Purusham Chaiva Kshetram Kshetrajñam Eva Cha. Aitad Veditum Ichchhāmi Jñānam Jñeyam Cha Keshava.

This means: Arjuna said, "I wish to understand the nature of *Prakriti* (the material nature), *Purusha* (the individual soul), *Kshetra* (the field of action), and *Kshetrajña* (the knower of the field)."(Note: This verse is not included in some versions of the Srimad Bhagavad Gita.)

1.Difference between body and soul (Shloka 1-19):- Arjuna wanted to understand the nature (*Prakriti*), the Supreme Power (*Purusha*), the *Kshetra* (the Field), and the *Kshetrajña* (the Knower of the Field).

Lord Shri Krishna explained that, "O Arjuna, this Body is called *Kshetra* (the Field), and the Soul that knows it is called *Kshetrajña* (the Knower of the Field). Understanding the nature with its qualities and the soul with its essence constitutes true knowledge. Now, I will explain the Field and the Knower of the Field briefly. The sages have described both these concepts in detail through various means such as Vedic mantras and the verses of Brahmasutra."

The Field (*Kshetra*) is characterized by the following prominent elements:

1. The five great elements (*Panch Mahabhuta*)
2. Ego
3. Intellect
4. Original nature
5. The ten senses
6. The mind

7. The five sense objects: sound, touch, form, taste, and smell
8. Desire, hatred, happiness, sorrow, and the gross body
9. Consciousness, retention power (Satvik, Rajasic, Tamasic qualities)

While the true knowledge includes:

- Simplicity in mind and speech, free from arrogance
- Control over the body, mind, and senses
- Devotion to the Guru through service
- Absence of attachment to worldly pleasures
- Acceptance of birth and death as natural
- Reflection on the pains and limitations of old age and illness
- Detachment from family, wealth, and material things
- Steady mind in the face of pleasure and pain
- Unwavering devotion to the Supreme Lord
- Living in solitude and purity
- Disinterest in the company of worldly pleasures
- Consistent engagement in spiritual knowledge, recognizing the Supreme Being as the essence of truth

This is true knowledge, and the opposite of it is ignorance.

Lord Krishna continued to explain the nature of the Supreme Being (*Param Brahma*):-That eternal Brahma is neither completely real nor completely unreal. He possesses hands, legs, eyes, and faces on all sides, and is present everywhere in the world. He is the knower of all sensory objects, yet He is without any sensory organs. He nourishes all beings but remains unattached. He enjoys all qualities but is free from qualities Himself. He is both very near and very far. He is complete inside and outside, present in all animate and inanimate beings, yet He transcends them. Extremely subtle, He cannot be comprehended by the senses.

In His form as Vishnu, He sustains all beings; as Brahma, He creates all things; and as Rudra, He destroys all. Despite being omnipresent like the boundless sky, He appears to be divided. He is the light of all lights and transcends illusion (Maya). He is the embodiment of knowledge and can be known and attained through the knowledge of truth (*Tatvagyan*). He resides in everyone's heart, and by understanding Him, one attains His divine form.

Thus, the Field and the Knower of the Field are both realms of knowledge, representing the Supreme Being. This brief explanation of my nature is given to you. By comprehending it fully, my devotee attains union with me. Recognize that both nature (*Prakriti*) and the soul (*Purusha*) are eternal. Understand that attachments, hatred, and all three Gunas (Satvik, Rajasic, and Tamasic) arise from nature.

2. **Nature And Purusha (Verse 20-35):-** The cause of creation, the effect, and the instrument is known as *Prakriti* (nature), while the soul is said to be the reason behind experiencing pleasure and pain. The soul, situated in nature, enjoys the three gunas (qualities) produced by nature, and these qualities determine the soul's birth in good or bad species. The soul in this body is essentially the Supreme Soul. It acts as the guide, being a witness; as the approver, providing correct guidance; as the sustainer, nourishing all beings; as the enjoyer, experiencing life; as Maheshwar, the master of Brahma; and as *Paramatma*, the repository of pure Sat-Chit-Ananda (pure existence, consciousness, and bliss).

It is said that the person who understands the relationship between *Purusha* (the soul) and *Prakriti* (nature), along with their qualities, attains liberation even while performing all duties. Many people realize the *Paramatma* through their purified intellect via meditation, seeing it in their hearts. Others attain it through *Gyan Yoga* (the path of knowledge) or *Karma Yoga* (the path of action). However, some people, with dull minds, without direct knowledge, worship according to the teachings of others—those who understand the truth. These individuals, devoted to hearing the truth, undoubtedly cross the ocean of worldly existence.

O Arjuna, all immovable and movable beings are born from the union of the field (*Kshetra*) and the knower of the field (*Kshetrajña*). The person who perceives the Supreme Lord as indestructible and equally present in all living and non-living beings—despite their perishable nature—sees the truth. This person recognizes that the Supreme Lord is equally present in all, and does not destroy himself. Such a person attains ultimate salvation.

The individual who sees all actions as being carried out by nature, while understanding that the soul is the non-doer, perceives the reality. The moment this person recognizes the separate nature of all beings situated in one God, and the expansion of all beings within that God, at that moment, they attain *Sachchidananda* (the embodiment of pure existence, consciousness, and bliss) in the form of *Brahman*.

O Arjuna, this indestructible Supreme Soul, although situated in the body, neither does anything nor becomes involved in any action, for He is eternal and without attributes. Just as the omnipresent sky remains unaffected due to its subtle nature, the soul, present throughout the body, is not affected by the qualities of the body because it is attributeless.

O Arjuna, just as a single sun illuminates the entire universe, similarly, a single soul illuminates the entire body. In this way, those great souls who understand the distinction between the field and the knower of the field, and who know how to transcend nature and its effects through the vision of knowledge, attain the Supreme *Brahman*, the Supreme Soul.

The Discussion

In the first verse of the first chapter of the Srimad Bhagavad Gita, the words *Dharmakshetra* and *Kurukshetra* are used. *Kurukshetra* refers to the land where the great war of Mahabharata was fought, while *Dharmakshetra* signifies the human body, through which a person can attain salvation by performing their *Dharma*. In the second chapter, it is stated that the living being is not the body but the soul. However, in the subsequent chapters, the body is necessary for practicing *Swadharma* (one's own duty) or *Bhakti* (devotion), which are the paths to salvation. Therefore, it is essential for the common people (whom Arjuna represents) to have the curiosity to understand the role of *Prakriti-Purusha* (nature and the Supreme Being) or *Kshetra-Kshetrajna* (the field and the knower of the field) in life.

As we have already learned, this body is referred to as *Kshetra* because its qualities are similar to that of a field. In spirituality, it is also called *Prakriti* (nature), as the natural qualities manifest from it. (Just as the fruit of the seeds sown in a field appears at the right time according to the conditions of the land, similarly, the fruit of the seeds of *sanskars* (impressions) sown in the body manifests over time. That is why it is also called the body's field.)

The soul that knows the body-like field is called *Kshetrajna*. The soul is considered the owner of the body. In spirituality, it is referred to as *Purusha* (the Supreme Being).

What we have learned up to the twelfth chapter is to perform work without attachment to its results, known as *Nishkama Karma*. However, the result of any action is inherently attached to the work, making it almost impossible to separate the fruit of work from the work itself. To address this, the system of *Rajyoga* has been introduced, which suggests that if the work is done for the welfare of others, the individual performs the action, and in such work, there is no attachment to the fruit of that work. But the truth remains that the fruit of work cannot be completely separated from the work itself. Similarly, it is impossible to understand the body and soul separately by isolating them from each other.

Everything in the world has two aspects: external and internal. For example, the external form of most fruits is the peel, while the internal form is the pulp. The real taste of the fruit lies in the pulp, which is what gives the fruit its identity. However, the fruit cannot be fully identified by its pulp alone; the identity of the fruit is found in both the pulp and the peel. Likewise, the external form of every living being is the body, while the internal form is the soul. The soul is the true essence of the being, but the identity of the living being is a combined form of both the soul and the body. The body serves as a means for the soul to achieve liberation.

Every action also has two forms. When a living being performs an action through the body, the result of that action directly affects the body. The soul's involvement in that action, which is reflected in the purity of the mind, remains unmanifest. The essence of this understanding is that the soul cannot be separated from the body; as long as life exists, the soul remains connected to the body. Death occurs when the soul departs from the body.

This raises the question: Is there a way to separate the soul from the body while still alive? The spiritual answer to this question is affirmative. Practically, to observe something, we need to maintain a certain distance from it so that it remains within our field of vision. For example, we cannot see a car while sitting inside it; we need to step out of it to observe it. Similarly, if we wish to observe the soul separately from the body, we must detach the soul from the body, all while ensuring the body does not die. Siddha Rishis and Munis are able to perform such tasks, as evidenced by the debate between Adi Shankaracharya and Mata Bharati (the wife of Mandana Mishra).

To achieve success in this practice, the scriptures recommend cultivating the *Sakshi Bhaav* (the witness state of mind), which can be attained through meditation. In this state, we observe our senses performing actions as if we are not involved in the work done by the senses, but are merely witnesses to the actions being carried out.

Now a question arises: if we cannot see the soul, what is the use of cultivating the *Sakshi Bhaav* (the witness state)?

The truth is that we cannot see the mind, intellect, and other subtle aspects of our being. To date, scientific research has recognized the existence of the mind, giving rise to the discipline of psychology. However, this field is still not fully complete, and the scientific understanding of the intellect remains unsatisfactory. Even the location of the mind and intellect within the body has not been definitively identified. Since the soul controls the mind and intellect, it is not possible to understand this from a purely scientific perspective.

Until the feeling of being a witness arises, we tend to identify ourselves with the body. When the body is harmed, we feel sorrow. We perform all our activities for the sake of the body. In essence, we become slaves to the body. However, according to spirituality, the body is a tool, not our master. Therefore, saints say that once we develop the *Sakshi Bhaav* (the witness attitude), we become the masters of our body.

There is a famous story about Socrates that illustrates this concept. When Socrates was about to be executed, some of his well-wishers, while meeting him, asked how he wanted his funeral to be conducted after his death. Socrates responded, saying, "One wishes to kill me, and another wishes to bury me. What is the difference between the two? Who is my friend and who is my stranger? Both are the same. One wishes to kill my body, and the other wishes to bury it. But I am not the body. Hence, no one can kill me, and no one can bury me." This was Socrates' witness attitude. And it is true that Socrates still lives among us through his wisdom.

Before we come to understand the soul within the body, we typically focus on work that gives us physical pleasure. In spirituality, a life focused solely on physical desires is considered similar to that of an animal, as the body serves as a trap for the soul. In life, whenever we fail to succeed in achieving what we desire for our physical well-being, despite our best efforts, we often feel the need for help. This is the moment when we can access our inner strength, which comes from the soul.

Once we start contemplating the soul, we realize that a living being is not just the body. The body belongs to the living being, but the living being is not the body itself. Through the witness state, a person can observe the actions of the body, seeing them as separate from the soul. Thus, it becomes clear that the field (the body) and the knower of the field (the soul) are distinct, but they exist together throughout life. To understand them separately, we require both the eye of knowledge and the witness state.

The importance of the witness state is also evident in our daily lives. The witness state always brings peace to the mind, as it enables us to detach ourselves from the fluctuations of worldly experiences and observe them with calm and clarity.

Conclusion

In this chapter, it has been clarified that the field and the knower of the field coexist in life. However, this reality can be realized by living in the witness state, through knowledge. Furthermore, the soul is considered a part of the Supreme Soul.

It is natural to raise the question: Since the Supreme Soul is beyond the three gunas (qualities), as Shri Krishna Himself declares, does that mean the soul, being a part of the Supreme Soul, is also beyond the three gunas? In the next chapter, the three gunas are further contemplated and discussed, offering deeper insight into this question.

-: Om Tat Sat:-

Chapter-14
Gunatraya-vibhag Yoga.

The fourteenth Chapter of Srimadbhagavad Gita At a glance	
Total Nos of verses	27
Nos of verses by lord Shree Krishna	26
Nos of verses by Arjuna	1
Nos of verses by sanjay	0
Nos of verses by Dritrastra	0
Main theam of the Chapter	Virtue of the Nature

श्री गणेशाय नमः

श्लोक

गोविन्द शंकर हरे गिरिजेशशम्भो
जनार्दन गिरीश मुकुन्द साम्ब।
नान्या गतिर्मम कथचनं वां विहायतस्म
आत्प्रभोमम गतिः कृप्या विधेया।।

दो0—भगवन बोले पार्थ सुनो ज्ञानो में उत्तम ज्ञान।
इसी ज्ञान से मुक्त हुए साधु ऋषिमहान।1।
दो0—प्रलयकाल व्याकुल नही धरते पुनः न रूप।
इसी ज्ञान आश्रय से ज्ञानी पाये मेरा स्वरूप।2।

ब्रम्ह मूल प्रकृति गर्भस्थाना। मैं करूं बीजस्थापन गर्भाधाना।।
प्रकृति पुरुष संयोग के कारण। सकल जीव करे तन धारण।।
जनक पुरुष जननी है प्रकृति। जिनसे जग चैतन्य आकृति।।
सत्व रज तम हे कुन्तिनन्दन। आत्मा को बान्धे तन बन्धन।।
सत्व निर्विकार विमल प्रकाशा। विमल ज्ञानी प्रारब्ध सुखाशा।।
रजस गुण राग रूप आसक्ति। कर्मफल में बाँधे यही शक्ति।।
तमस मोह अभिमान अज्ञाना। आलस प्रमाद निद्रा दोष नाना।।

सत्व बढ़े रज तम करी उना। प्रेम ज्ञानादि पार्थ सत्वगुणा।।
सत्वगुण बढ़े तो चेतना जागे। विवके बढ़े सब दूर्गुण भागे।।
रजस बढ़े सत्व तम घट जाए। सकाम कर्म में यही लगाए।।
सत्व रज मर्दन तमस बढ़ाए। आलस्य प्रमाद दूर्गुण भरमाए।।

दो0—प्रयाणकाल चित्त सत्व तो जीवात्मा स्वर्ग को जाए।
रजस अवसान काल रहे मनुष्ययोनी पुनि पाए।3।
दो0—तमस अन्त काल रहे जो जीव मति अति मूढ़।
कीट पतंग पशु रूप धरे यह रहस्य अति गूढ़।4।

श्रेष्ठकर्म वैराग्य सुख ज्ञाना। निर्मलचित्त सात्विक गुण नाना।।
राजस कर्म सुख दुःख परिणिति।तामस फल भय की अनुभुति।।
सत्वगुण उत्पन करत है ज्ञाना। रजस जनित लोभ मद् नाना।।
तमस जनित अति मोह प्रमादा।भय अज्ञान दूःख रोग बिषादा।।
सत्व दिलाए स्वर्गसमउच्चलोका।सुखशान्तिसह ज्ञान आलोका।।
राजसी गुण मध्यलोक ले जाए।पार्थ यही मृत्युलोक कहलाए।।
तामसी जीव अधोगति अपनाये।कीटपशु आदि योनी वह पाऐ।।
त्रिगुणयुक्त ही कर्म के कारण। प्रयाण परे जीव करे तनधारण।।
त्रिगुण अतिरिक्त नही कछु कर्ता।ज्ञान सदा सकल दुःख हर्ता।।
सच्चिदानन्द पार्थ त्रिगुण रहिता। परम शक्ति करे जग हिता।।

दो0—जगत के सुखदूःख भाव होवे त्रिगुण के कारण।
त्रिगुणातीत करे नही सुख दूःख कछु भी धारण।5।

पाई ज्ञान कहे पार्थ मृदु वचना।त्रिगुण छाडि प्रभु कैसी रचना।।
त्रिगुणरहित जीवन क्या लक्षण।पाये जीव कैसे त्रिगुण संरक्षण।।
मुक्ति हेतु गुण क्या अपनाये। त्रिगुणातीत प्रभु कौन उपाय।।
सुनहु पार्थ प्रिय कहे कृष्णा। ज्ञान पाई करहूँ दूर तृष्णा।।
सत्वगुण देवत अन्तःप्रकाशा। रजोगुण दे कर्मफल अभिलाषा।।
तमोगुण सदा मोह की जननी। अहंकार द्वेष है इनकी करनी।।
इन्द्रियों करे बिषय विचरण। आत्मा करे मर्यादित आचरण।।
परमात्मा घ्यान करे एकीभावा। साक्षी सदृश आसक्ति अभावा।।
करे साक्षी स्थिति को धारण। विचलन का हो जाये निवारण।।
अविचलित प्रकृति त्रिगुणातीता। निर्विकार कर्म करे पुनिता।।

दो0–आत्मभाव स्थिती निरंतर सुख दुख रहे समान।
जग सकल सम लगे उसे मृदा स्वर्ण पाषाण।6।
दो0–निन्दा स्तुति प्रिय अप्रिय ज्ञानी बैरी अरू मित्।
सदा भाव अविचलित रहे हार मिले या जीत।7।
दो0–सदा भजन करे हरि काहो कर्तापन रहित।
मान अपमान सम प्रतीत तो मनुज गुणातीत।8।
दो0–त्रिगुणातीत सच्चिदानन्द सम लाँघे त्रिगुणविकार।
अव्यभिचारी भक्तियोग परमात्मा करे स्वीकार।9।
दो0–मैं आश्रय आनन्द का एकरस नित्य अखण्ड़।
अविनाशी परब्रह्म अपि सुधारस यही ब्रह्माण्ड़।10।

।।इति चर्तुदश् अध्याय।।

The fourteenth Chapter of Srimadbhagavad Gita

The Essence

The 14th Chapter of the Srimad Bhagavad Gita is known as *Gunatrayavibhag Yoga*. This chapter contains a total of 27 shlokas. For the convenience of study, it can be divided into three parts.

1. **Origin of the world from Prakriti-Purusha (Shloka 1-4):-**

Shri Bhagwan said, "I will again speak about that supreme knowledge, which is the best of all knowledge. By knowing this, all the sages have been freed from this world and have attained supreme success. Those who adopt this knowledge and attain my form are not born again at the beginning of creation. My original nature, in the form of Mahat Brahma, is the womb of all beings. I establish a conscious womb within that womb, and from the union of the inanimate and the conscious, all beings are born. The living beings born in various species of life are conceived by nature, which is their mother, and I am the father who establishes the seed."

2. **Subject of Triguna (Shloka 5-18)**:-

The three gunas, born from nature, bind the immortal soul within the body. Satvaguna is free from all defects; it binds the soul with happiness and knowledge, leading to pride. Rajoguna binds the soul to action and its results because it is the cause of attachment. Tamoguna, characterized by ignorance, binds the soul in negligence, laziness, and sleep. Satvaguna is the cause of happiness, Rajoguna is the cause of action, and Tamoguna is the cause of ignorance, which obscures knowledge and leads one into negligence.

Satvaguna increases by suppressing Rajoguna and Tamoguna; Rajoguna increases by suppressing Satvaguna and Tamoguna, and Tamoguna increases by suppressing Satvaguna and Rajoguna. When consciousness and the power of discrimination arise in the body, mind, and senses, Satvaguna should be considered to have increased. When Rajoguna predominates, greed, desire for sensual pleasures, selfishness, and unrest arise. When Tamoguna increases, negligence, useless efforts, and the mind's tendency to sleep or become enchanted emerge.

At death, if Satvaguna is predominant, one attains heaven. If Rajoguna prevails, one is reborn in the human form, attached to karma. However, if Tamoguna is dominant, the soul is born in a lower form, such as an insect or animal. The result of Satvik karma is happiness, the result of Rajasic karma is sorrow, and the result of Tamasic karma is ignorance. Knowledge is born from Satvaguna, greed from Rajoguna, and attachment from Tamoguna. Those situated in Satvaguna attain heaven, those in Rajoguna remain in the human realm, and those in Tamoguna face downfall, reaching hell.

3. **Ways to go beyond Gunas (Shloka 19-27):-** When the seer knows me in essence, beyond the three gunas, he attains my form. In other words, he is freed from sorrow and attains supreme bliss.

After this, Arjuna asks what the characteristics of one who is beyond the three gunas are, and how such a person conducts themselves.

In response, Shri Bhagwan explains that the person who, despite being influenced by the light of Satvaguna, the tendency of Rajoguna, and the attachment of Tamoguna, does not hate or desire any of them, is one who has transcended the gunas. Such a person, situated like a witness, is not disturbed by the qualities. He recognizes that the qualities only operate within the qualities themselves, and thus remains in oneness with the Supreme Being, undisturbed by them.

The person who is always centered in self-consciousness and maintains equal feelings towards praise and criticism is beyond the gunas. Such individuals, by constantly worshipping me, transcend the three gunas with ease. This is because I am the shelter of the indestructible Supreme Brahman, the source of unbroken, constant bliss, and eternal truth.

The Discussion

To understand whether the soul is beyond the three gunas, we first need to understand the origin of living beings. Lord Shri Krishna explains that living beings are born into various species, with nature as their mother, carrying them in the womb, and He Himself as the father, who establishes the seed. Since the seed is divine, the being born is inherently divine, but the development of the body follows the laws of nature. Nature is composed of the three gunas—Sattva, Rajas, and Tamas. Therefore, it is natural for the soul to be influenced by these gunas.

Thus, although the soul is beyond the three gunas, it becomes influenced by them due to its existence in the body. However, the soul has the capacity to change the influence of the three gunas through its actions. As Lord Krishna explains, upon death, the soul, influenced by the increased presence of a particular guna, attains different results:

- A soul influenced by an increase in Satvaguna (goodness) attains heaven.
- A soul influenced by Rajoguna (passion) is reborn in a human body, attached to action.
- A soul influenced by Tamoguna (ignorance) is reborn in lower forms, such as insects or animals.

Therefore, one can adopt any of the three gunas through their actions. As stated, those situated in Satvaguna attain heaven, those in Rajoguna remain in the human realm, and those in Tamoguna fall into degradation. However, by practicing Nishkam Karma (selfless action), a person rises above the three gunas, thus becoming Trigunatita (beyond the gunas). Lord Krishna says, "When the seer knows me in essence beyond the three gunas, he attains my form," meaning that such a person is freed from sorrow and attains bliss.

From a practical perspective, to be free from the three gunas, one must master Satvaguna, Rajoguna, and Tamoguna. The primary result of Tamoguna is laziness, so to master Tamoguna, one must overcome laziness through physical labor. While many consider sleep to be the effect of Tamoguna, sleep, within limits, is important for health. The disturbance caused by dreams results in incomplete sleep, which can lead to restlessness. Deep sleep, however, provides peace and requires physical exertion to achieve. Therefore, overcoming laziness and taming Tamoguna involves engaging in physical activity.

Rajoguna is characterized by endless desires, which destabilize the mind. To stabilize the mind, one must act according to one’s own dharma (duty), which can be challenging to determine. However, one's dharma is inherently tied to one’s nature and life circumstances. Some saints believe that service is an essential part of one’s dharma, such as serving one’s parents or working for the betterment of society. By working within the limits of one's dharma, desires become limited, and the mind becomes concentrated.

When we manage to control Tamoguna and Rajoguna, Satvaguna naturally remains. As long as we are alive, we cannot be entirely separated from nature, and some influence of nature, including Satvaguna, will always remain with us. However, if Satvaguna causes ego, it can hinder progress, as it might lead to attachment to one's good deeds. Thus, it is crucial to control Satvaguna and remove any ego tied to it. A person can do this by making good deeds a part of their nature, so that they no longer feel pride in their actions. This can be achieved through self-knowledge.

In conclusion, a person who is free from ego, selflessly fulfills their duties, and transcends the influence of the three gunas becomes Trigunatita. Such a person becomes the embodiment of the divine, realizing their true nature beyond the limitations of the gunas.

The Conclusion

This chapter illuminates the journey from birth to liberation. Prakriti is likened to the mother, while Parameshwar is like the father. Just as the father's seed grows in the womb of the mother, it is natural for the qualities of the mother to be passed on to the child. Triguna (the three qualities) is the nature of Prakriti, and the soul, which is a part of Parameshwar, takes a body in the womb of this mother, Prakriti. It is natural for the body to possess a part of Triguna.

However, a living being has the ability to change the proportion of the three gunas through their actions. By performing good deeds, a living being can control Tamoguna (ignorance) and Rajoguna (passion), and practice living with humility and selflessness in Satvaguna (goodness), which leads to becoming Trigunatita (beyond the three gunas).

To transcend the three gunas completely, self-knowledge is required. After learning about the state of being Trigunatita, a natural curiosity arises: What is self-knowledge, and how can it be attained? The solution to this curiosity is provided in the next chapter.

-: Om Tat Sat: -

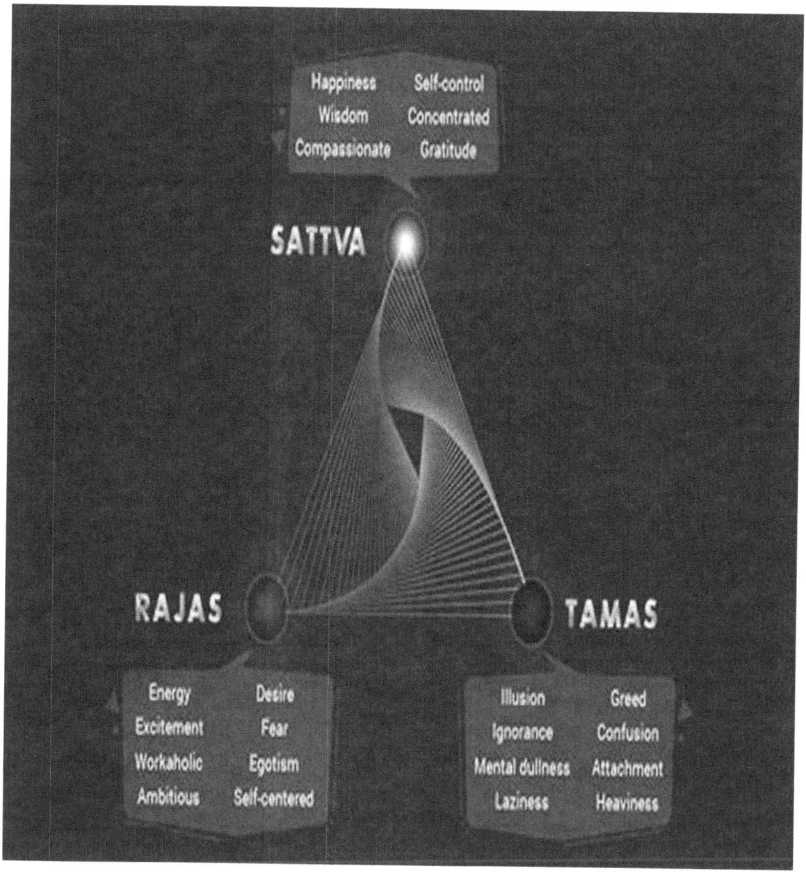

Chapter-15
Purushotam Yoga

Fifteenth Chapter of Srimadbhagavad Gita At a glance	
Total Nos of verses	20
Nos of verses by lord Shree Krishna	20
Nos of verses by Arjuna	0
Nos of verses by sanjay	0
Nos of verses by Dritrastra	0
Main theam of the Chapter	The Super-Soul

श्री गणेशाय नमः

श्लोकः

त्वं वायुरग्निरवनिर्वियदम्बुमात्राः
प्रणेन्द्रियाणि हृदयं चिदनुग्रहश्च।
सर्वं त्वमेव सगुणो विगुणश्च भूमन्
नान्यत् त्वदस्त्यपि मनोवचसा निरूक्तम्।।

दो0—कहे मुरारी पार्थ सुनो कौन है वेद का ज्ञाता।
भवतरू को जो समझ ले तो सकल द्वन्द्वमिट जाता।1।
दो0—भवतरू आश्चर्य है नीचे तना वृहद उर्ध्वमूल।
पते छन्द है वेद के अव्यय निवास अनुकूल।2।
दो0—भवतरू के मूल में सच्चिदानन्द करते वास।
ज्ञान श्रोत परमात्मा करे अज्ञान विनाश।3।

संसार वृक्ष वट् वृक्ष समाना। अतिमूल तना से निकले नाना।।
त्रिगुण जल सिंचित जग वृक्षा। विस्तृत चहूँओर जगाए ईच्छा।।
तनाप्रस्फूटित कोपल अपि मुला।बृहदतरू मुख्यमूल जग भुला।।
वासना विषय कोपल तरूअंगा। ज्ञानीनके अपि करे ध्यानभंगा।।
देव मनुज सम व्याप्त उपशाखा।ममता अहंता पाश मूल राखा।।
भवतरू स्वरूप बुद्धि सीमातीता।यह अन्तहीन कहे वेद पूनिता।।

तरूवर मौलिक मूल परमेश्वर। ब्रह्म मौलिक शाखा सृष्टिकर।।
अतिमूल शाखा व्याप्त जगमाही।मौलिकज्ञान सहज जग नाहीं।।
जो चाहे जीव परमेश्वर संगा।वैराग्यकुठार से काट अतिअंगा।।
आदिपुरुष से योग यही युक्ति।वैराग्य दिलाये पार्थ जगमुक्ति।।

दो0—दृढ़ निश्चय वैराग्य है काटे विषय वासना मूल।
अव्यय ब्रह्म को प्राप्त करे मिट भवबन्धन शूल।4।
दो0—मान अपमान मोहमुक्त आसक्ति दोष रहित।
परमात्मा में नित्य स्थिति मनबुद्धि कर्म पुनित्त।5।
दो0—नष्ट सम्पूर्ण कामना सुख दूःख द्वन्द्व न व्याप्त।
सकल मुढ़ता अन्तहो अविनाशी लोक हो प्राप्त।6।

मम परमधाम है स्वयं प्रकाशा। पाये ममभक्त जो करे प्रयासा।।
परमधाम नही कोई उद्दिपक। नही रवि चन्द्र सम अग्निदीपक।।
परमधाम मम भक्त प्रिय जाए। जन्म—मरण बन्धन बिसराए।।
जीवात्मा है मम अंश सनातन। प्रकट होए धरे तन नुतन।।
षष्टइन्द्रि जीवात्मा आकर्षित। मन ज्ञानेन्द्रि हो सुखहर्षित।।
जिमी वायुगन्ध विचरे जगमाही। आत्मा संग षष्टइन्द्रि जाहीं।।
आत्मा नुतन शरीर जो पाए। षष्टइन्द्रि समाहित हो जाए।।
स्थुल देह कर्मेन्द्रिय संयोजन। चैतन्य षष्टइन्द्रि देहि योजन।।
जीवात्मा करे बिषय का सेवन।सहयोग करे बुद्धि इन्द्रिय मन।।
षष्टइन्द्रि सदा प्रारब्ध युक्ता। प्रारब्ध कारण जीव नही मुक्ता।।

दो0—जीवात्मा भोगे विषय चैतन्य शरीर करे बास।
दुस्कर रहस्य है जानना बिना प्रभु विश्वास।7।

बिन जीवात्मा नही जग प्राणी। रहस्य जाने विवेकशील ज्ञानी।।
निज उर स्थित पार्थ है आत्मा।यत्नपुर्वक तत्त्व जाने महात्मा।।
जाके शुचित अन्तःकरण नाही।तत्त्व ज्ञान कवन विधी पाहीं।।
कोटी नक्षत्र जो दिखे अकाशा। रवि शशी अरू अनलप्रकाशा।।
सकल महूँ मम तेज विराजत।दृश्यादृश्य जग जे कछु राजत।।
मैं ही धरा की धारणशक्ति। जिससे घरा—भूत रहे व्यवस्थित।।
मैं शशि सुधा औषधि पुष्टकर्ता। मैं अग जग का जीवन धर्ता।।
मैं सकल प्राणि का प्राण अपाना। जठराग्नि पाचक विधिनाना।।

मैं अन्तर्यामी सकल उर बासी। मैं बुद्धिरूप सकल भ्रम नाशी।।
मैं ज्ञान स्मृति अपि अपोहन। पार्थ सकल भ्रम करूं दोहन।।

दो0—वेद मेरा हीं खोज करे मैं वेद वेदान्त का रचनाकार।
ज्ञान कर्म भक्ति मुझसे मैं सकल जगत आधार।8।

जगत पुरुष के हैं द्विभेदा। नित्य अनित्य कहत है वेदा।।
देह अनित्य आत्मा अविनाशी। दोनो पुरुष सकल भूतबासी।।
एक पुरुष दोनो से उत्तम। वेद जिसे कहता पुरूषोत्तम।।
सकल लोक का पालनहारा। जग अविनाशी भगवान पुकारा।।
नित्य आत्मा से मैं अपि उतम। परमात्मा आदि देव पुरूषोत्तम।।
अनित्य मूल जड़ से मैं अतिता। सर्वदा नित्य पुनीत प्रतीता।।
पुरूषोत्तम वेदान्त प्रतिष्ठित। सकल जगत है उनमें स्थित।।
तत्वज्ञानी मुझे पुरूषोत्तम जाने। करे भजन मुझको सन्माने।।
सर्वज्ञ भजन करे नित मोरा। जिससे मिटे अज्ञान अतिघोरा।।
ईश्वर के ईश्वर जान नरोत्तम। मैं सृष्टि रचनाकार पुरूषोत्तम्।।

दो0—रहस्य युक्त अपि गोपनीय शास्त्र का समझो अर्थ।
जिसे जान हो ज्ञानवान अपि सब प्रकार कृतार्थ।9।

।।इति पंचदश अध्याय।।

FifteenthChapter of Srimadbhagavad Gita

The Essence

The 15th chapter of Srimad Bhagavad Gita is known as Purushottamyoga. This chapter consists of 20 shlokas. For the convenience of study, it can be divided into 4 parts.

1. Sansar Vriksha – The tree of Universe (Shloka 1-6): - Shri Bhagwan said, "This world is like a banyan tree, with its roots upward and numerous secondary roots emerging from its trunk. God is the root of this world tree, and its main branch, in the form of Brahma, is indestructible. The Vedas serve as its branches, and one who understands their true meaning is never confused by the verses of the Vedas. This world tree is nourished by the water of the three gunas, and the buds that sprout from it represent objects and enjoyments. In addition to the main branch, the tree's branches spread everywhere in the form of gods, humans, and creatures with three forms. The roots of ego, attachment, and lust that bind the human world stretch both above and below. The form of this world tree cannot be fully perceived, as it is endless. Its far-reaching roots and branches are so vast that the main root, God, and the primary branch, Brahma, are difficult to distinguish. Therefore, God can only be realized by cutting off the extreme roots and branches with the sword of renunciation.

Those who take refuge in the first being, Narayan, are liberated. Those who conquer attachment and remain eternally in the form of God, free from the dualities of pleasure and pain, attain the supreme, eternal position. This supreme position, which once attained, ensures that a person does not return to the cycle of birth and death, is my supreme abode. It is self-illuminated, and thus the sun, moon, and fire do not illuminate it."

2. The subject of the soul (Shloka 7-11):- The soul within this body is my eternal part, which attracts the mind and senses that are situated in nature. Just as air absorbs the fragrance from its surroundings, similarly, the soul absorbs the senses along with the mind and enters a new body. The soul experiences objects with the help of the senses and the mind. When leaving the body or consuming material things, the ignorant do not recognize the soul, but the wise understand the essence of the soul through their discernment. The diligent yogis know the soul in its true essence. However, those who have not purified their inner being are unable to know the soul, even with effort.

3. Form of the Supreme Lord (Shloka 12-15):- I am the original source of the light that fills the entire world, including the Sun. I am the sustaining power of the Earth, and the nectar of the Moon, which nourishes the plants, is also my form. I am the life force of all living beings, and I am the fire that digests food in four ways. I reside in the hearts of all living beings as Antaryami. It is from me that memory, knowledge, and thoughts arise. I am the one who can be known through all the Vedas. I am the doer of Vedanta and the knower of the Vedas.

4. The subject of Kshar, Akshar Purushottam (Shloka 16-20):- In this world, there are two types of Purushas: the perishable and the imperishable. Among these, the bodies of all living beings are perishable, while the soul is imperishable. The Purushottam, who is superior to both and sustains the world, is the imperishable Supreme Soul, or God. Since I am completely beyond the perishable and inanimate realms, and I am also superior to the imperishable souls, I am known in the Vedas by the name Purushottam. O Arjuna, the wise man who knows me as Purushottam in essence, that omniscient one continuously worships me. Thus, this secret and profound knowledge has been imparted by me, and by knowing it, one becomes knowledgeable and fulfilled.

The Discussion

In the previous chapter, when we contemplated the Triguna, one thing became clear: to go beyond the Triguna, self-knowledge is essential. Self-knowledge means understanding the Almighty. Just as we know about our earthly father, we should also know the Supreme Father. However, this does not happen easily because we become confused for various reasons. In this chapter, this confusion is presented through a metaphor. The world is compared to a Banyan tree, whose roots grow upwards, while its stem, leaves, and fruits grow downwards. The tree is irrigated by the water of the three gunas, and the Vedas, or knowledge, are its leaves. As the water of the gunas nourishes the tree, buds sprout from it, which take the form of roots of desires (Vasanas). When a Banyan tree grows old, it becomes difficult to distinguish between the main root and the numerous secondary roots that spread out.

Through this metaphor, it is explained that the main root points to the Supreme Father, the Almighty. However, when the secondary roots also appear similar to the main root, confusion naturally arises. Due to this confusion, a person becomes entangled in sensory desires and is deprived of supreme knowledge, or self-knowledge. To attain self-knowledge, detachment is essential. Indian sages have compared renunciation to a lotus flower, which lives in water but remains detached from it. Therefore, to achieve freedom by surrendering to the Supreme Lord, one must strive in that direction. Knowledge, attained through devotion and renunciation, leads us to a point where we can differentiate between the material and the spiritual—this is self-knowledge.

In practical life, it is impossible to separate karma, knowledge, and devotion. However, when karma is performed with the understanding that it is service (love) to the Lord, the karma itself becomes an act of devotion and helps us draw closer to the Supreme Lord. Some saints have said that love, karma, and knowledge are the three main pillars of a devotee's life, which always protect the devotee from falling and guide them closer to God. Thus, self-knowledge is a harmonious combination of love, action, and knowledge.

Self-knowledge = Love for the Supreme Father + Action for the Supreme Father + Knowledge without ego.

At the end of this chapter, it is explained that in this world there are two types of creatures: the perishable and the imperishable. The Supreme Father, the Supreme God, is superior to both because He is provider for the both. Therefore, the Vedas refer to Him as Purushottam. This signifies that in Sanatan Dharma, Advaita (non-duality) holds great importance, and Purushottam represents the embodiment of Advaita. In practical life, our goal is to reach the state of Purushottam, but along the way, many sub-roots and sub-branches, in the form of illusions, arise, making it difficult to achieve the goal. These sub-roots and sub-branches are misleading ideas that appear to be the truth, but confuse us at every step.

Conclusion

In this chapter, the path to reach Purushottam through self-knowledge has been contemplated. It becomes clear that self-knowledge is the only way to reach Purushottam, the Supreme Truth. There is a natural curiosity that arises: if we can live happily in this beautiful world, then why and to whom does the desire to reach the Supreme Father, the Supreme God, arise? This curiosity is addressed and explored in the next chapter.

-:Om Tat Sat :-

Chapter-16
The Daivasur –Sampadvibhag -Yoga

Sixteenth Chapter of Shrimadbhagavad Gita At a glance	
Total Nos of verses	24
Nos of verses by lord Krishna	24
Nos of verses by Arjuna	0
Nos of verses by sanjay	0
Nos of verses by Dritrastra	0
Main theam of the Chapter	Virtue from Destiny by birth

श्री गणेशाय नमः

श्लोक

मनोजगर्वमोचनं विशाललोललोचन।
विधूतगोपशोचनं नमामि पद्मलोचन।।
करारविन्दभुधरं स्मितावलोकसुन्दर।
महेन्द्रमानदारणं नमामि कृष्णवारणम्।।

दो0–प्रारब्ध प्राप्त जीव सम्पदा जानो पार्थ धीमान।
दैवी आसुरी सम्पदा कहे जिसे वेद विज्ञान।1।

इन्द्रियदमन दान यज्ञ ध्याना। लोभमुक्त सहृदय धिमाना।।
निर्भय शान्त विगत अभिमाना। स्वध्यायलीन रहे विधी नाना।।
स्वधर्मपालन योग व्यवस्थित। करे सत्कर्म प्रभु प्रेमस्थित।।
अहिंसक सत्यवादी अक्रोधी। सरलबुद्धि मन विचलन रोधी।।
दयावान अनासक्त सत्चारी। धैर्य क्षमा तेज शुद्धता धारी।।
रहे अविचलित आये जब विपदा।यही पार्थ है दैवीय सम्पदा।।
दम्भ घमण्ड़ क्रोध अभिमाना। अज्ञानी करे निन्दा विधि नाना।।
यहीमनुज की आसुरी सम्पदा।अत्याचारी पाए जग विपदा।।
दैवीसम्पदा दे मुक्तिअभिनन्दन।आसुरीसम्पदा करे जगबन्धन।।

प्रारब्ध पार्थ तव दैवीसम्पदा। शोक न कर मिटा मन विपदा।।

दो0–दो भाँती की सम्पदा से भरी पूरी जग सृष्टी।
दैवी सम्पदा मुक्त करे आसुरी अपावन दृष्टि।2।
दो0–दैवी धन विस्तार कहा सुनो आसुरी पहचान।
मिथ्याभाषी अत्याचारी हो शोक युक्त अज्ञान।3।
दो0–आसुरी सम्पदायुक्त हो अशुद्ध आचरण हीन।
प्रवृति निवृति ज्ञान नही अपि विचार से दीन।4।

आश्रयरहित है यह जग सारा। हे पार्थ यही आसुरी विचारा।।
ईश्वर का अस्तित्त्व न कोई।प्रकृतिजनित जगत सब होई।।
जग जब संयोग करे नर नारी। स्वयं उत्पन्न हो सृष्टी सारी।।
अवलम्बन करे मिथ्या ज्ञाना। जगतनाश क्रुर कर्म नाना।।
वह मन्दबुद्धि जगत्अपकारी।ईश्वर उपहास करे अपि भारी।।
काम को समझे सुखसाधना।दम्भीअभिमानी न करे अराधना।।
दुष्पूरक कामना का ले आश्रय।आचरणभ्रष्ट हो सदानिराश्रय।।
मिथ्या सिद्धान्त जग में फैलाये। करे कामपुरण हेतु अन्याय।।
विषय भोगरत रहे मृत्युपर्यन्ता। अशान्तचित्त के काम अनन्ता।।
कामभोगार्थ करे संचय नाना।करे अन्याय कुचेष्टा अधिमाना।।
अनन्त आशा पडे जगबन्धन। असुर वहीं जग कुन्तीनन्दन।।

दो0– आज अर्जित कल अर्जन इच्छा नही मनोरथ अन्त।
आज हना कल अपि हनुगाँ बनने को धनबन्त।5।
दो0–मैं ईश्वर सब भोग मेरा सिद्धि युक्त बलवान्।
धनी कुटुम्बबली जग में कोई न मेरे समान।6।
दो0–आमोद प्रमोद अधिकार मेरा दूसरे दया अधीन।
यज्ञ दान अहंकारबस जाने जग समीचिन।7।
दो0–नीति विरूद्ध कर्म सदा अज्ञानी मोह फँस जाए।
अति आसक्त ही असुर है सदा नरक ही जाये।8।

अहंकारी क्रोधी कामआसक्ता। छली लोभीपाखण्ड़ी अभक्ता।।
अन्तर्यामी प्रभू से करे विद्वेषा।बिन कारण नित करे क्लेशा।।
निज धर्म को अतिश्रेष्ट बखाने। दूजा धर्म कभी ना सन्माने।।
परकार्य सदैवदोष निहारे। अहंकारी द्वेषी पाप आचारे।।

क्रूर नराधम जन्मे बारंबारा। पाए वह आसुरीयोनी संसारा।।
आसुरीवृति बन्धन का कारण। बारंबार योनी आसुरी धारण।।
होय मूढ़ कवहूँ नही मुक्ता। जीवन बने सदा शोक युक्ता।।
करे कर्म नीच यही संसारा। भवसागर भटके पाये न पारा।।
अस प्राणीको कवहूँ ना शान्ति। अज्ञान बढ़े रहे चित्त भ्रन्ति।।
लोभक्रोध कामासक्ति संसारा। यही त्रिदोष नरक मुख्य द्वारा।।

दो0– चाहे सुख समृद्धि शांती सिद्धि जगत उद्धार।
त्याग त्रिदोष कर्तव्यकर्म करहो भवसागर पार।9।
दो0– शस्त्रविरूद्ध कर्म मनमानी सुखशान्ति न पाए।
त्रिदोषमुक्त शुद्ध आचरण परमधाम नर जाए।10।
दो0–कर्तव्य अकर्तव्य कर्म को शास्त्र सिद्ध प्रमाण।
शास्त्र नियत कर्म करे मनुज बनते जगतमहान।11।

।।इति षोडश अध्याय।।

Sixteenth Chapter of Shrimadbhagavad Gita

The Essence

The 16th chapter of Srimad Bhagavad Gita is known as Daivasur Sampadvibhag Yoga. This chapter consists of a total of 24 verses. For the convenience of study, it can be divided into 3 parts.

1. Divine and demonic wealth (verses 1-5): - Shri Bhagwan said: Fearlessness, purity, knowledge, self-control, endurance in hardships for the sake of righteousness, performing sacrifices in accordance with the scriptures, serving teachers, non-violence, love for truth, freedom from anger, humility, peacefulness, non-judgment, mercy, detachment, radiance, patience, and similar qualities are the characteristics of those born with divine attributes. On the other hand, arrogance, pride, arrogance, anger, cruelty, ignorance, and similar traits are the characteristics of those born with demonic qualities. Divine qualities lead to liberation, while demonic qualities lead to bondage. O Arjuna, you need not grieve, for you are born with divine qualities. You have been blessed with these virtues.

2. Characteristics of those with demoniac qualities (Shloka 6-20):- In this world, there are only two types of humans: those with a divine nature and those with a demoniac nature. Those with a demoniac nature neither understand their own nature nor the world's true nature. They are ignorant of the concept of renunciation, and as a result, they have neither purity within nor without, nor good conduct, nor truthful speech. They believe the world is shelterless, untrue, and without a divine power, existing solely as a result of the union between man and woman. In other words, they consider nothing in the world except sensuality to be of any significance. This false knowledge corrupts their nature. Their intellect is clouded, they are cruel, and they harm others, even to the point of causing destruction in the world. Filled with arrogance, pride, and conceit, they mislead themselves and others by clinging to unattainable desires, adopting false principles born of ignorance, and practicing corruption. They remain burdened by innumerable worries until death, viewing material enjoyment as the highest form of happiness. They live without hope, bound by countless attachments, overwhelmed by lust and anger, and strive to amass wealth and pleasure unjustly. They think, "Today I have gained this, and I will gain even more tomorrow. I have wealth, and it will only increase. I have defeated my enemies, and I will defeat more. I am powerful, I am blessed with strength, I am rich, I have a great family, and there is no one like me. I will perform rituals, give charity, and indulge in pleasures."

Such individuals, deluded by ignorance and addicted to sensual pleasures, fall into hell. Those who consider themselves superior, intoxicated by wealth and status, perform only nominal rituals. Their sacrifices are mere formalities, not in accordance with the scriptures. Driven by ego, power, pride, desire, and anger, they criticize others and hate the divine presence within themselves and others. I condemn such malicious, sinful, and cruel people to demoniac births in this world. O Arjuna, these fools, instead of attaining me, are repeatedly born into demoniac forms and descend into even lower states, eventually falling into a terrible hell.

3.Inspiration to behave in accordance with the scriptures (Shloka 21-24):- Lust, anger and greed - These are the three gates to hell that destroy the soul and lead to its degradation. Therefore, these three should be abandoned. One who is free from these three acts in their own welfare and attains ultimate salvation. A person who disregards the rules of the scriptures and acts arbitrarily neither achieves success, nor ultimate salvation, nor true happiness. Therefore, it is your duty to act according to the scriptures. In determining what should not be done, the scriptures serve as the guiding authority. You must understand that only actions prescribed by the scriptures are truly worth undertaking.

The Discussion

If we read carefully, from Chapter 1 to Chapter 15, the path to attaining the essence of Sanatan Dharma (the proximity of the Supreme Father God and the attainment of supreme bliss) has been described. This is a wonderful path that can be achieved through selfless work. However, a common person might wonder: Why should people follow the path of Sanatan Dharma and strive to attain the Supreme Father God? Moreover, who are those in the world who desire the proximity of the Supreme Father God more than worldly pleasures? This curiosity is addressed in this chapter.

As in Chapter 13, the human body is described as a field. Just as a field is evaluated by its produce, similarly, there must be a way to evaluate human life. Practically speaking, the wealth we accumulate through our deeds in life must eventually be left behind in this world. However, the deeds done for charity, the virtues, and good conduct we experience in life accompany us and are known as divine wealth. In contrast, the evil deeds, bad conduct, and selfish qualities accumulated in life remain with us as demonic wealth. After rebirth, the struggle between the wealth earned by destiny continues throughout life.

This struggle is what we call the battle of the Dharmakshetra, introduced in the first verse of the first chapter of the Srimad Bhagavad Gita. Just as there is preparation for war between the Kauravas and Pandavas in Kurukshetra, similarly, the war between divine and demonic wealth continues throughout life in the mind of man. Thus, in our conscience, virtue and vice are always ready for battle. Both sides have a commander. The commander of virtue is called Abhay (fearlessness), while the commander of vice is represented by fear.

Abhay equips his army with three main weapons:

1. Truth
2. Non-violence
3. Humility

On the other hand, the army of vice is equipped with three main weapons:

1. Arrogance
2. Ignorance
3. Anger

In this way, two armies stand ready in the battlefield of life, the Dharmakshetra, each moment, battling for supremacy.

A distorted form of non-violence can often be seen in life. Those who follow the vow of non-violence prefer to die rather than commit violence. For example, in the first chapter of the Bhagavad Gita, when the thought of violence and non-violence arises in Arjuna's mind, he considers non-violence to be in alignment with dharma and believes it is better to abandon the war. However, in our worldly life, non-violence is often misunderstood as a sign of weakness.

National poet Ramdhari Singh Dinkar, in his reflections, considers forgiveness as the result of true non-violence. In a dialogue between Bhishma Pitamah and Arjuna, he poignantly expresses this sentiment, highlighting the complex relationship between non-violence and moral strength.

क्षमा ,दया, तप, त्याग ,मनोबल सबका लिया सहारा।
पर नरव्याघ्र सुयोधन तुमसे कहो कहाँ कब हारा ?
क्षमाशील हो रिपु –समक्ष तुम विनित हुये जितना ही।
दुष्ट कौरवों ने तुमको कायर समझा उतना ही।।
अत्याचार सहन करने का कुफल यही होता है।
पौरूष का आतंक मनुज कोमल होकर खोता है ।।
क्षमा शोभती उस भुजंग को जिसके पास गरल हो ।
उसको क्या जो दन्तहीन विषरहित विनीत सरल हो।।

Forgiveness, kindness, penance, sacrifice, and moral integrity were once taken for granted. But tell me, Suyodhana, the warrior of men, when did you lose? You believe that by forgiving and showing humility before your enemies, you are upholding righteousness. Yet, the more the evil Kauravas have seen you as a coward, the more you forgive. This is the unfortunate consequence of tolerating atrocities. The terror of masculinity is lost when a man becomes too soft. Forgiveness is fitting for a cobra with poison, but what of one who is toothless, without poison, humble, and simple?

The underlying message here is that when weak people talk about non-violence, it becomes laughable. Non-violence is the hallmark of heroes. In India, many of our generations have been bound in the chains of slavery under the guise of following the vow of non-violence. The truth is, only those who are brave can practice non-violence effectively; they are the ones who can triumph over violence. Violence cannot be conquered by violence alone. Throughout history, many wars have been fought, but the result has always been destruction.

The reality is that when a man endowed with divine qualities commits violence, it is to protect society from the influence of demonic forces. This type of war is known as *Dharmayuddha* (righteous war). Non-violence means causing no harm to others by thought, word, or deed. However, for the brave, protecting society from those who cause harm—whether by mind, speech, or action—also falls within the realm of non-violence.

To understand this better, we must first identify demonic qualities. Without recognizing them, how can we avoid them? The outcome of demonic qualities is lust, anger, and greed.

The message of this chapter is clear: a man should cultivate his divine qualities and stay away from the influence of demonic qualities. Those who are destined to possess more divine qualities (such as truth, non-violence, humility, etc.) will naturally seek to increase them. As a result, they will feel a strong desire to take refuge in the Supreme Lord. On the other hand, those whose destiny is dominated by demonic qualities (such as lust, anger, greed, etc.) will seek to increase these negative qualities, leading to their attachment to worldly things.

Conclusion

In this chapter, we have explored the curiosity of why some people become involved in worldly activities while others detach themselves from worldly life. This shows that, due to destiny, different people have different inclinations. Some are drawn towards the world, while others are inclined towards God. It is natural for ordinary people to wonder that if destiny itself determines human inclinations, what then are the Shastra-based methods? These methods are said to lead one to salvation when life is lived according to their guidance. This curiosity is answered in the next chapter.

Chapter-17
Shraddha-traya-vibhag Yoga

Seventeenth Chapter of Srimadbhagavad Gita At a glance	
Total Nos of verses	28
Nos of verses by lord Krishna	27
Nos of verses by Arjuna	1
Nos of verses by sanjay	0
Nos of verses by Dritrastra	0
Main theam of the Chapter	The adopted degree of Devotion

श्री गणेशाय नमः

श्लोक

गुणाकरं सुखाकरं कृपाकरं कृपापर।
सुरद्विषनिकन्दनं नमामि गोपनन्दन।।
नवीनगोपनागरं नवीनकेलिलम्पट।
नमामि मेघसुन्दरं तडित्प्रभालसत्पटम्।।

दो0—शास्त्र विधि त्यागी करे सुमिरण श्रद्धा के साथ।
रजस तमस सात्विकी कैसी यह श्रद्धा है नाथ।1।
दो0—कहे कृष्ण शास्त्र परे स्वभावजा श्रद्धा है तीन।
सात्विकी राजसी अरू तामसी जाने वेद प्रवीण।2।

श्रद्धा नही है शास्त्र आधारित। श्रद्धा सकल प्रारब्ध सवँारित।।
श्रद्धा सदैव हो आत्मअनुरूपा।जस श्रद्धा तस पाये स्वरूपा।।
सात्विक श्रद्धा आश्रय देवपूजा।आचरणशुद्ध विश्वास न दूजा।।
राजस श्रद्धा पूजे राक्षस यक्षा। करे सदा सुख काम की ईच्छा।।
तामसी करे भूत प्रेत अराधन। भ्रमित आलसी माँगें साधन।।
शास्त्रविरूद्ध तप मनकल्पित। करे कामासक्त कर्म संकल्पित।।
शास्त्रविरूद्धयज्ञ तप दर्शन। दम्भजनित अभिमान प्रदर्शन।।
अज्ञानी शास्त्र विरूद्ध उपवासा।हो धर्म हानि करे देह नाशा।।

कल्पित यज्ञ हेतु करे कृश देहा। पाखण्ड यही नही प्रभू नेहा।।
अन्तःकरण परमात्म निवासा। कृश परमात्म न पूर्ण हो आशा।।
नाना पाखण्ड़ न ईश्वर भावा। यही अज्ञानी असुर स्वभावा।।

दो0—ज्ञानार्जित प्रकृतिस्वरूप होता जप तप दान।
सात्विक राजसी तामसी प्रकृतिनुसार पहचान।3।
दो0—भोजन के अपि तीन रूप निज प्रकृति अनुसार।
प्रकृतिनुसार भोजन रूचे भोजन प्रभाव व्यवहार।4।

जग सरस पुष्टकारी आहारा।सात्विक भोजन शुद्धविचारा।।
रसयुक्त स्थिर अपि प्रीतिकारी। स्वस्थ रखे चित देह हमारी।।
कटु खट्टा उष्ण हरता आयु। असंतुलित करे कफपीत वायु।।
अस भोजन राजस कहे लोगा।बढ़े अप्रीति चिन्ता अरू रोगा।।
अर्द्धसिद्ध निरस अरू बासी। अशुद्ध जुठन तामस भोजराशि।।
शास्त्रोक्त विधि अनासक्त कर्मा। रखे सेवा भाव निर्वाहे धर्मा।।
जन प्रसन्न बढ़े अगजग नेहा। अस यज्ञ सात्विक विगत संदेहा।।
जो यज्ञ भाव हो भौतिक बृद्धि। करे दम्भ अभिमान की सिद्धि।।
असयज्ञ पार्थ राजस प्रकारा।निज स्वार्थहित करे बिचारा।।
तामस यज्ञ शास्त्रविधिहीना।बिनश्रद्धा कल्पित मात्र प्रविणा।।

दो0—न वेदमंत्र का उच्चारण नही पुरोहित दक्षिणा।
तामस यज्ञ है श्रद्धाहीन कल्पित प्रदक्षिणा।4।

देवद्विज गुरु ज्ञानी पुजा। जनक जननी अपि देव है दुजा।।
सरल अहिंसक पवित्र ब्रम्हचारी।अस मनुज सात्विक तप धारी।।
पठनपाठन वेद शास्त्र अभ्यासा।परमेश्वर नाम जप हरे निराशा।।
अनुद्वेगकर प्रियबचन अनुशासीत। वाणीतप यथार्थ जगभाषित।।
मन प्रसन्न भगवतचिन्तन पुष्टी।मनतप सरलस्वभाव सन्तुष्टि।।
मनतप तनतप अरू तपबचना।यही हैसात्विक तप संरचना।।
स्वार्थ दम्भ पाखण्ड़ जनित तप।करे सम्मान हेतु मिथ्याजप।।
अस तप फल रहे अनिश्चिता। राजस तप हेतु निज हिता।।
पीडित करे निज देहमन वाणी। हठी मूढ़ करे सकल नादानी।।
पर अनिष्ट की रखे मन भावा। तामस तप हो फलाभावा।।
देश कालपात्रानुसार उपकारा। सात्विकदान इसे कहे संसारा।।

करे दान प्रत्युपकार फलआशा। राजस दान की यही परिभाषा।।

दो0–श्रद्धारहित दान कुपात्र को देश काल प्रतिकूल।
तामस दान यह दान है हिय उपजाय शूल।5।

ऊँ तत्सत् पार्थ मौलिक त्रिबचना।इनसे वेद ब्रम्हण यज्ञ रचना।।
ये त्रिशब्द सच्चिदानन्द नामा। जहाँ पाये अग जग विश्रामा।।
शास्त्र सम्मत् यज्ञ तप दाना। सकल कर्म परमेश्वर ज्ञाना।।
श्रेष्ठपुरुष करे जब पावनकर्मा।आरम्भ ऊँ उच्चारण सत्धर्मा।।
तत् अर्थ सबकुछ परमात्मा। अनासक्त कर्म करे महात्मा।।
यज्ञ तप दान करे कल्याणा। तत्काल मोक्षदाता कहे धिमाना।।
परमसत्य जग सत् कहलाए। दैवीय त्याग जिसका है उपाय।।
सत् सात्विक यज्ञतपदाना। कर्म ईश्वर हेतु सत् समाना।।
श्रद्धा सहित जग कर्तव्य कर्मा। सबही सत् कहे शश्वत धर्मा।।
श्रद्धारहित सब यज्ञ तप दाना। असत् कहे मुनि योगी धीमाना।।

दो0–असत् मन भ्रमित करे बढ़े जग बाद विबाद।
असत् सदा हानि करे जीवन या जीवन बाद। 6।
दो0–श्रद्धारहित यज्ञ दान तप फल चिन्ता अरू शोक।
असतकर्म निष्फल सदा इहलोक अपि परलोक।7।

।।इति सप्तदश् अध्याय।।

Seventeenth Chapter of Srimadbhagavad Gita

The Essence

The seventeenth chapter of Srimad Bhagavad Gita is known as Shraddhatrayavibhag Yoga. This chapter contains a total of 28 shlokas. For the convenience of study, it can be divided into three parts.

1. **Shraddha (Shlok 1-6):-** Arjun said, "O Krishna! Those who abandon the Shastra Vidhi and worship the gods with devotion, what is their state? Are they Satvik, Rajasi, or Tamasi?"

Shri Bhagwan replied that the faith of men, born solely from nature without the influence of Shastra, can be of all three types—Satvik, Rajasi, and Tamasi. Faith aligns with one's conscience, so it reflects the nature of the person. Satvik individuals worship the gods, Rajasic individuals worship Yakshas and demons, and Tamasic individuals worship ghosts and spirits. Those who perform severe penances purely in their minds, without adhering to the rules of scriptures, and are filled with arrogance, ego, desire, attachment, and pride of power, and who insult the spiritual presence within both the body and me, the Supreme Soul in the heart, should be considered of demonic nature.

2. **Types of food, sacrifices, penance and donations (Verses 7-22):-** Food is also liked by individuals according to their nature, and therefore, food is categorized into three types. Similarly, sacrifices, penance, and donations are also of three types.

Satvik individuals prefer food that enhances longevity, intelligence, strength, health, happiness, and love. Such food is juicy, smooth, stable, and naturally pleasing to the mind. Rajasic individuals, on the other hand, prefer food that is bitter, sour, salty, very hot, pungent, dry, or burning, as well as food that leads to sorrow, worry, and disease. Tamasic individuals favor half-cooked, tasteless, foul-smelling, stale, or impure food.

Satvik individuals consider yajna (sacrifice) as a duty. Rajasic individuals perform yajnas with the hope of obtaining fruits or rewards. The yajna done without following the Shastra rituals, without charity, without mantras, and without faith is called Tamasic yajna.

Penances also differ according to nature. Physical penance includes the worship of God, Brahmins, Gurus, and learned individuals, as well as purity, simplicity, celibacy, and non-violence. Speech-related penance includes practices such as reading and reciting the Vedas and chanting the name of God, which are beneficial and true. Mind-related penance involves cultivating happiness, calmness, thinking about God, controlling the mind, and purifying inner feelings. These three types of penance are called Satvik penance.

Rajasic penance is done for respect, honor, worship, or other selfish motives, often driven by nature or hypocrisy, and its results are uncertain or temporary. Tamasic penance is done foolishly, stubbornly, with pain to the body, speech, or mind, or to cause harm to others.

Donations are also categorized based on their nature. A donation given according to the country, time, and the deserving recipient, with the understanding that it is a duty and not a favor, is considered Satvik. A donation given with pain, with the expectation of reciprocation, or with the desire for reward is Rajasic. A donation given to an unworthy or undeserving person without respect is Tamasic.

3. **Explanation of the use of Om Tat Sat (Shloka 23-28):-** Om and Tat Sat are the names of Brahman. With these names, at the beginning of creation, Brahmins, the Vedas, and yajnas were also created. Therefore, the yajnas, penance, and charitable activities prescribed in the scriptures always begin with the name of the Supreme Lord, Om. Those who seek welfare perform penance and charity with the name of Tat Sat, which signifies truth and the highest devotion to God. Any sacrifice, penance, or charity performed without faith is false; it brings no benefit, either in this world or the next.

The Discussion

Whatever work a person does in the world, their motivation is influenced by three factors:

1. Our body
2. Social sanskars (the values imparted by parents, teachers, and society)
3. Geographical situation (the environment or creation)

By destiny, we are born with divine and demonic wealth, as well as natural qualities (Satva, Rajas, and Tamas), which are reflected in our worldly activities. However, the primary objective of the Indian Vedas is the welfare of the entire human race. Therefore, the sages have outlined certain symbolic practices in the Vedic texts, which, when followed, elevate human life. The main ones among these are Yajana, Tapa, and Daan. The symbolic purpose of Yajana is to guide life along a path of progress without causing harm to natural resources. Daan refers to fulfilling one's social duties, while Tapa emphasizes maintaining the health of both the body and mind.

As discussed in the previous chapters, a living being is born with natural qualities due to being within the womb of nature. Therefore, the effect of these natural qualities is also reflected in practices like Yajana, Tapa, and Daan. Each of these activities can be categorized into three types—Satvik, Rajasi, and Tamasi. Since food is essential to maintain the health of the body, a person's preferences for food vary according to the influence of their Gunas. Hence, food also falls into three categories: Satvik, Rajasi, and Tamasi. Similarly, each individual's nature determines their interests, which is referred to as Shraddha.

As we have learned in previous chapters, whatever deeds we perform, if offered to God, lead to salvation. This is why the sages propounded the symbolic mantra "Om Tat Sat" for the welfare of people, advising its use during Yajana, Tapa, and Daan. The literal meaning of this mantra is as follows: Om (God), Tat (the one detached from creation), Sat (with true faith). In other words, "I offer my deeds (Yajana, Tapa, Daan) with true faith to the God who is detached from this creation."

To understand this message from a practical perspective, the Shastra-guided rituals serve as a code of conduct for us. By following them, human life becomes more beneficial. Our deeds in the world are influenced by the wealth given by destiny and the three Gunas of nature, which govern our worldly existence. These are like the oars of the boat of life, which can steer it. However, a rudder is needed to ensure the boat moves in the right direction. The rules and regulations prescribed by the scriptures act as that rudder, providing the necessary direction.

The primary aim of these rules is to ensure that our actions are beneficial to the body, society, and the environment. Yajana, Tapa, and Daan are symbolic forms of such deeds. Due to our ignorance, we may sometimes misunderstand the purpose of practices like Yajana, Tapa, and Daan, thinking that they are about receiving fruits without effort, but this view is not supported by either the practical or spiritual aspects of life. This chapter clearly demonstrates that deeds performed according to the prescribed rules of the scriptures play a crucial role in both the practical and spiritual upliftment of an individual.

In Sanatan culture, a great emphasis is placed on the worship of God, which signifies the purity of mind and helps an individual focus on performing their duties. We can sum up the virtue of Shastra-based conduct in one sentence: The Shastra-based method is like a rudder that provides direction to the boat of life, while karma, influenced by destiny and nature, is like the oar that steers the boat.

Conclusion

In this chapter, the characteristics of Yajana, Tapasya, Daan, and food have been contemplated according to their nature. This demonstrates that a person should follow the Shastra-based method, which helps an individual progress on the path of public welfare. The reflections in this chapter also address the question of why we should follow the Shastra-based method. However, the proper answer to the question posed by Arjuna in the first chapter of the Srimad Bhagavad Gita—whether war is justified or not—has not yet been clearly provided by the teachings in the chapters so far. Therefore, it is natural for ordinary people to be curious about the relevance of war in Arjuna's context. The next chapter, which is the final chapter of the Srimad Gita, contemplates this curiosity of the common people.

-:Om Tat Sat:-

Chapter-18
Moksha-Sanyas Yoga.

The Eighteenth Chapter Srimad Bhagavad Gita At a glance	
Total Nos of verses	78
Nos of verses by lord Krishna	71
Nos of verses by Arjuna	2
Nos of verses by sanjay	5
Nos of verses by Dritrastra	0
Main theam of the Chapter	**The decision making Asset.**

श्री गणेशाय नमः

श्लोक

स्थाने हृषीकेश तव प्रकीर्त्या
जगत्प्रहृष्यत्यनुरज्यते च।
रक्षांसि भीतानि दिशें द्रवन्ति
सर्वे नमस्यन्ति च सिद्धसंघा ।।

दो0—श्रवण करि अमिय बचन उपजा मन विश्वास।
पार्थ जिज्ञासा किये भेद क्या त्याग सन्यास।1।

मोहन कहे अति गूढ़ बचना। कर्मव्यकर्म को हीं तन रचना।।
त्याग काम्य कर्म विधि नाना। संन्यास इसे कछु कहे धिमाना।।
पूर्ण त्याग जो कर्मफल त्यागे। कहे विद्वान ज्ञान जब जागे।।
कछु कहे कर्ममात्र में दोषा। त्याग सकल कर्म नही भरोषा।।
कछु कहे कर्तव्यकर्म पुनिता। त्याग इसे जग होय अहिता।।
जानो अर्जुन अब त्याग स्वरूपा। सकल त्याग अपि हो त्रिरूपा।।
सात्विक राजस तामस त्यागा। कहे विस्तार ज्ञानी मुनिजागा।।
त्यज्य नही पार्थ कर्तव्यकर्मा। अतिपुनित यही मानव धर्मा।।
कर्तव्यकर्म करे आसक्ति त्यागी। पार्थ वहीं जग में बड़भागी।।

कर्तव्य कर्म अनिवार्य नरोत्तम। यही धिमान् निश्चित मत् उत्तम।।

दो0—कर्तव्य कर्म नही त्यज्य है उत्तम् जीवन भाग।
भ्रमवश कोई छोड़े इसे तो कह तामस त्याग।2।

सकल कर्म जग है दुःखरूपा। छोडे अगर यह मानी नर भूपा।।
त्याग कतर्व्यकर्म क्लेश अनुमानी। जिससे ना हो निज तनहानि।।
अस त्याग पार्थ है राजस त्यागा। मन बुद्धी कर्मफल में लागा।।
त्याग आसक्ति करे कर्तव्यकर्मा।जगहितकारी निर्वाहे निजधर्मा।।
आसक्ति त्याग है सात्विकत्यागा।मन शास्त्रोक्त कर्म में लागा।।
अकुशल कर्म से करे न द्वेषा। अनासक्त कर्म पर करे भरोषा।।
सकलकर्म त्याग तनधारी असंभव। फलत्याग मात्र है जगसंभव।।
कर्मफल त्याग करे शुद्ध त्यागी। रहे चिन्तामुक्त वही बड़भागी।।
शुद्ध चित्त संशयरहित देहा। सात्विक त्यागी करे जग नेहा।।
जो न त्यागे कर्मफल मनुदेहा। भोगे कर्मफल न कछु संदेहा।।

दो0—कर्मफल निश्चित भोगे यदि हो फलासक्ति।
कर्मफल भोगे नही जाके अनासक्त कर्मभक्ति।3।
दो0— कर्मफल के रूप है तीन अपावन मिश्रित पावन।
कछु फल जीवन बाद कछु जीवन जस भावन।4।

जाको रहे कर्मफल आसक्ति। कहाँ करे वो जग में भक्ति।।
कर्मानुसार मिले दुःख शोका। फल नियत इहलोक परलोका।।
कर्मफल वह कवहुँ नही पाता। जिसने फल आसक्ति निपाता।।
कहे वेदान्त करी पावन जाँचा। कर्म सिद्धि हेतुयुक्ति पाँचा।।
हे पार्थसकल ले मुझसे ज्ञाना। सस्मित बोले कृष्ण भगवाना।।
प्रथम सिद्धि हेतु कर्मअधिष्ठाना। जाको शरीर सब कहे धिमाना।।
द्वितीय सिद्धि हेत ुकरण कहलाता। इन्द्रिय विषय से रखेनाता।।
तृतिय सिद्धि हेतुजगत प्रयासा। कर्म सिद्धि की यही मूकभाषा।।
चतुर्थसिद्धि हेतुकर्ता कहे ज्ञानी।इसे अहंकार वेदान्त ने मानी।।
पंचमसिद्धि हेतुदैव कहे लोगा। यह प्रारब्धप्राप्त प्रेरण संयोगा।।

दो0— जस कर्म करे मानव शास्त्रोचित या वीपरीत।
पंच हेतु हीं कारण है जिससे जग हित अहित।5।

अज्ञानी कहेआत्मा ही कर्ता। भ्रमित क्या जाने पंचअहर्ता।।
हो जाके विचार अकर्ता भावा। न पड़े कर्मबन्धन के प्रभावा।।
कर्म प्रेरणा अपि तीन प्रकारा। करे प्रेरित कर्म हेतु संसारा।।
प्रेरणा भेद ज्ञेय ज्ञान ज्ञाता। रखे सदा मनबुद्धि से नाता।।
कर्मसंग्रह अपि है तीन भेदा। कर्ता करण क्रिया कहते वेदा।।
ज्ञान कर्ता कर्म प्रकृति अनुसारा।कहे तीन है शास्त्र साख्यधारा।
सात्विकराजसतामसी ज्ञाना। सर्वशास्त्र यही करे वखाना।।
सकल भूत महूँ एक अविनाशी। भाव सात्विक ज्ञान की राशी।।
पृथक भाव पृथक भूत को धारे। राजस ज्ञान कहे श्रुतिसहारे।।
तुच्छ अर्थरहित युक्तिहीन ज्ञाना। तामस ज्ञान इसे कहे धिमाना।।

दो0– निज तन आसक्ति कहे निजतन को सम्पूर्ण।
तत्त्व अर्थ जाने नहीं वह तामस ज्ञान अपूर्ण।6।

शास्त्र विधी नियत जग कर्मा। कर्ता अभिमान विगत करे धर्मा।।
बिन राग द्वेष अपि बिन आसक्ति।करे कर्म यथा निज शक्ति।।
हो कर्म सुफल मिले युक्तिनाना। सात्विककर्म इसे कहे धीमाना।।
अतिश्रमयुक्त कर्म करे अहंकारी।अतिभोगइच्छा लिए मनसारी।।
अस कर्म पार्थराजस कहलाता। जो रखे मात्र स्वार्थ से नाता।।
कर्म का परिणाम यदि हानि। वह शास्त्रविरूद्ध कर्म मनमानी।।
अज्ञान हिंसा जाकर पहचाना । बिना बिचारे कर्म है तामस नाना।।
जो करे कर्म त्यागी आसक्ति। सहित उत्साह करे यथाशक्ति।।
रखे धैर्य छाड़ि मिथ्याहंकारा।असकर्ता सात्विक संसारा।।
करे कर्म हो कर्मफल लिप्ता। लोभ आनन्द सुख दुःख दीप्ता।।
सदा सर्वदा स्वार्थ पे मरता। पार्थ इन्हे कह राजसकर्ता।।

दो0– शस्त्र विरूद्ध कर्म करे कपट आलस दिखलाये।
हो छल हिंसा कर्म में तामसी कर्ता कहलाये।7।
दो0– पार्थ सुनो अब ध्यान लगा बुद्धि धृति बिस्तार।
जिसे जान बढ़े आत्मबल हो भव बाधा निस्तार।8।
दो0– बुद्धि धृति के भी तीन भेद प्रकृति गुण अनुसार।
राजस तामस सात्विकी यह ज्ञानी कहेसुबिचार।9।

अनासक्त जगत गृहस्थ प्रवृति। जगज्ञानी कहते इसे ही धृति।।
संन्यास अपनाये जो मुक्ति हेतु। इसे कहे शास्त्र निवृति सेतु।।
प्रवृति निवृति जग भेद जो जाने। कर्तव्य अकर्तव्य वही पहचाने।।
जो समझे बन्धन मोक्ष सच्चाई। भय अभय अपि शत्रुता मिताई।।
अस बुद्धि को है सात्विक कहते। चित् भ्रमित कभी नही रहते।।
जो जाने न धर्म अधर्म विभेदा। कर्तव्य कर्म अनुशासन वेदा।।
कर्तव्य अकर्तव्य यथार्थ न जाने। असबुद्धि ज्ञानी राजस माने।।
वेदोक्त अधर्म अपि धर्म ही माने। पाप पुण्य का भेद न जाने।।
चले सकल जग बुद्धि वीपरीता। अस बुद्धि ही तामस है मिता।।
राजसी तामसी सात्विक बुद्धि। मनुज जो जाने करे सो शुद्धि।।

दो0—धारण शक्ती धृति है कर्म पर करे प्रभाव।
सुख दूःख होता धृति से नही प्रमाण अभाव।10।
दो0—भगद्वचिंतन छोड़कर रखे भौतिक कामना प्रीति।
व्यभिचारदोष यही वीपरीत अव्यभिचारिणी धृति।11।

मनप्राणक्रिया को ध्यान में धारे। भगवद् प्राप्ती कर्म करेसारे।।
अव्यभिचारिणी धृति ही सात्विकधृति।करे ध्यान मय भगवद्स्मृति।।
धर्म अर्थ काम क्रोधे धारण।हो फलइच्छा आसक्ति कारण।।
हो सदा सकाम धारणा आवृति। शास्त्र कहे उसे राजस धृति।।
रखे भय चिन्ता प्रमाद उन्मादा। निद्रा दुःख भ्रम अति बिषादा।।
हो प्रकृति विरूद्ध कर्म से प्रीति। शास्त्र कहे इसे तामस धृति।।
मानव सुख अपि तीन प्रकारा। प्रकृति अनुसार जाने संसारा।।
आरम्भ जो विषतुल्य होय प्रतीता।अन्त सुधा सम लगे पूनिता।।
जो मिटा भ्रम आत्मज्ञान जगाए। यही सात्विक सुख कहलाए।।
विषय इन्द्रिय संयोग सुख कैसा। आदि अमृत अन्त विष जैसा।।
है राजस सुख इन्द्रिय विलासा। अति क्षणिक बान्धे भवपाशा।।

दो0—निद्रा आलस्य प्रमाद जनित मिथ्या सुख वेबात।
तामस सुख मोहित करे भोग प्रति दिन रात।12।
दो0—त्रिगुण मुक्त है सत्व नही धरा गगन देवलोक।
त्रिगुण प्रकृति युक्त सकल कर्म बुद्धि मन शोक।13।

प्रारब्ध प्राकृतिक गुण अनुरागा। ब्राह्मण क्षत्रि वैश्य शूद्रविभागा।।
शान्तक्षमाशिल अरू धर्मपालक।सहनशील सौम्य इन्द्रियघालक।।
करे वेदशास्त्र अध्ययन अध्यापन।ईश्वर श्रद्धा सबसे अपनापन।।
सकलब्राह्मण गुण स्वभाविक।बढ़े ज्ञानबुद्धि मान चतुर्दिक।।
रहेवीरता धीरता तेज चतुरता। हिम्मत नेतृत्व दान आतुरता।।
युद्धकौशल दृढ़ स्वाभिमाना। बल बुद्धिशाली क्षत्रिय पहचाना।।
कृषि गोपालन अनेक व्यापारा। व्यवहारकुशल जग दे आहारा।।
धनअर्जन वैश्य कर्म स्वभाविक। बढ़े धनबल से मान चतुर्दिक।।
कर्मकौशल सेवा मानव कल्याणा। यही शूद्र प्राकृतिक पहचाना।।
तत्परता से स्वभाविक कर्मा। मिले परमसिद्धि माने निजधर्मा।।

दो0–स्वभाविक गुण प्राकृतिक है कोई उच्च न नीच।
कर्म प्रकृतिक गुण अनुसार लिक कोई ना खीच।14।

प्राकृतिकगुण कारण जनधर्मा। निज गुणानुसार करे जग कर्मा।।
करे धर्मनिर्वाह पावे जनमुक्ति। स्वभाविक कर्म ही इनकी युक्ति।।
स्वभाविक कर्म सकल तनधारी। परम सिद्धि मिले कहे मुरारी।।
परमेश्वर से सकल प्राणी उत्त्पति। उनके बल जगगति स्थिति।।
करे कर्म स्वभाविक और न दूजा।स्वभाविककर्म जग सम पूजा।।
करे नित स्वभाविक कर्मअभ्यासा।पाए परमसिद्धि करो विश्वासा।।
परमसिद्धि पाए पार्थ जनमुक्ति।स्वभाविक कर्म ही मुक्तियुक्ति।।
परधर्म श्रेष्ठ सदैव निजधर्मा। मनबुद्धि निर्द्वन्द्व न करे अधर्मा।।
यदिनिजधर्म प्रतीत युक्त दोषा। तौ परधर्म न कवहूँ भरोषा।।
धर्म सकल कछु दोष अच्छादित। जिमि पावक धुम्र से छाजित।।

दो0–अनासक्त बुद्धि सीमितमन करे त्याग अभ्यास।
साधक पाये सिद्धि जो रखे स्वधर्म विश्वासा।15।
दो0–नैष्कर्म्यसिद्धि साख्ययोग से करता साधक प्राप्त।
परमसत्य को जानो पार्थ जो सर्वत्र है व्याप्त।16।

स्पृहारहित अनासक्त जो बुद्धि। अन्तःकरण साधक की शुद्धि।।
नैष्कर्म्यसिद्धि परानिष्ठा ज्ञाना। हो कैसे प्राप्त नही जन जाना।।
तु सुनो पार्थ संक्षिप्त विचारा। जो करे सकल भरम के पारा।।
नैष्कर्म्यसिद्धि से आत्मअनुभूति।जग पाए इसे अनासक्त विभूति।।

सात्विक आहार रखे बिशुद्ध बुद्धि। विषय त्यागी हो आश्रयशुद्धि।।
हो सात्विक धृति इन्द्रियनियंत्रित। शुन्य रागद्वेष घ्यानयंत्रित।।
अल्पाहारी अपि अहंकारहीना। मोहरहित कर्म ही करे प्रविणा।।
साधक प्राप्त परम नैष्कर्म्यसिद्धि। हो सदा भक्ति की अभिबृद्धि।।
नैष्कर्म्यसिद्धि शान्ताकार ब्रह्मयोगा।है ईच्छा शोक अन्त संयोगा।।
प्राप्त परमसुख प्राणि समभावा। पार्थ वहीं नैष्कर्म्यसिद्धि पावा।।
जानी परम्तत्त्व पाए पराभक्ति। हो प्राप्त मुझे वो पाये मुक्ति।।
करे सकलकर्म हो मेरा परायण।वो करे प्राप्त शाश्वतनारायण।।
सकल कर्म करे मुझमें अर्पण। समबुद्धि चित हो करे समर्पण।।

दो0—करे कर्म चित मुझमेंचैतन्ययोगी सउल्लास।
मम्कृपा से भक्त के संकट मिटे अनायास।17।
दो0—जो रमें भौतिक सुख में रखे मन अहंकार।
परमार्थ भ्रष्ट नष्ट हो अपि उसका ना उद्धार।18।

अहंकारी चित्तहो अति चंचल। हो नष्ट भ्रष्ट कर्म सब निष्फल।।
अहंकारवश यदि चाहे संन्यासा। उसको जग में मिले निराशा।।
तव प्राकृतगुण क्षत्रिय स्वभावा। स्वभावजन्य रण ही तोहे भावा।।
यदि युद्ध छोड़े तुमोह कारण। प्रारब्धवश क्षत्रिय धर्मधारण।।
प्रारब्धवश तु कभी युद्ध न छोड़े। युद्ध से क्षत्रिय मुख ना मोड़े।।
परमात्मा सकल ह्रदय में स्थित। मम माया करे कर्म व्यवस्थित।।
पार्थ परमेश्वर शरण में जायो। भगवद्कृपा शश्वत शाँति पायो।।
पार्थ कहा गोपनिय ज्ञान सारा। करो कर्म निज मति अनुसारा।।
तु है अतिशय भक्तप्रिय मोरा। यह गूढ़वचन सकल हित तोरा।।
पार्थ करो मेरी घ्यान अरू भक्ति।करो कर्म हो चित्त अनाशक्ती।।

दो0—ममप्रिय हे पार्थ तु मैं हूँ सर्वत्र ही व्याप्त।
पूजन ध्यान भक्ति मेरी करे मुझे ही प्राप्त।19।

छोडो पार्थ सकल आड़म्बर। कर्तव्यकर्म मुझको अर्पणकर।।
छाडीशोक आयो मम शरणा। जो इच्छा हो पापउवरना।।
पार्थ यह गूढ़ रहस्य पुनिता। न कहो उसे जो भक्तिरहिता।।
जो तपरहित रखे भगवद्द्वेषा। न दे ताकोगूढ ज्ञान उपदेशा।।
जो करे यह गूढरहस्य प्रचारा। मैं करू भक्त जगत्त उद्धारा।।

नही भक्त कोई तुझसे बढ़कर। भविष्य अपि न होय धरा पर।।
धर्ममय संवाद ज्ञानयुक्त नाना।पठनपाठन ज्ञान यज्ञ समाना।।
होउ पूजित ज्ञान गीता द्वारा। हो सकल सिद्धि यही संसारा।।
श्रोता जो शास्त्र सुने श्रद्धायुक्ता।पाये श्रेष्ठलोक होये पापमुक्ता।।
पार्थ हुआ क्या तव भ्रम अन्ता। क्या मिटा मोह पूछे भगवन्ता।।

दो0—क्या एकाग्रचित किया श्रवण यही पावन ज्ञान।
बता तेरा क्या मिट गया मोह जनित अज्ञान।20।
दो0—पार्थ कहे हृषीकेशसे मोह हुआ मम नष्ट।
संशयरहित आज्ञापालन को मम दृष्टि स्पष्ट।21।
दो0—हर्षित संजय हो रहे सुन कृष्ण अर्जुन संवाद।
अद्भुत कथन श्री कृष्ण के हितकारी र्निविवाद।22।
दो0—मैंने सुना अद्भुत संवाद जो कहे स्वयं भगवान।
व्यास कृपा दिव्य दृष्टि का करूं बड़ा सम्मान।23।
दो0—राजन मैं अति हर्षित सुन गीता गूढ़ ज्ञान।
हरिद र्शन संभाषण से मिटा सकल अज्ञान।24।
दो0—राजन अर्जुन जान गये धर्म अधर्म का भेद।
साथ परमेंश्वर कृष्ण स्वयं जिनको गाये वेद।25।
दो0—अचल नीति श्री विजय विभूति अपि धर्म का सार।
सकल वहीं हैं कृष्ण जहाँ राजन सुसिद्ध विचार।25।

।।इति अष्टदश अध्याय।।

The Eighteenth Chapter Srimad Bhagavad Gita

The Essence

The 18th Chapter of the Srimad Bhagavad Gita is known as Moksha-Sanyas Yoga. This chapter consists of a total of 78 shlokas. For the convenience of study, it can be divided into 7 parts.

1. **Topic of Renunciation (verse 1-12):-** Arjun said, "O Vasudev, I wish to understand the essence of renunciation and the difference between renunciation of actions and renunciation of their fruits."

Lord Shri Krishna replied that many scholars consider renunciation to be the abandonment of desired actions, while others define it as the renunciation of the fruits of actions. Some scholars believe that all actions are flawed and should be renounced, while others do not consider actions like yajna, daan, and tapasya as renunciable. Therefore, O Arjun, first listen to the explanation of renunciation.

Renunciation can be categorized into three types: Satvik, Rajasi, and Tamasi. Yajna, daan, and tapasya should not be renounced; they are compulsory duties because they purify the mind. However, attachment to the fruits of these deeds must be renounced. Renouncing these duties out of confusion is considered Tamasi renunciation. If one renounces duty out of fear of physical pain, it is Rajasi renunciation. Satvik renunciation, on the other hand, is when one performs prescribed duties with a sense of detachment from their fruits.

The person who neither hates bad deeds nor clings to good deeds, and who is endowed with pure sattva guna, is considered a true renunciant—doubtless, intelligent, and virtuous. It is impossible for any human being to renounce all actions entirely. Therefore, the one who renounces attachment to the results of actions is the true renunciant. A person who does not relinquish attachment to the fruits of their actions will inevitably reap the results, either in this life or the next. However, one who remains detached from the fruits of their actions is never affected by them.

2. **Sankhya Siddhanta (Verse 13-18):-** In Sankhya Shastra, five causes are identified for the success or failure of all actions: 1. Adhishthan (the body), 2. Karan (the organ of action), 3. Cheshta (effort), 4. Karta (the ego or doer), and 5. Destiny (fate). Whatever a person does with their body, mind, and speech, whether in accordance with the scriptures or against them, the causes for these actions are rooted in these five factors. However, some ignorant individuals, due to delusion, believe that the soul is the sole cause of actions because they are unaware of the true reality. The person

who does not harbor the belief of being the doer is not bound by their actions.

The knower, knowledge, and the knowable form the threefold motivation for karma, while the doer, the instrument, and the action itself constitute the threefold structure of karmasamgrah.

3. **Knowledge, deed, doer, intelligence, patience, happiness (Verse 19-40):-** In Sankhyashastra, three types of knowledge, doers, and actions are described.

The knowledge by which a person perceives the one indestructible Supreme Being present equally in all separate elements, without division, is known as Satvik knowledge. The knowledge that leads a person to generate distinct feelings about separate elements is called Rajasi knowledge. The knowledge that is attached to the physical body as a whole, illogical, devoid of essential meaning, and trivial, is referred to as Tamasi knowledge.

The work that is in line with the scriptures, done without pride of being the doer, and performed without attachment or hatred, by a person who does not desire the result, is called Satvik work. However, work that involves excessive effort and is performed by someone desiring pleasures or driven by ego is Rajasi. Work done out of ignorance, driven by considerations of results, loss, violence, or personal ability, is Tamasi.

The doer who is free from attachment, does not speak egoistic words, is patient, enthusiastic, and unaffected by the joy or sorrow related to the completion or non-completion of the work, is called a Satvik doer. The doer who is attached, desires the fruits of the work, is greedy, and causes harm to others, is called Rajasi. The doer who is unreasonable, uneducated, arrogant, deceitful, destroys others' livelihoods, causes grief, and is lazy or procrastinating, is called Tamasi.

Intelligence and patience are also categorized into three types. The intellect that understands the paths of action and renunciation, duty and non-duty, fear and fearlessness, bondage and liberation, is Satvik. The intellect that is confused about Dharma and Adharma, duty and non-duty, is Rajasi. The intellect enveloped by Tamoguna, which considers Adharma to be Dharma and sees everything in opposition, is Tamasi.

Attachment to worldly things, excluding devotion to God, is the fault of Vyabhichar. Dharana free from this fault is called Avyabhicharini Dharana. A person endowed with the power of pure concentration, who controls the actions of the mind, soul, and senses through meditation, is a Satvik practitioner. The concentration by which a person, driven by desires, holds onto Dharma, Artha, and Kama with intense attachment, is Rajasi concentration. The concentration of a person with an evil intellect who remains immersed in sleep, fear, worry, and sorrow to the point of madness, is Tamasi concentration.

Happiness is also classified into three types. The happiness experienced by a seeker practicing Bhajan, meditation, and service, which ultimately leads to the end of sorrow, appears difficult at first but its result is like nectar. This type of happiness, born from the grace of the intellect subject to God, is Satvik. The happiness that arises from the union of the subject and the senses, which appears like nectar during enjoyment but leads to suffering in the end, is called Rajas happiness. The pleasure that captivates the soul both during enjoyment and in its aftermath, originating from sleep, laziness, and negligence, is Tamasi happiness.

There is no being on earth, in the sky, or among the gods, and nowhere else, that is devoid of these three qualities born of nature.

4. **Varna-dharma (Verse 41-48):-** O Arjuna, Brahmins, Kshatriyas, Vaishyas, and Shudras are distinguished by the qualities born from their nature and actions. The natural duties of a Brahmin include controlling the conscience, suppressing the senses, enduring hardships for the sake of religion, maintaining purity both inside and outside, forgiving others' wrongs, keeping

the mind, senses, and body simple, having faith in the Vedas, scriptures, God, and the afterlife, studying and teaching the Vedas, and experiencing the essence of God.

For a Kshatriya, the natural duties include valor, brilliance, patience, cleverness, courage in battle, giving charity, and a sense of leadership. The natural duties of a Vaishya include farming, cattle rearing, trade, and conducting oneself truthfully. The natural duty of a Shudra is to serve the other castes according to one's ability.

A person who diligently performs his natural duties attains the ultimate success of reaching God. Listen to how such a person, by following his natural duties, can attain this success. The God from whom all beings have originated, and by whom this entire world is pervaded, is worshipped through the performance of one's natural duties. By doing so, a person attains the ultimate success.

One's own duty, even if it seems lacking in qualities, is better than the duty of others, if performed with dedication, because a person who follows their own natural duty does not commit sin. Therefore, O Arjuna, one should not abandon their natural duty, even if it has flaws, because, like fire with smoke, all deeds contain some imperfections.

5. **Gyan-nishtha (Verse 49-55):-** A person with a mind free from attachment to everything, devoid of desires, and with a conquered conscience, attains the ultimate self-action through Sankhya Yoga. The way a person reaches Brahman after attaining the perfection of non-action, which is the ultimate goal of Jnana Yoga, can be briefly understood from me. A person with a pure intellect, one who eats light, sattvic, and regular food, who renounces all worldly objects such as words and other distractions, and lives in a solitary, pure place, controls his mind, speech, and body. By mastering his conscience and senses through sattvic concentration, such a person completely destroys attachment and hatred and takes shelter in firm detachment. He renounces ego, pride, lust, anger,

and possessions and is always devoted to meditation. A person who is without attachment and full of peace is eligible to be situated in the **inseparable state of Sachchidanandaghan Brahman.**

Then, the yogi, united with the Sachchidanandaghan Brahman, with a joyful mind, neither grieves for anyone nor desires anything. Such a yogi, who views all beings with equal feelings, attains my supreme devotion. Through this supreme devotion, he comes to know me, the Supreme Soul, exactly as I am and to the full extent of my being. By knowing me in essence through this devotion, he immediately enters into me.

6. **Karmayoga with devotion (Verse 56-66):-** A Karmayogi who is devoted to me, even while constantly performing all actions, attains the eternal and indestructible supreme position by my grace. By surrendering all actions to me with a focused mind and adopting the yoga of equal understanding, be devoted to me and remain constantly focused on me. By being focused on me in this way, you will easily overcome all difficulties through my grace. But if, due to ego, you choose not to heed my words, you will be destroyed—that is, you will be deviated from the path of spirituality. If you take shelter in ego and believe that you will not fight, then this resolve of yours is false, for your nature will compel you to fight.

O Arjuna, the actions that you do not wish to perform due to attachment, you will still do, bound by the nature of actions performed before. The omniscient Supreme God resides in the heart of all beings, directing their actions through His Maya, causing them to wander according to their deeds. O Arjuna, you should take refuge in that Supreme God in every way. By His grace, you will attain supreme peace and the eternal Supreme Abode.

In this manner, I have shared with you this profound secret knowledge. Now, after contemplating this mysterious wisdom, you should act as you wish. Listen again to my most secret words. You are very dear to me, so I will tell you the most beneficial truth: O Arjuna, fix your mind on me, become my devotee, surrender to me. By doing so, you will surely attain me. I promise you this truth because you are very dear to me.

Relinquish all duties and religions, and take refuge only in me, the all-powerful, all-supporting God. I will free you from all sins. Do not grieve.

7. **Importance of Shrimad Bhagavat Gita (Verse 67-78):-** O Arjuna, this ultimate secret of the Gita should never be shared with someone who is devoid of penance, devotion, or interest in listening, nor with someone who has a fault-finding attitude towards me. However, whoever will impart the secret knowledge of this Gita among my devotees will surely attain me, without a doubt. There is no greater service to me than this. I believe that the person who meditates on this Gita Shastra and shares its wisdom will be worshipped by me through the sacrifice of knowledge. The person who listens to this Gita with faith and without any fault-finding attitude will also be freed from sins and will attain the highest realms reserved for those who perform righteous deeds.

O Partha, did you listen to the Gita Shastra with concentration? Has your delusion born of ignorance been dispelled?

Arjuna said: By your grace, I have regained my clarity of mind, for my delusion has been destroyed. Now I am free from doubts and will follow your guidance.

Sanjaya said: In this way, I heard this wonderful, mysterious, and thrilling conversation between Shri Vasudev and the great Arjuna. By the grace of Shri Vyas ji, I, having been granted divine sight, heard Lord Shri Krishna himself speak the profound Yoga of the Supreme to Arjuna. O King, I am delighted again and again as I recall this auspicious and wondrous conversation between Krishna and Arjuna. I am also filled with great awe as I remember the unique form of Shri Hari repeatedly, and my heart rejoices anew each time.

O King, in my opinion, wherever there is Lord Shri Krishna, the lord of Yoga, and wherever there is Arjuna, the wielder of the Gandiva bow, there too are wealth, victory, glory, and unshakable righteousness.

The Discussion

Renunciation and abandonment:-

Arjuna's last question is, what is the difference between renunciation and sacrifice?

In a general sense, there is no difference between renunciation and sacrifice. However, in spirituality, sacrifice refers to the detachment from worldly attachments, while renunciation signifies the absence of the sense of doership. In the *Shrimad Bhagavad Gita*, Arjuna represents the ordinary person. In worldly life, an ordinary person may abandon their duties under the influence of negative emotions such as fear, anger, or worry, mistakenly considering this to be true renunciation. We see countless examples of this in the world: someone might leave home out of fear of punishment for a crime and proclaim themselves a sannyasi, while another might abandon their household due to frustration with domestic disputes. Similarly, Arjuna, troubled by the possible outcomes of the war, wanted to give up the battle, believing this to be renunciation.

In reality, true renunciation does not happen spontaneously; it requires significant effort and discipline to gain control over the mind. After learning about the true meanings of renunciation and sacrifice, Arjuna realizes that what he had been considering renunciation is, in fact, neither true renunciation nor genuine sacrifice. He understood that his desire to abandon his duty was rooted in attachment, not spiritual detachment. When Shri Krishna asks him to make a decision based on knowledge, Arjuna acknowledges that his ignorance—mistaking the abandonment of duty for renunciation—has been dispelled. Free from confusion, Arjuna no longer hesitates. He now comprehends that abandoning one's duty does not constitute true renunciation. Empowered by this understanding, he resolves to perform his duty and prepares for battle.

Relevance of War

Any human action, including war, is not merely a mechanical process; it requires the application of discretion and skill. Therefore, making a decision about an action as dreadful as war is never easy. Arjuna's dilemma—whether to fight or not—is a profound question that even Lord Krishna does not answer directly. Instead, in the final chapter of the *Bhagavad Gita*, Krishna imparts practical and spiritual wisdom, leaving the ultimate decision to Arjuna. He advises him to reflect deeply on this profound knowledge and act according to his understanding.

This signifies that the justification for war depends on one's perspective; it cannot be decided solely based on the destruction it causes or its outcomes.

First, we must consider the *war of Dharmakshetra* that constantly takes place within the human mind—a battle between demonic tendencies (*asuric sampatti*) and divine virtues (*daivic sampatti*). When demonic tendencies prevail, we become trapped in the worldly web of lust, anger, greed, and ego. Conversely, when divine virtues triumph, qualities like non-violence, goodwill, and humility arise, leading to detachment and spiritual liberation.

From a spiritual perspective, it is up to the individual to decide whether to cultivate demonic tendencies or nurture divine virtues. To increase demonic tendencies, one sharpens the "weapons" of lust, anger, and greed while engaging in actions that feed the ego. Similarly, to foster divine virtues, one must strengthen "weapons" like non-violence, goodwill, and humility.

The inner war between demonic and divine qualities is inevitable and ongoing. However, if the mind becomes inactive—neither enhancing divine virtues nor demonic tendencies—it falls into a state of *tamoguna* (inertia). Tamoguna leads to grief, which is contrary to the ultimate goal of human life: attaining happiness.

This interpretation emphasizes that the relevance of war, whether external or internal, is rooted in one's perspective and intent.

Man is born with two types of wealth: divine and demonic. Since the beginning of creation, there has been an ongoing conflict between two opposing forces—selfishness and altruism. War can only be postponed by avoiding it, but it cannot be eliminated entirely. Those with divine wealth wield weapons like non-violence and compassion, while those with demonic wealth resort to violence and aggression.

Becoming non-violent out of fear is a false pretense, not a virtuous act. In contrast, adopting non-violence for a just cause, even when one possesses the power to act violently, is a hallmark of divine wealth. Violent wars are typically driven by selfishness and ego, whereas the goal of a non-violent war is often altruistic and rooted in philanthropy.

In practical terms, a purely non-violent approach may not be effective against a violent adversary. To a violent person, non-violence may appear as weakness or surrender. Therefore, when a war is waged with violent means but for a philanthropic purpose, it is considered a righteous war (*dharma yuddha*) and not an act of adharma (unrighteousness). This is because the essence of dharma lies in selflessness and service to others.

Just as water is needed to extinguish a fire, peace is essential to end a war. Violent means, when used in a righteous war, aim to crush the root cause of conflict—ego. Once the cause is eliminated, peace naturally follows. Peace, like water, must be abundant and powerful enough to overcome the fire of war. Even if peace is inherently stronger, it must still confront unrest until the ego, the source of conflict, is subdued.

Thus, peace and non-violence are not the domains of cowards. True peace requires strength, resilience, and the courage to confront the forces of ego and unrest.

After listening to the entire teachings of the *Bhagavad Gita*, Arjuna realizes that even if he chooses to abandon the war, the conflict cannot be stopped. The Kauravas have entered the battle driven by selfishness and ego, making it clear to Arjuna that his participation in the war is necessary. He understood that peace can only be achieved by crushing the ego of the Kauravas, especially since all attempts at peaceful negotiation before the war have failed.

The question of whether war is right or wrong depends entirely on perspective. Such a decision cannot be made based solely on the outcome of the war. Most wars arise from ignorance, and ego is a visible manifestation of this ignorance. To end such ego-driven conflicts, knowledge is essential, and the primary source of knowledge is experience.

History demonstrates that there are two types of wars:

1. **Ideological War:** This is a battle of ideas, requiring knowledge rather than weapons. Such a war does not involve loss of life and is fought on the plane of intellect and understanding.
2. **Wars Born Out of Ignorance:**This type of war arises from negative emotions such as anger, greed, jealousy, and ego. Unlike ideological wars, weapons are necessary to fight wars born out of ignorance. These conflicts often result in significant loss of life and various forms of physical destruction.

Is War Right or Wrong?

The truth is that war or conflict is a fundamental law of nature. Survival depends on one's willingness to fight; those who avoid conflict are more likely to face destruction. Therefore, the question of whether war is right or wrong is irrelevant. War is simply war, and when it arises, it must be fought.

If the war is ideological, it is fought with reason, logic, or knowledge. However, when a war is driven by ignorance, it cannot be resolved through reasoning or knowledge alone—such wars require weapons. This principle is reflected in the *Vidur Neeti*, which states:

कृते प्रतिकृतिं कुर्याद्विंसिते प्रतिहिंसितम्।
तत्र दोषं न पश्यामि शठे शाठयं समाचरेत्।।

Krite Pratikriti Kuryad Vinsite Pratihinsitam.
Tatra Dosham Na Pashyami Shathe Shathayam Samacharet.

(Translation: "Respond to action with appropriate action and to aggression with retaliation. In dealing with the deceitful, one must use deceit. I see no fault in this.")

This wisdom underscores the necessity of adapting one's approach to the nature of the conflict, whether it demands knowledge or force.

This means that one’s response should align with the nature of the action taken against them. If someone commits violence, there is no fault in responding with equal force, as foolishness cannot be countered with wisdom. This is why it is said:

उपदेशो हि मूर्खाणां प्रकोपाय न शान्तये।
पयः पान भुजंगानां केवलं विषवर्धनं ।

(Translation: "Giving advice to fools does not pacify them but rather intensifies their anger, just as feeding milk to a snake increases its venom.")

It can be concluded that Conflict and war are laws of nature, inherently uncertain. They can arise at any time, in any place, and in any form. Therefore, every individual must always be prepared for such uncertainty. A war fought to satisfy one's ego falls into the category of *Adharma* (unrighteousness). However, a war fought to protect one's existence and uphold righteousness is not considered *Adharma*; it is a *Dharmayuddha* (righteous war).

Conclusion

The *Bhagavad Gita* offers numerous teachings that are deeply relevant to our daily lives. Its most significant message is the importance of staying in the company of a guide or a capable Guru, like Shri Krishna, who can help us make the right decisions in every situation. Fortunately, such a detached and capable Guru is always with us in the form of our soul. By taking refuge in our soul, we gain self-confidence, find solutions to our problems, and resolve the conflicts of the mind.

A calm and composed mind is essential for making decisions aligned with *Dharma*. Such decisions can only be made when we let go of ego and selfishness. The victory of divine virtues (gentle and righteous) over demonic tendencies (arrogant and unrighteous) symbolizes the triumph of *Dharma* over *Adharma*. The purpose of God's incarnation on earth is to subdue demonic forces and promote divine power. As Shri Krishna declares in the *Bhagavad Gita*:

यदा यदा ही धर्मस्य ग्लानिर्भवति भारत,
अभ्युत्थानमधर्मस्य तदात्मानं सृजाम्यहम्।
परित्राणय साधूनां विनाशाय चदुष्कृताम्,
धर्मसंस्थपनार्थाय सम्भवामि युगे युगे।।

"Whenever there is a decline in righteousness (Dharma) and a rise in unrighteousness (Adharma), O Bharata, I manifest Myself. For the protection of the virtuous, the destruction of evildoers, and the re-establishment of Dharma, I incarnate Myself, age after age."

Goswami Tulsidas expresses a similar idea in simpler terms:

जब जब होई धरम के हानि। बाढ़े असुर अधम अभिमानी।।
तब तब धरि प्रभु विविध शरीरा। हरहिं दयानिधि सज्जन पीरा।।

Many interpret these verses to mean that whenever unrighteousness dominates the earth, God incarnates to restore balance. While this may be true, through the *Shrimad Bhagavad Gita*, Maharishi Ved Vyasa also conveys a deeper message: every individual can strive to become a *Sthitapragya* (person of steady wisdom) or a *Karmayogi* (person devoted to selfless action). With practice, any person can embody divine qualities and uphold the dignity of Dharma, which is the ultimate duty of a human being.

The qualities of a *Karmayogi* are beautifully described in the following shloka:

विपत्ति धैर्य धनं अभ्युदये क्षमा,
सदसी वाक्पटूता युद्धि विक्रमा।

"Vipati Dhairya Dhanam Abhudaye Kshama,
Sadasi Vakpatuta Yuddhi Vikrama."

(Translation: "A *Karmayogi* remains patient in adversity, becomes forgiving when blessed with wealth and power, demonstrates wisdom in the assembly of scholars, and shows valor when war is necessary.")

The *Shrimad Bhagavad Gita* inspires every individual to embrace the path of a *Karmayogi*—a life marked by equanimity, duty, and inner balance. A *Karmayogi* does not succumb to mental stress but approaches life's uncertainties with enthusiasm, consciousness, and composure. By following this path, one can face challenges effectively and contribute meaningfully to the preservation of Dharma.

In the *Mahabharata* war, Shri Krishna's decision to serve as Arjuna's charioteer symbolizes that God always stands by the *Karmayogi*, guiding them in the war of *Dharma*. It shows that God remains with those who fight for righteousness, offering guidance in every moment of uncertainty.

The eternal message of the *Shrimad Bhagavad Gita* is that a person should continue performing their duties, staying within the boundaries of their own *Dharma* (in an egoless state). Here, duty refers to actions carried out with consideration for the four *Purusharthas—Dharma, Artha, Kama,* and *Moksha*—the fundamental pursuits of human life. Through this effort, an individual transforms into a God-like being of steady wisdom, capable of facing or embracing every uncertainty without mental stress or disturbance.

In Sanatan Dharma, non-violence is considered the ornament of the brave, which they use with patience to establish peace. However, when war is necessary for the welfare of others, they do not shy away from it. Cowards, in an attempt to hide their fear, mistakenly label the abandonment of their duties as non-violence. In reality, following Sanatan Dharma, or one's own duties, is the proven path to happiness and salvation.

Following *Sanatan Dharma*—one's true, righteous path—is a proven way to attain inner bliss. There is no place for fear or grief in this path. The wisdom imparted in the *Shrimad Bhagavad Gita* is the key to a successful human life. Its study and contemplation lead a person to self-realization and the fulfillment of life's goals, i.e., the pursuit of *Dharma, Artha, Kama,* and *Moksha*, all while remaining full of enthusiasm and consciousness throughout life.

Om Tat Sat

|| Jai Shri Krishna ||

AFTERTHOUGHT

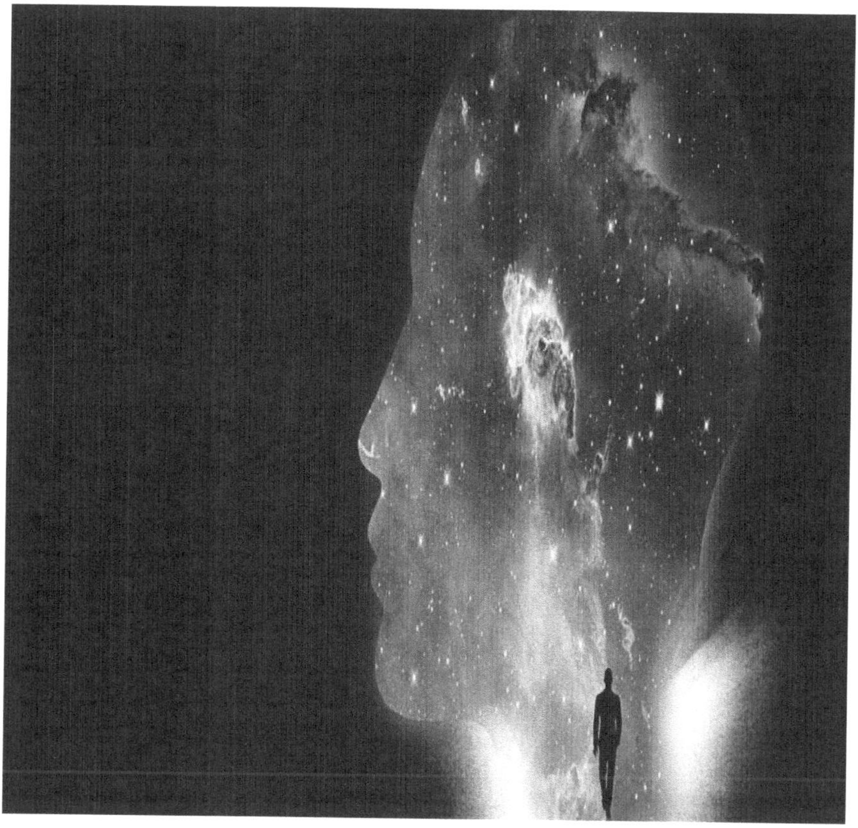

Appendix-A
Significance of the Title ShrimadbhagwatGita

It is important to discuss the naming of the *Shrimad Bhagavad Gita*, the pillar of *Sanatan Dharma*, because the title of any subject often reveals the essence of its content.

Sanatan Dharma teaches the practice of four main types of *yogas*:

1. *Karmayoga*
2. *Sakhyayoga*
3. *Bhaktiyoga*
4. *Rajayoga*

Rajayoga is considered most suitable for householders. It is a combination of *Karmayoga* (selfless action) and *Bhaktiyoga* (devotion), which in common terms we call good deeds done for the welfare of others.

No person in the world desires trouble in life. Everyone seeks happiness. The ultimate experience of happiness is known as the attainment of *bliss*, which, according to *Sanatan Dharma*, is synonymous with the attainment of God.

The essence that a person adopts is called their *Dharma*—the core quality or nature of that person. The true essence of every individual is the attainment of supreme bliss.

Arjuna, due to his attachment, became sad on the battlefield of Kurukshetra. Lord Shri Krishna dispelled his sadness by imparting profound knowledge. Once sadness is removed, happiness naturally follows. Thus, Arjuna found joy even in the midst of the war.

In a state of happiness, even a person's ordinary movements seem like a dance, and simple words appear as an enjoyable song. Due to Arjuna's sense of duty, even in such dire circumstances as war, the conversation between Krishna and Arjuna takes on the form of an uplifting and harmonious song. Therefore, this conversation between Shri Krishna and Arjuna is known as the *Shrimad Bhagavad Gita*. Which is like a joyful song uttered by Sri Krishna to attain awareness irrespective of circumstances.

The simple meaning of the *Shrimad Bhagavad Gita* is "the divine song for human welfare, spoken by the God." Thus the title SrimadbhagvatGita specificify correctly the outline of informations covered in the subject.

Om Tat Sat

Appendix- B
Karmanyewadhikaraste Ma Phaleshu Kadachan

कर्मण्येवाधिकारास्ते मा फलेषु कदाचन्

This is a famous quotation of Srimadbhagwat Gita. Most of the people, think that its meaning is – We have authority only to do our duty but never authority over the outcome of our action . Such an interpretation of this verses creates disappointment in the common people, because people usually perform there duty with the hope of the outcome of duty. Therefore so many people think that if the outcome of action is uncertain, then why do karma or duty for uncertain outcome.

For the correct interpretation of the above verse, the words used in the verse have to be deeply considered. There are three main words in this verse: karma – the action, Adhikar – the control , and phal(produce)- the outcome.

Karma(The Action):-The result of any deed is certain, but the success of the deed depends on the dedication of the doer. The dedication of the doer depends on his efficiency. And efficiency depends on the knowledge generated by experience. Knowledge is the basis of success of any deed. Man can gain knowledge through his efforts. That is why it is said that man has complete authority over his deeds (Action). The Deed (Action) is a subject of **present**.

Adhikar(The Control):- Adhikar means under one's own control. In general any type of action by humanbeing is usually motivated by the imagination of its outcome.But the outcome is always in the womb of future.**It is fact that nobody has control over the past and the future.** Now it is clear that we have control only over our present not over the past and future. As the karma is a matter of present, hence we can control our karma only by our dedication.

Karmaphala(The produce):- It is fact that our action is always motivated by the produce. but the produce is a matter of future . As nobody has control over his future . Hence nobody can control result of Action.

Hence the simple massage of the verse is that focus in the present and do action with dedication , and be ready to accept the result of the action.because nobody can change the result because it is produce of Action taken in the past . The past is also beyond our control. We can even reach a state where our actions become non-reactive—where instead of fearing the outcome, we find joy in the action itself. The result lies in the future, which is uncertain. If we focus on performing our actions to the best of our ability and let go of attachment to the outcome, success is certain. All the successful individuals of present believe in the present, not in the future.

Thus, the meaning of the verse *Karmanyevadhikarastha Maa Faleshu Kadachana* is that we have control over our actions because they are in the matter of present moment. we have no control over past and future.

Om Tat Sat

Appendix- C
Radha-Krishna & Saptpadi

In recent times, curiosity and controversy have led to confusion among people about the relationship between Radha and Shri Krishna, who are often worshipped together in temples.

It is said that there is no direct mention of Radha in the scriptures related to Krishna Leela, such as *Shrimad Bhagwat Mahapurana*, *Mahabharata*, *Harivansh Mahapurana*, and *Vishnupuran*.

Shrimad Bhagwat Mahapurana and *Mahabharata* mention Shri Krishna as having 16,000 and 8 queens, respectively, while *Harivansh Purana* and *Vishnupuran* refer to Shri Krishna as having 16,108 queens. Radha's name is not found in these texts.

Some scholars believe that the word "Radha" is a corrupted form of "Aaradhya," meaning "the one who is worshipped by Shri Krishna." Others argue that Shri Krishna, as described in the *Vishvarupa* in *Shrimad Bhagwat Geeta*, is a yogi in whom everything is contained, and therefore, separate identity of Radha is not logical.

According to *Garg Samhita* (authored by Maharshi Garg, the family guru of Shri Krishna), Shri Krishna and Radha were married. In this tradition, Shri Krishna is regarded as the incarnation of Adi Purush (the primordial being), while Mother Radha is considered the incarnation of Adi Shakti (the primordial energy).

Some well-known storytellers describe Radha as the lover of Shri Krishna to make their relationship more romantic and enjoyable for the audience.

These various accounts and interpretations have led to numerous contradictory folklores about the relationship between Radha and Shri Krishna, creating confusion among devotees.

However, according to the 13th chapter of *Shrimad Bhagwat Gita*, every conscious being is born from the union of nature and spirit. Both nature and spirit are eternal. For any action, the doer requires inspiration. Shri Krishna symbolizes the soul, the doer, while Radha is seen as the symbol of nature, the inspiration behind the actions. The 13th chapter of the *Shrimad Bhagwat Gita* also tells us that the soul resides in the body, and the body cannot exist without the soul, nor can the soul exist without the body with any identity. Similarly, Radha and Shri Krishna are inseparable.

Many scholars believe the fundamental reason for these contradictions is our attempt to understand the relationship between Radha and Shri Krishna from a purely physical perspective. However, despite these varying interpretations, devotees are generally ready to accept that there was a supernatural connection between Radha and Shri Krishna. Whether Radha was his lover, wife, or both, or whether they are essentially the same, remains a matter of devotion and faith.

According to the *Garg Samhita*, Mother Radha and Shri Krishna were married. Thus, Mother Radha is considered the better half of Shri Krishna. It is believed that their love was not sensual but supernatural.

The essence of supernatural love is that two beings become one, and therefore neither has a separate identity. This is similar to how the body and soul cannot have distinct identities—they are inseparable.

If, as stated in the *Garg Samhita*, Radha and Krishna were married, their love must have been supernatural. And since their love was supernatural, their identities cannot be different.

After this discussion, a question arises: the idols of Radha and Krishna are installed in temples, where they appear to have two distinct identities.

At this point, it is relevant to mention a statement by Swami Vivekananda. He said that he feels joy when he sees children heading toward the temple, but sadness when he sees elderly people going there. This is because people approach the temple and the spiritual messages in the same way they learn the alphabet in primary school. Unless the spiritual teachings are actively practiced, worshiping the idols in the temple has no real benefit.

The idols of Mother Radha and Shri Krishna in the temple serve as a symbol for transitioning from duality to non-duality. However, it is essential that we put this lesson into practice. Just as it is appropriate for children to go to primary school to learn, it is illogical for adults to continue learning at the same level. Similarly, adults must move beyond merely worshiping idols and strive to understand and embody the deeper spiritual teachings.

In material life, the love between a husband and wife is often considered sensual. However, the goal of *Sanatan Dharma* has always been human welfare. Therefore, in *Sanatan Dharma*, the wife is called *Dharmapatni*, which signifies a relationship grounded in divine love, not sensuality. This love between husband and wife becomes a means of liberation rather than bondage. Keeping this goal of *Sanatan Dharma* in mind, Maharishi Shvetketu, the father of the Indian marriage system and the son of Uddalak Aruni, proposed certain principles. These principles brought about an unprecedented change in society at the time, and we know them today as *Saptapadi*. While *Saptapadi* has now become a traditional marriage ritual, it originally symbolized a profound transformation in the nature of the marital bond.

Typically, married life begins with the marriage ceremony, which is based on natural attraction of a couple. However, over time, this attraction can sometimes degrade. But, If the principles of

Saptapadi are embraced, the marriage bond transforms into a harmonious, supernatural relationship. In a *Sanatan* marriage, Agnidev (the fire god) is taken as a witness, and both the bride and groom take a pledge to uphold essential promises for a successful married life.

In *Sanatan* marriages, the bride accepts the marriage bond through the groom's commitment to seven vows. These vows are as follows:

The Seven Commitments

1. *तीर्थ–व्रतोद्यापन यज्ञकर्म मया सहैव प्रियवयं कुर्याः* **(Tirtha-vratodyapan yajnakarma maya sahaiva priyavayam)**– The first vow is that you will make me your partner in religious duties, including pilgrimage, vows, and rituals.

2. *पुज्यो यथा स्वौ पितरौ ममापि तथेशभक्तो निजकर्म कुर्याः* **(Pujyo yatha svau pitarau mamaapi tatheshabhakto nijkarma kuryaah)** – The second vow is that you will respect my parents as you respect your own.

3. *जीवनम् अवस्थात्रये पालनां कुर्यात* **(Jeevanam avasthyatrey palanam kuryat)** – The third vow is that you will support me through all the stages of life—youth, adulthood, and old age.

4. *कुटुम्बसंपालनसर्वकार्य कर्तु प्रतिज्ञां यदि कान्त कुर्याः* **(Kutumb sampalana sarvakarya kartu pratigyam yadi kant kuryaah**) – The fourth vow is that, while you were once free from the responsibilities of maintaining a family, after marriage, you will bear the responsibility of supporting and maintaining the family.

5. *स्वसद्यकार्ये व्यहारकर्मण्ये व्यये मामापि मन्त्रयेथा* **(Swasadyakarye vyahaarkarmanye vyayae maamapi mantrayetha**)– The fifth vow is that you will take my advice on household matters, including expenditures and other important decisions.

6. न मेपमानमं सविधे सखीना द्यूतं न वा दुर्व्यसनं भंजश्वेत **(Na mepamanamam svidhe sakhina dyutam na va duvryasanam bhanjshvet)** – The sixth vow is that you will never insult me in front of friends or at any function. Additionally, you will avoid gambling and other vices.

7. परस्त्रियं मातुसमं समीक्ष्य स्नेहं सदा चेन्मयि कान्त कूर्या **(Parastriyam Matusam Samikshya Sneham Sada Chenmayi Kant Kurya)** – The seventh vow is that you will always treat other women with the respect as a mother, and will never let anyone come between our love as husband and wife.

After these vows are accepted, both the groom and the bride take further vows to maintain a sweet and harmonious relationship in marriage. These vows are as follows:

Promises by the Groom

1 धर्मपत्नी मिलित्वैव , ह्येकं जीवनमावयोः।अद्यारभ्य यतो में त्वम् अर्द्धांगिनीति घोषिता **(Dharampatni militvaiva, hayekam jimaamavayoh. Adyarabhya yato mein tvam ardhanginiti ghoshita)** – By declaring you as my half-wife from today onwards, I pledge that in my new life with you, I will take care of you as I do my own body.

2 स्वीकरोमि सुखेन त्वां, गृहलक्ष्मीमीन्ततः। मनयित्वा विधास्यामि, सुकार्याणि त्वया सह **(Swikaromi sukhen twam, Grihlaxmimintatah. manyitwa vidhasyami, sukaryani tywa sah)** – From today, I accept you as *Grihalakshmi* (the goddess of the household) and promise to value your advice in every decision I make in life.

3 रूप– स्वास्थ्य, गुणदोषादीन्सर्वतः।रोगज्ञान– विकारांश्च तव विस्मृत्य चेतसः **(Roop swasthya, Gunadoshadin Sarvath. Roggyan - Vikaransch Tav Vismritya Chetasah**)– I will not focus on your physical appearance, health, or any defects or disorders caused by

ignorance. I promise to not express dissatisfaction and will maintain our intimacy with affection, aiming for improvement.

4 सहचरो भविष्यामि,पूर्णस्नेहः प्रदास्यते । सत्यता मम निष्ठा च, यस्याधरं भविष्यति **(Sahacharo Bhavishyami, Purnasneh Pradasyate. Satyata Mam Nishtha Cha, Yasyadharam Bhavishyati)** – I promise to remain devoted and keep my word with full sincerity. I will nurture a friendly and affectionate bond with you, and my commitment to you will be unwavering.

5 पवित्रचित्तेन पातिव्रत्य त्वया धृतम । तथैव पालयिष्यामि पत्नीव्रतमहं ध्रुवं **(Pavitrachiten Pativratya twya dritam,Tathayav Palayishyami Patnivratamah Dhruvam)** – Just as the dignity of husbandry has been stated for the wife, I will also uphold the duties of a husband with the same determination. In both my thoughts and actions, I will refrain from any lustful relationship, remaining loyal to my wife.

6 गृहस्यार्थव्यवस्थायां मन्त्रयित्वा त्वया सह। सञ्चालनं करिष्यामि गृहस्थोचित. जीवनमं **(Grihsyarthvyavsthayam Mantraiyatva Tvaya Saha. sanchalanam Karishyami Grihasthochit. Jeevanmam)** – I will prioritize you in all household matters. I will manage our family life, including income and expenses, in harmony with your consent.

7 समृद्धि. सुख. शान्तिनां रक्षणाय तथा तव। व्यवस्थां वै करिष्यामि स्वशक्ति वैभवादिभिः **(Samridhi, shukam, Shantinam Rakshanaya tatha Tav. Vyavastam Vai Karishyami Swashakti vaibhavadibhi)**– I will use my strength and resources with full sincerity to ensure your happiness, peace, and security, and will continue to work towards our shared prosperity and well-being.

8 यत्नशीलो भविष्यामि सन्मार्गसेवितुं सदा। आवयोः मतभेदांश्च दोषान्संशोध्य शान्तित **(ytanashilo bhavisyami lanmarg sevitum sada . aavayo matbhedasaya doshansanshodhya shantitah)** – I will strive to maintain good approach and good behavior from my side. I will make every effort to peacefully resolve differences and mistakes to maintain peace.

9 *भवत्यामसमर्थायां विमुखायाञ्च कर्मणि। विश्वासं सहयोगञ्च मम प्राप्स्यसि त्वं सदा* **(Bhavatyaamsamarthayaan vimukhayaanch karmani. Vishwasam Sahayognch Mam Prapsyasi Tvam Sada** – Even if my husband becomes incapable or turns away from his duties, I will not withdraw my support or cooperation in any way, and will remain committed to fulfilling my responsibilities.

Promises by the bride

1.स्वजीवनं मेलयित्वा भवतः खलु जीवने। भूत्वा चार्द्धाङ्गिनी नित्यं निवत्स्यामि गृहे सदा **(Swajivanam melayitva bhavat khalu jeevne. Bhootva Chadradhangini Nityam Nivatsyami Grihe Sada)** – I will create a new life by uniting my life with yours, and in this way, I will always remain your true better half within our home.

2.शिष्टतापूर्वकं सर्वैः परिवारजनैः सह। औदार्येण विधास्यामि व्यवहारं च कोमलम् . **(shishtapurvakam sarveh parivarjaneh sah Audarayen Vidhyasyami Vyavaram Cha Komalam)** – I will treat my husband's family members as part of one body, serving them with courtesy, generosity, and kindness.

3. त्यक्त्वालस्यं करिष्यामि गृहकार्ये परिश्रमम् । भर्तुर्हर्षं हि ज्ञास्यामि स्वीयामेव प्रसन्नताम् **Tyktvalasyaam karishyami grihakaryaye prasharanam. Bharturharsham hi jyasyami swiyameva prasannatam** – I will abandon laziness and dedicate myself diligently to household work. In doing so, I will contribute to my husband's happiness and the overall development of our lives.

4.श्रद्धया पालयिष्यामिए धर्मं पातिव्रतं परमं । सर्वदैवानुकूल्येन पत्युरादेशपालिका **Shraddhaya Palayishyamiye Dharmam Pativratam Paramam, sarvdaivanukulyen praturadespalika).:**– I will follow the highest dharma of *pativrata* (devotion to my husband). I will always maintain a friendly and loving attitude towards him, following his guidance without hesitation or doubt.

5.सुश्रूषणपरा स्वच्छा मधुरं प्रियभाषिणी। प्रतिजाने भविष्यामि सततं सुखदायिनी **(Sushrushanpara Swachha Madhuram Priyabhashini. Pratijane Bhavishyaami Santatam Sukhdayini)** – I will serve with cleanliness, loving speech, and kindness. I will avoid jealousy, grudges, and negative emotions, always striving to be a source of happiness.

6.मितव्ययेन गार्हस्थ्य. सञ्चालने हि नित्यदा। प्रयतिष्ये च सोत्साहं तवाहमनुगामिनी (**mitvyen garhaSThay sachalne hi nityada. Prayatishye Cha Sotsahan Tavahamnugamini)** – I will manage our household efficiently, avoiding wasteful expenditure, and will enthusiastically support my husband in all his endeavors.

7. देवस्वरूपो नारीणां भर्त्ता भवति मानवः। मत्वेति त्वां भजिष्यामि नियता जीवनावधिम् (**Devaswaroopo Naarinam Bhartta Bhavati Manavah. Matveti twan bhajishyami niyata jivanavadhim** – I will treat my husband as a god. With this understanding, I will remain devoted to him throughout my life, forgetting any differences and never insulting him.

8. पूज्यास्तव पितरो ये श्रद्धया परमा हि मे। सेवया तोषयिष्यामि तान्सदा विनयेन च **(pujyastav pitro ye shrdhya parmahi me . Sevaya Toshayishyami Tansada Vinayen Cha)** – I will keep my husband's revered ancestors and those worthy of respect always satisfied through service and humility.

9. विकासाय सुसंस्कारैःए सूत्रैः सद्भाववर्द्धिभिः। परिवारसदस्यानां कौशलं विकसाम्यहम् **(Vikasaya susanskaaraih e sutraih sadbhavarddhibhi. Parivarasadsyanam Kaushalam Vikasamyham)** – I will develop the skill of fostering good values and nurturing a spirit of goodwill within the family, guiding them to live in harmony.

Even in present era context, if the vows and promises mentioned above are followed throughout life, the bond of marriage will transform from a worldly connection into a supernatural harmony. Its relevance remains just as significant today.

In modern times, truth is often debated and considered invalid without logical arguments. However, the story of Mata Radha and Shri Krishna belongs to a time long past, and no logical explanation can fully encapsulate it. Instead of getting caught in futile reasoning, it is wiser to embrace the divine message of love that Mata Radha and Shri Krishna convey. By internalizing this message and practicing it, one can lead a fulfilling and harmonious life—both physically and spiritually.

A natural question arises: How can a husband and wife be one with each other, especially when their times of death may differ? Scholars suggest that when love is supernatural, it transcends the physical body. The bond between the bodiless soul and the embodied soul remains intact, thus transforming duality into non-duality. The two bodies continue their shared journey towards a common goal. The embodied body performs karma, while the soul within provides the inspiration for action.

The love story of Mata Radha and Shri Krishna can be seen as symbolic. According to the Shrimad Bhagwat Gita, God incarnates to establish righteousness on earth. For Lord Krishna, nature itself is the divine inspiration for establishing this dharma. Mata Radha, in turn, is believed to embody Adishakti, the power of God. Many scholars also believe the name Radha originates from the word *Aaraaghya*, meaning the worshipped one, signifying Radha as the divine goddess revered by Krishna.

The essential takeaway from the stories of Radha and Krishna is that Shri Krishna represents the Karmayogi (the one who engages in selfless action), and Radha serves as the inspiration for those actions. Their union is inseparable. In Sanatan culture, the wife is considered the "better half" of the husband, symbolizing the supernatural harmony between the two. This harmony can be achieved by adhering to the vows and promises outlined in the Sanatan marriage tradition.

| | Shri Radha Krishna Namo Namah | |

Appendix- D
Mourning for whom

According to Srimad Bhagavad Gita, Lord Krishna explains to Arjuna that those present in battle are not worthy of mourning, because death is certain, which is just like eternal sleep. The soul is immortal and has two motions:

1. Liberation of the soul from rebirth

2. Rebirth of the soul

All these things of knowledge are from before the war. In this, Shri Krishna advises Arjuna not to be fascinated. But in ordinary life man is fascinated. People have the sorrow of separation from their loved ones. On this subject, the sages say that we should mourn when someone dies, when it seems that after death, the soul will not be liberated but will wander in the cycle of birth and death. To identify this, Goswami Tulsidas, through Guru Vashishta, has expressed the decision of mourning through the following lines to remove the sorrow of Bharat after the departure of King Dashrath to the next world:

सुनहू भरत भावी प्रवल बिलखि कहेउ मुनिनाथ।
हानि लाभ जीवनु मरनु जसु अपजसु बिधि हाथ।।
अस बिचारि केहि देइअ दोसू। ब्यरथ काहि पर कीजिअ रोसू।।
तात बिचारू करहु मन माहीं। ब्यरथ काहि पर कीजिअ रोसू।।
तात बिचारू करहु मन माहीं । सोच जोगु दसरथु नृपु नाहीं ।।
सोचिअ बिप्र जो बेद बिहीना। तजि निज धरमु बिषय लयलीना।।
सोचिअ नृपति जो नीति न जाना। जेहि न प्रजा प्रिय प्राण समाना।।
सोचिअ बयसु कृपन धनवानू । जो न अतिथि सिव भगति सुजानू।।
सोचिअ सुद्रु बिप्र अवमानी । मुखर मानप्रिय ग्यान गुमानी ।।
सोचिअ पुनि पति बंचक नारी । कुटिल कलहप्रिय इच्छाचारी।।

सोचिअ बटु निज ब्रतु परिहरई । जो नहिं गुर आयसु अनुसरई।।
सोचिअ गृही जो मोह बस करई करम पथ त्याग।
सोचिअ जती प्रपंचरत बिगत बिबेक बिराग।।
बैखानस सोइ सोचै जोगु। तपु बिहाइ जेहि भावइ भोगू।।
सोचिअ पिसुन अकारण क्रोधी। जननी जनक गुर बंधु बिरोधी।।
सब बिधि सोचिअ पर अपकारी । निज तनु पोषक निरदय भारी।।
सोचनीय सबहीं बिधि सोई । जो न छाड़ि छलु हरि जन होई ।।
सोचनीअ नहिं कोसलराउ। भुवन चारिदस प्रगट प्रभाउ।।
भयउ न अहइ न अब होनिहारा।भूप भरत जस पिता तुम्हारा ।।
बिधि हरि हरु सुापति दिसिनाथा। बरनहिं सब दसरथ गुन गाथा।।
कहहु तात केहि भँति कोउ करिहि बड़ाई तासु।
राम लखन तुम्ह सत्रुहन सरिस सुअन सुचि जासु ।।

The meaning of these lines is very simple which tells that you have to follow your worldly religion/religion. The soul of those who are detached from responsibility is not liberated, but who selflessly follow their worldly religion/religion. They should not grieve for the responsibility they are responsible for, because they have done the work for which they were born on this earth, so they deserve salvation and there is no need to mourn for them. One should understand the hidden sentiment in these lines which is as follows:

King Dashrath is not worthy of sorrow, because he has not given his religion/religion. Have fulfilled the responsibility. Worthy of grief are the ignorant Brahmanas who are disgusted with their worldly religion. The mourner is a king who has no knowledge of policy, which makes his subjects unhappy. Worthy of grief is a rich but gracious merchant who does not serve his guest. Worthy of sorrow is he who ridicules the learned and does not increase his knowledge and considers himself to be the most knowledgeable. A woman worthy of grief is who is not a believer in her husband and is always engaged in unreasoned crookedness. In the same way, we should grieve for them.

Appendix- E
Mental Emotions and Physical Diseases

The results of our actions are always in the womb of the future. Hence, we cannot do anything whether our results are in our favour or against. This is the opinion of almost all Sanatan scriptures that we should have an equal attitude towards the results of our actions. When we can do our work only in the present, then we have to be prepared for any situation that may arise in the future. Generally, a common human being gets disturbed by not keeping an equal attitude in both situations of success and failure. The feeling of deviation due to his results of actions appears in the following three basic forms. Which are called Emotion.

1. The Anger:- A man gets angry when he does not get the desired result, and it is very common that no ordinary man considers himself responsible for his failure, he considers someone else responsible for his failure. As a result, he gets angry with others without any reason. According to Ayurveda, due to anger, the **Pitah** in the body often becomes unbalanced. And this causes Pitah related diseases. Which is responsible for cronic diseases .

2. The Fear:- When a person has to take a decision for any work. Then due to ignorance, he become indecisive result in development of conflict in mind. This conflict is the cause of fear. According to Ayurveda, due to fear, the **Cough** of the body becomes unbalanced. And this causes cough related diseases. It causes breathing related problems in the body.

3. The Worry:- Due to not being able to start any work at the right time, there is always a doubt about the result of the work or the success of the work. Such doubts gives rise to worry. According to Ayurveda, due to worry, the **Vayu** (air element) of the body becomes unbalanced. And it causes air related diseases. It appears in the form of pain in the body.

So for a happy, joyful and disease free life, it is necessary to control the emotional . And for this, it is very important to be honest towards one's duty. it is very important to take the right decision at the right time with dedication. Still, if the desired result is not achieved, then it is our duty to pay attention toward the shortcomings of the effort and try again. Shrimadbhagwat Gita teaches us to do our duty with dedication and awareness with control over the Emotion.

-:Om Tat Sat:-

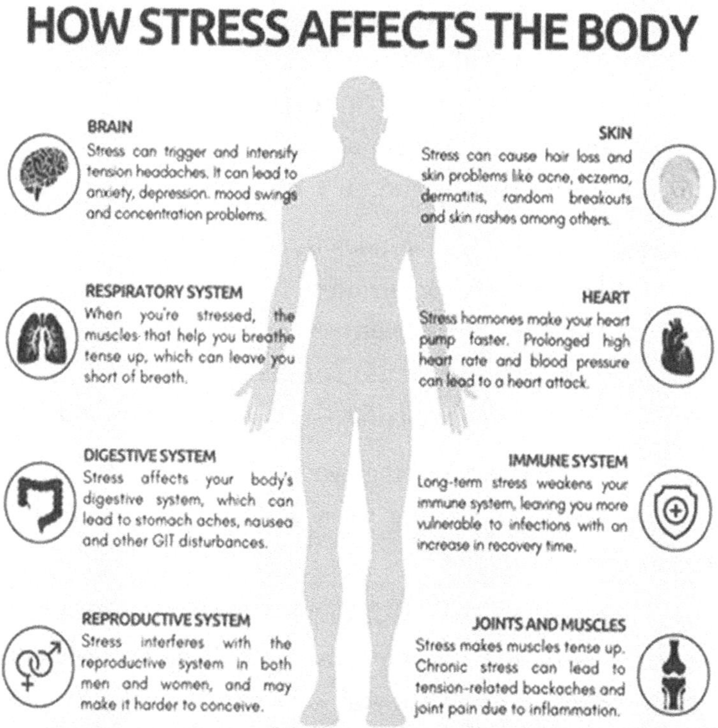

Appendix- F
Ashtanga Yoga and Yoga presented in Shrimad Bhagwat Geeta

The *Shrimad Bhagavad Gita* contains 18 chapters, and the word "Yoga" appears in the title of each chapter. Yoga, in its essence, means the union of the soul with the Supreme Soul. When the term "Yoga" is mentioned, the *Ashtanga Yoga Sutras* of Maharishi Patanjali often come to mind, which are divided into two parts:

1. **External Yoga**: This includes five practices:
    1. Yama (Moral restraints)
    2. Niyama (Observances)
    3. Asana (Physical postures)
    4. Pranayama (Breath control)
    5. Pratyahara (Withdrawal of senses)
2. **Internal Yoga**: This includes three practices:
    1. Dharana (Concentration)
    2. Dhyana (Meditation)
    3. Samadhi (Absorption or union)

    These three are collectively called *Sanyama*.

A question often arises: Is the yoga described in Patanjali's *Ashtanga Yoga* the same as the yoga described in the chapters of the *Shrimad Bhagavad Gita*?

To understand this, we must reflect on a profound teaching from the sixth chapter of the *Chandogya Upanishad*. The Mahavakya (great statement) is: **Tat Tvam Asi** – "You are That" (i.e., God is not separate from you, He is you).

If the soul and the Supreme Soul are not separate, how can yoga be described as the union of the soul with the Supreme Soul? The modern misunderstanding of yoga, promoted through popular culture, often limits it to just Pranayama and Asanas, which are external aspects of yoga as per Patanjali's Sutras. However, without the inner journey—without self-control—the ultimate goal of yoga, *Samadhi*, cannot be attained.

In the *Shrimad Bhagavad Gita*'s 11th chapter, Lord Krishna reveals His universal form, encompassing everything in the cosmos, which is also explained in the *Purusha Suktam* of the Vedas. This implies that nothing in the universe is separate from Him, thus proving that the soul and the Supreme Soul are one. Therefore, when we say that the Supreme Soul is within everyone or that the soul resides in everyone, both statements are true because the soul and the Supreme Soul are one. But the question remains: how does the soul unite with the Supreme Soul?

What is Yoga?

The practical meaning of yoga is the effort to add something positive to the present situation with the aim of improving the future. Our body is governed by three *Gunas* (qualities): Tamas (inertia), Rajas (passion), and Sattva (goodness). Through the guidance of a Guru, a person's Tamas decreases, and the Rajas increases. Likewise, the Rajoguna of an individual is reduced, and Sattvaguna increases. As the level of Sattvaguna increases, the soul moves closer to liberation.

Maharishi Patanjali defines yoga as: **Chitta Vritti Nirodha** – the cessation of the fluctuations of the mind. The mind can be pacified only when it is focused, and the intellect is that part of the being capable of directing the mind when it is calm. Therefore, the use of intellect is essential for achieving Chitta Vritti Nirodha.

According to the *Ashtanga Yoga Sutras* of Patanjali, the mind can be easily concentrated by practicing the external aspects of yoga. This leads to a peaceful state of mind. When the mind is peaceful, the intellect forms perceptions based on its capacity. However, without a capable Guru, these perceptions may be incomplete or distorted.

Dharana (concentration) is the first stage of internal yoga, followed by **Dhyana** (meditation). Dhyana enhances the intellect, allowing it to direct the mind inward. The combination of these three practices —**Dharana, Dhyana, and Samadhi**—is collectively called *Sanyama.*

According to the Mahavakya **Tat Tvam Asi**, the Guru is also God, and the disciple is also God. Hence, the Guru and the disciple are one, but due to ignorance, we fail to hear the voice of our inner Guru. As per Maharishi Patanjali, through meditation, a person can strengthen their belief and make their intellect more capable. This process removes the veil of ignorance and leads to the attainment of *Samadhi*. At this point, the intellect expands to infinity, merging with the infinite, which is God. This is the state of yoga. In *Samadhi*, duality ends, and the non-duality of **Tat Tvam Asi** is experienced.

Yoga in the *Shrimad Bhagavad Gita*

The *Shrimad Bhagavad Gita* is a dialogue between Lord Krishna (God) and Arjuna (the devotee). The first chapter, **Arjuna Vishada Yoga**, reflects Arjuna's sorrow and confusion, symbolizing the first step in internal yoga. In the subsequent chapters, Lord Krishna explains four primary forms of yoga—**Karma Yoga, Bhakti Yoga, Jnana Yoga**, and **Raja Yoga**—to refine Arjuna's perception. These represent the methods of meditation, the second step of internal yoga.

As Arjuna's intellect expands, he attains divine vision, seeing Krishna's cosmic form in Chapter 11. This marks the highest goal of Arjuna's internal yoga: *Samadhi*. Thus, Arjuna's experience of Krishna's universal form symbolizes the end of duality and the realization of oneness with the infinite.

The last chapters (12th to 18th) of the *Gita* compile esoteric knowledge in the form of Krishna-Arjuna dialogue to further refine human perception. In this way, every chapter of the Gita represents a step in internal yoga. Therefore, the use of the word "yoga" in each chapter's title signifies the human welfare intention behind the teachings of Krishna to Arjuna.

Patanjali's Yoga and Gita's Yoga

Both Patanjali's internal yoga and the yoga in the *Shrimad Bhagavad Gita* have the same objective: to stabilize the mind through **Chitta Vritti Nirodha** (the cessation of mental fluctuations), to concentrate the mind through the intellect, and to reach *Samadhi*, thus becoming one with the infinite.

Benefits of Yoga for an Ordinary Person

A common question is: What benefit does an ordinary person gain from the yoga presented by Patanjali? The simple answer is that yoga has the power to make an ordinary person extraordinary. Through yoga, the mind becomes stable and concentrated, ending the confusion about duties. Once this confusion is eliminated, a person is freed from the main disorders caused by the results of karma, such as fear, anger, and sorrow. These disorders stem from attachment, which is a form of illusion (Maya). When *Samadhi* is achieved through yoga, Maya is destroyed, and the person attains liberation.

Many people in India believe that liberation (moksha) occurs only after death. However, through yogic practice, a person can experience liberation during their lifetime. After death, the soul merges with the infinite, freeing itself from the cycle of birth and death. The reason for the soul to take on a physical body is dissatisfaction with the material world. Through yoga, the soul achieves liberation even while in the body.

Om Tat Sat

Appendix- G
Significance of Esoteric Principles of Sanatan Dharma - Yajna

Every living being is born with three essential components of life, which influence their entire existence. These components are:

- **Body**
- **Society** (parents, siblings, and other close ones)
- **Natural wealth**

The core principle of *Sanatan Dharma* is to embark on a journey of continuous development without causing harm to these three components. This principle is the foundation of *Sanatan Dharma*, and its relevance remains unquestioned even today. In fact, contemporary scientists are increasingly acknowledging its significance.The sages and saints of ancient India devised a method for such continuous development, which they termed *Sanatan Paddhati* (the eternal path). They viewed their blessings as a form of debt, and they prescribed three key measures to repay this debt:

- **To repay the debt of the body**: *Tapasya* (spiritual austerity)
- **To repay the debt of society**: *Daan* (charity)
- **To repay the debt of natural wealth**: *Yajna* (sacrifice)

To fully understand *Sanatan Dharma*, one must grasp the significance of *Yajna*, *Daan*, and *Tapasya*. These concepts are discussed in detail in the *Bhagavad Gita*, where Vedic duties—*Yajna*, *Tapas*, and *Daan*—are emphasized. In Indian culture, *Yajna* serves as a symbolic expression of these three principles:

- Fasting, as part of *Tapasya*, symbolizes the purification of the body.
- *Havan* (sacrificial fire) symbolizes the process of repairing the damage caused by the exploitation of natural wealth.

- The donations made during a *Yajna* represent *Aparigraha* (non-possessiveness), ensuring the maintenance of socio-economic balance.

After the *Upanayan Sanskar* (the sacred initiation ccrcmony) in *Sanatan Dharma*, it is customary for the individual to wear the *Yajyopavit*—a sacred thread with three strands. This thread serves as a reminder for an individual to always remember and honor the three debts throughout their life, living in accordance with their duties.

These principles of *Sanatan Dharma* are elaborated upon in the *Shrimad Bhagavad Gita.* One of the unique features of the original scriptures is their use of symbolic explanations (*Sankhya*) to present esoteric knowledge. This approach not only makes the knowledge interesting and accessible but also ensures its universality and timelessness. However, the symbolism can sometimes lead to varying interpretations, which, over time, may cause the esoteric truths to be distorted or misunderstood.

In contemporary times, *Yajna* is often reduced to a mere religious ritual, with a greater emphasis on the rituals themselves. Scholars suggest that the relevance of these rituals should be explained in the context of modern era. It is possible to adapt the form of *Yajna* while preserving its core essence of human welfare (such as the use of sacred fire, etc.), ensuring its continued significance in the present world.

The philoshophy of the Yajana in the Sanatan Dharma may be summeries as : **The Yajana is eternal path to attain the suprime bliss is to perform selfless prime duty with awareness of sustenable development. Sustenable development is the moral responsibility of human being irrespective of creed or caste.**

-: Om Tat Sat:-

References

1. Shreemadbhagvat Gita – Gita press Gorakhpur
2. Shreemadbhagvat Gita(as it is) – ISKCON
3. Shreemadbhagvat Gita (Gita rahsya) – Lokmanya Bal Gangadhar Tilak
4. ShreemadbhagvatGita –Dr. Radhakrishnan (Former President of India)
5. Shreemadbhagvat Gita(Gita Mata) –Rastrapita Mahatma Gandhi
6. Shreemadbhagvat Gita(Gita pravachan) –Aacharya Vinoba Bhabe